ANTICIPATE

ANTICIPATE

THE ART OF LEADING
BY LOOKING AHEAD

ROB-JAN DE JONG

AMACOM

AMERICAN MANAGEMENT ASSOCIATION

New York • Atlanta • Brussels • Chicago • Mexico City • San Francisco
Shanghai • Tokyo • Toronto • Washington, D.C.

Bulk discounts available. For details visit: www.amacombooks.org/go/specialsales
Or contact special sales: Phone: 800-250-5308 E-mail: specialsls@amanet.org
View all the AMACOM titles at: www.amacombooks.org
American Management Association: www.amanet.org

LIBRARY OF CONGRESS CATALOGING-IN-PUBLICATION DATA
De Jong, Rob-Jan.
Anticipate : the art of leading by looking ahead / Rob-Jan de Jong.
pages cm
Includes index.
ISBN 978-0-8144-4907-3 -- ISBN 0-8144-4907-7 1. Leadership. 2. Creative ability in business.
3. Strategic planning. I. Title.
HD57.7.D4 2015
658.4'092--dc23   2014024651

About AMA

American Management Association (www.amanet.org) is a world leader in talent development, advancing the skills of individuals to drive business success. Our mission is to support the goals of individuals and organizations through a complete range of products and services, including classroom and virtual seminars, webcasts, webinars, podcasts, conferences, corporate and government solutions, business books, and research. AMA's approach to improving performance combines experiential learning—learning through doing—with opportunities for ongoing professional growth at every step of one's career journey.

Printing number

10 9 8 7 6 5 4 3 2 1

Dedicated to my father, whose life stance continues to inspire me—
I wish you were still here to witness.

Contents

Preface

When I graduated from high school some thirty years ago, the school's principal—who had also been our draconian German class teacher—subtly criticized my attitude of continuous challenge during the diploma ceremony. After putting in a few nice words for my parents, he mentioned that he would remember me as a vigilant student who was always willing to point out a different perspective. I think he was just trying to tell me that I had behaved like a wiseass know-it-all more often than he had liked.

I was raised in Europe (the Netherlands) and went through high school in the early eighties, amid vivid political debate about the pros and cons of capitalism vs. those of socialism, the madness of the nuclear arms race both sides had entered, Ronald Reagan's Star Wars protection program, the birth of Poland's Solidarity union and many other Cold War–related West vs. East themes. The school's principal was known to uphold right-of-center opinions, and I would oppose him with leftish arguments. But when we moved to our next class and found ourselves discussing the same themes with a left-wing-oriented teacher, I'd just as easily morph into the right-of-center rationale. Just for argument's sake.

This was probably more than just a teenager trying to make sense of the world around him. I was fascinated by the debate, and my curiosity about the other side of an argument—any argument—withheld me from committing to one worldview. The issues seemed too complex for that. The curiosity remained; later in life, I transformed it into an interest in exploring and challenging what is seemingly taken for granted (keeping the annoyance factor in check).

This book emerged from that same fascination with questioning what might seem simple and mundane, clear and understood, but on second thought isn't that easy at all. As we progress to discover the art of anticipating the future, we'll go in depth, exploring the seemingly straightforward concept called *vision,* a word often and readily used in the domain of business and political leadership. Some scholars call it the hallmark of leadership, others list it among the three or four central themes, and yet others put it on a different pedestal—you'll rarely find anyone who does not deem it an important leadership theme. In real life, the importance of vision is easily acknowledged as well. In business, for example, we frequently find people criticizing their superiors for their lack of it.

But then, when it comes to developing our *own* vision, it's suddenly no longer duck soup. We wonder if it's really that important, and even if we are convinced, it's not clear to us how we should actually go about foretasting the future. It seems to come naturally to the larger-than-life kind of leaders who seemingly effortlessly inspire with a compelling big-picture story. But for us mortal souls, artfully looking ahead, anticipating the future, and inspiring others with a gripping vision does not come easy. Nor does it top our to-do list of important matters to work on in terms of growing our leadership persona.

I find such contradictions fascinating. Theoretically top of the list, in practice bottom of the list. It got me wondering why we struggle with this issue. How do we concretely engage with the future? We're all fascinated by it; we all have dreams and ambitions. We all make plans, and most of us like to be part of something that's fascinating and energizing. So engaging with the future, and the things it might have in store for us, should by definition be of interest to us. But where does it disconnect? Or better, what could we do to make it better connect?

To get a deeper understanding of how this process of engagement with the future works (or doesn't work) with leaders and aspiring leaders, I ran a survey several years ago to test this phenomenon. The survey used a four-level scale that indicated the degree of someone's "future engagement." I gathered answers from 210 people from a wide range of different industries.

When I asked people what they do, concretely, to stay in touch with relevant future developments, the answer always included "reading newspapers," "talking with customers/colleagues," and other methods of "staying up-to-date." These are all smart things to do—and I encourage you to continue doing them—but they're level 1 activities in terms of future engagement and developing visionary capacity. News facts and developments in your industry are mostly concerned with what *has been,* or at most *what is.* The bulk of what you find in the newspaper is about what happened yesterday, not about what will happen tomorrow. Monitoring the news therefore marks level 1. I found a near 100 percent score for activities at this level. As every professional can be expected to actively follow the news, this high score was unsurprising.

Since level 1 is concerned with today and yesterday, level 2 involves consciously seeking out sources that specialize in covering *future* developments. Reading industry analyst reports and attending conferences with a focus on the future are examples of level 2 activities. The positive responses halved: 47 percent reported to have attended a conference or seminar focused on their industry's future in the last six months. About a third (36 percent) had in recent months asked a team member to make an analysis of developments in the sector, and 24 percent had outsourced that kind of analysis to an outside expert. Averaging these statistics would not be appropriate, but gut feeling tells us the amount of level 2 engagement is at least half of level 1. (See Figure P-1.)

What the first two levels have in common, and what sets them apart from levels 3 and 4, is that they are both levels of *passive* engagement with the future. You're merely a consumer of other people's brainwork. Confucius clearly understood the significant difference between passive and active engagement when he said:

"I hear and I forget, I see and I remember, I do and I understand."

Fresh ideas, new insights, and real learning are rooted in *active* engagement with the future, which is therefore the distinctive feature of the levels

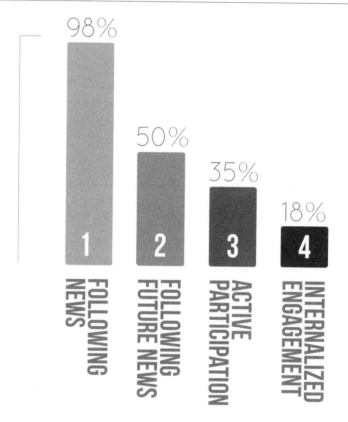

Figure P-1. Levels of future engagement.

3 and 4. At level 3 you are actively engaged in future-oriented activities, such as trend analysis, modeling, and simulation, or some of the other tools and techniques that support you at this level. Your active participation in these active forms of exploring "what might be" will provide you with *self*-generated insights. These insights are much more likely to have a profound impact on your ability to anticipate and look ahead.

Notwithstanding this promising return on investment, when the respondents to my survey were asked about their level 3 engagement activities, the percentage took another free fall and landed at 35 percent.

The reason most often mentioned is time consumption. Many leaders report that they lack the time to "do the Vision Thing." So they outsource it, leaving a strategy department or project (or even worse, a consultant) to do the work. This effectively puts the leader back at level 1 or 2: passively reading findings that have been produced by others.

So we would benefit from a fourth—and most heightened—level of future engagement: active, systematic visionary development on an ongoing, somewhat effortless basis. Level 4 would be the ideal to strive for: You reap the insightful benefits of level 3, yet without its drawback of substantial time and effort that hamper your active participation. It requires an internalized way of working with the future through habits and practices that continually nurture your visionary capacity. I found that only 18 percent of people operate at this most productive level.

In conclusion, despite the widespread acknowledgment of its importance, there is a steep downward slope in how leaders fruitfully engage with the future to develop their forward-oriented perspective.

My ongoing exploration of this topic over the years has led me to believe that anyone can improve their visionary side. Substantially, even. This also—and especially—applies to those who do *not* aspire to become larger-than-life heroes, but who *do* want to be a source of inspiration to their followers and want to lead their teams and organizations with energizing direction and purpose.

The first step on this journey is a personal one; one that helps you develop the various dimensions of your visionary self through an integrated perspective, bringing together your rational mind, your imagination, your emotions, your character, your values, your behavior, and your words.

This is what is in store for you. With this work, I intend to bring out the best future-oriented leader you could possibly be by helping you reach levels 3 and 4: productive—and often effortless—engagement with the future. So you will lead by looking ahead, and your views, expressions, and deeds will ignite and inspire others to see an alluring perspective to actively work toward. I trust this interests you, because, to paraphrase the futurist Adam Kahane, the future is where you will spend the rest of your life.

READING SUPPORT

In contemplating this book, I noticed I kept going back and forth between providing academic concepts and readily applicable, practical ideas. I didn't want to write yet another shallow "how to" book that lacked academic solidity. At the same time, overburdening largely practical readers with heavy academic concepts was not my intention, either.

Developing a powerful vision calls for the integration of various fields of expertise, including creative, psychological, strategic, behavioral, and narrative disciplines. So there is a lot to tap into. As a result, I have included solid academic research concepts in combination with practical ideas, tools, and approaches that I know from experience will help you develop your visionary swing. I have grouped them into four different parts (see Figure P-2), marking the key stops we will make:

Part 1: Visionary Content

The first stop focuses on important elementary matters in the art of looking ahead, such as the essential ingredients a powerful vision consists of and the notions that define, form, and shape it (Chapter 1). To generate resourceful ideas that constitute your vision, you will need the ability to tap into your imagination, which is why we will spend time exploring what it takes to unlatch your creative, imaginary side (Chapter 2).

Part 2: Visionary Practices

In this second part the focus is on understanding and building a developmental framework to nurture your visionary capacity constantly and deliberately (Chapter 3). We will discover that there are two key developmental dimensions that direct your growth: your ability to see change early (Chapter 4) and your ability to connect the dots (Chapter 5). We cover practical, real-life approaches to enact on these dimensions, starting with a novel one

Figure P-2. Four parts of visionary development.

called FuturePriming in Chapter 4. In Chapter 5, we work on the ability to responsibly create coherence in your vision while keeping an eye on the risk of tunnel vision.

Part 3: Visionary Self

At the third stop, your visionary self, we move on to the personal and behavioral dimension of visionary capacity; we look at mindsets, attitudes, and values to ensure the crucially important authenticity of your vision (Chapter 6) as well as productive behaviors and practices to allow your personal growth to take place (Chapter 7).

Part 4: Visionary Communication

Finally, we arrive at the critical ability to verbalize and communicate your vision powerfully. This marks our fourth and final stop, visionary communication (Chapter 8), which aims to make your vision speak not only to the heads, but also to the hearts of your followers.

MASTERY

The journey we'll be taking together in this book isn't the one you will undertake to absorb these ideas. That will be an individual journey. It will lead you to find opportunities in your own life, your own reality; it will lead you to work with your own challenges and potential, to put these ideas to work, to play with them, experience them, struggle with them, and transform them into something you can make your own.

Mastery follows a familiar route. (See Figure P-3.) Developing your visionary side is similar to other things you've learned, from biking to mathematics, technical to management skills. You will need to build your awareness and understanding of the various concepts involved. Next, you will need to step onto the practice field and start exploring your talents—possibly even your hidden talents. This deliberate exposure should help you figure out what works well for you and what doesn't. You'll gradually migrate from experimenting to deliberately integrating your newly developed practices into your leadership repertoire (implementing). Even-

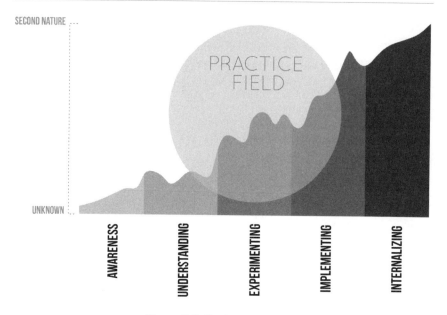

SECOND NATURE

PRACTICE FIELD

UNKNOWN

AWARENESS

UNDERSTANDING

EXPERIMENTING

IMPLEMENTING

INTERNALIZING

Figure P-3. Route to mastery.

tually, they'll become second nature to you, in ways that fit your personal style and preferences (internalizing).

To make sure you'll move beyond awareness and understanding, and actually get your feet wet and try things out, I've included various "practices" throughout. These practices are simple ideas and exercises for you to experiment with, to take from the pages of this book, and to incorporate into your daily leadership reality.

I strongly encourage you to actively engage with these practices. They can be found on the website www.visionarycapacity.com, which complements this book and includes many other resources for you to engage with. To make this as practical as possible, QR codes have been inserted to create easy access and provide further detail, background, references, video, and other media, using your smartphone as a QR code scanner. If QR scanning is not for you, you can visit the site and enter the practice number below the QR image. You will be able to explore a wealth of ideas to experiment with and that you can access whenever real life calls for it.

Collectively, this book and the digital support will provide you with what you need to create habits that will improve your visionary swing.

Practice P-1.
Sample QR Code

Many of these practices will stretch you into your *discomfort* zone. They might require some effort at times. But as our lives are already busy enough, most of them are focused on doing things differently rather than doing more things. They will help you make the move from intellectually grasping the ideas to developing routines that will make them work for you in the daily leadership practice called *life*.

Acknowledgments

First and foremost, a work like this could not have come to life without the home front support that allowed me the many hours away from my fatherly duties—thank you, and I promise to catch up now.

Taken as a whole, this book has benefited tremendously from the comments and insights given to me by Jim Keen over the years. I extend my deepest gratitude to him for our conversations, and my appreciation for our friendship. In the same vein, Tom Cummings has been instrumental in my personal transformation from the strategy to the leadership field. Without his support, and his nerve to put me in front of his clients, I would not have developed the insights laid out in this book. Thank you for our enduring friendship as well.

My agent Steve Harris has provided invaluable support to get this work noticed—thank you.

Many colleagues and friends made the book a lot better. I'm particularly thankful for the patience of Jeanine Jansen and Jaap de Jonge, who scrutinized drafts of the text and provided very helpful suggestions for improvement. The multidisciplinary angle I have taken on the subject was made possible by the numerous talented people I have met and worked with over the years. They helped me develop an understanding and appreciation for the subject that reached far beyond what I could have imagined by myself. Here's the roll call of great people, in no particular order: Jack Pinter, Nick

Van Heck, David Pearl, Thomas ten Kortenaar, Alison Peirce, Josh Patel, Paul Schoemaker, Bruce van Barthold, Didier Marlier, Elizabeth Lank, Beatrijs Verploeg, Lizzy Allen, and Eric Vogt. I'd like to add to this list those brave souls who allowed me a chance to voice my ideas in front of their clients, providing me with a great platform to get feedback, confront questions, identify my blind spots, and receive the encouragement to pursue. The continued roll call of people I'm grateful to: Lizette Cohen, Selma Spaas, Samantha Howland, Griet Ceuleers, Marianne van Iperen, Nel Hildebrand, Dave Heckman, Deb Giffen, Stan Steverink, Joris De Boulle, Claire Teurlings, Angelica Thijssen, Gonca Borekci, Esin Akay, Anna Osterlund, Saskia Vos, Ron Ettinger, and the many other clients who gave me a chance to play.

Lastly, I am deeply indebted to my editors, Lauren Starkey and Maud Bovelander, whose masterly skills—and gentle ways of treating my shortcomings—did wonders to this manuscript; my illustrator, Jet Steverink, for her artful creative interpretations; and to Teun Steverink for his skill and diligence in putting together a beautiful short movie of this book.

ANTICIPATE

Introduction

Everything is the same until it is not.

—ELLEN LANGER

UNRAVELING THE MYSTERY

"What's the one word you find in every definition of leadership?" I've asked that question many times to various audiences of senior executives around the world at the start of leadership sessions I run with them. I know what's coming. The word *vision* is almost always fired back at me. Apparently it's a no-brainer that leaders should, first and foremost, be skilled in the art of looking ahead and have a vision.

But then something interesting happens. I point out that they are all leaders and ask them if *they* have a vision. Surprisingly (or maybe not), only a few, if any, of the executives raise their hands.

This remarkable response got me thinking. If vision is one of the first things we think of when it comes to leadership—at least in theory—why is it so hard to find in practice? It can't be because there's no need for vision. In fact, a frequently heard complaint in the lower ranks of organizations is that their top leaders lack a clear vision. There's a strong desire for leadership that anticipates the future and brings direction, meaning, and inspiration. So if leaders and followers alike believe in its importance, why do so few leaders practice it?

For some, a compelling vision is like a fine work of art: it's admired, but considered out of reach for mortal souls like ourselves to create. Or it's a luxury, something we'll get to once we've got the time; right now we're just too busy with the more immediate issues, overwhelmed by our managerial responsibilities. But is the absence really due to a perceived lack of ability or time? Or is something else going on here?

As I thought about an answer, I started to explore the art of looking ahead and its expressions such as vision and anticipation. You'd think something as universally acknowledged as a critical leadership quality would be the subject of countless books, tools, and required MBA courses designed to help you grow your ability to become more visionary and future-oriented. We all recognize the importance of good health, and we find thousands of books devoted to helping us develop a healthy lifestyle. But that's not true for visionary leadership. There's almost nothing that explains how to develop and nurture our visionary capacity. At least not with the soundness, rigor, and practicality you would look for with such an important leadership quality.

So maybe we can attribute the lack of visionary leadership to an absence of knowledge and understanding about how to grow this quality. That absence would explain the lack of developmental guidance. After all, how would you be able to develop your visionary self if you don't have a clear idea of what it consists of? And subsequently, how would you know where to start and what to focus on if you wanted to become better at the art of leading by looking ahead? If this lack of understanding is true, then the start point toward visionary leadership depends on knowledge and developmental guidance. Waiting for inspiration to strike just isn't working.

This book is about unraveling the mystery of the thing called vision, in its broadest sense. From increasing our ability to look ahead and anticipate the future to turning that ability into a compelling story that ignites your followers. It's about demystifying the thing leaders, and their followers, say is so important, but that they struggle with to put into practice. We'll take vision from the realm of the mysterious into the real world, providing guidance for those who wish to become a more visionary and inspirational leader. Hopefully that includes you.

THE VISION THING

The January 26, 1987, issue of *Time* magazine featured an article on George H. W. Bush, who was serving as vice president under Ronald Reagan. It was common knowledge that he would run for president in the upcoming election. In "Where Is the Real George Bush?" journalist Robert Ajemian explored what the candidate-to-be stood for, what inspired him, what motivated him, and—above all—where he would take the United States if elected.[1] A close friend of Bush confided to the reporter that he had urged the vice president to step back, retreat to Camp David for a few days, and reflect upon these important questions. Unimpressed, Bush responded with exasperation: "Oh, you mean for 'the vision thing.'" Unconvinced, he ignored the advice.

Depending on your political views, you might wince or even chuckle at this story. You might remember that it haunted Bush throughout his career. In fact, nowadays the unfortunate quote is part of his official biography on the United States Senate website.[2] Some argue that his inability and unwillingness to create a vision was one of the main reasons Bush lost to Bill Clinton in the 1992 election.[3]

It is tempting to ridicule him for this quote. To be fair, though, it's not easy to be good at the Vision Thing. Of course we want the world's most powerful man to be more inspired in his ideas about the future, but we also need to acknowledge that creating and communicating a vision—especially a powerful, compelling one—is incredibly challenging. Even for those who aspire to lead a nation.

Creating a vision requires ideas, ideally intriguing and refreshing ideas that trigger people's interest, curiosity, and excitement. It requires engagement with your imagination and an ability to think outside the clichéd box. It requires an open mind and willingness to listen to others' unconventional ideas and, in a responsible way, incorporate these ideas into your own perspectives. It requires clarity of thought on what you fundamentally stand for: the values you maintain, the beliefs that are dear to you, the enduring commitments you have set out for yourself.

Finally, it requires the courage to voice your vision, to stand up for it, and to battle the resistance you'll inevitably face in return. Because an effective vision by definition has to be original, and therefore to some degree be provocative, maybe even slightly controversial. After all, there's very little "vision" in more of the same. And because a vision deals with the future, which is by definition unknown, it is surrounded by uncertainty. Here's where a fear factor enters the equation: Your vision could turn out to be wrong. And since we've evolved with the notion that being wrong is a bad thing, it hampers our ability to stand out with something creative and different. But as the educationalist Ken Robinson once said, "If you are not prepared to be wrong, you'll never come up with something original."

So, as much as we agree that leaders need the ability to look ahead, there's very little understanding of how to develop this competence and improve visionary capacity. It's also typically misunderstood. The reason might stem from the belief that it takes too much time. Or that our overwhelming short-term focus can't prioritize it. Or that someone is either born visionary or not. It's this same confusion Harvard Business School professor John P. Kotter observed in his landmark article, "What Leaders Really Do." He writes: "Most discussions of vision have the tendency to degenerate into the mystical. The implication is that vision is something mysterious that mere mortals, even talented ones, could never hope to have."[4] But developing a powerful vision isn't magic. It's not easy, but neither is it magic.

The truth—the premise of this book, in fact—is that *all of us* can become more visionary. My take on the term *visionary* (which we'll get to later) isn't larger-than-life, born-with-it-or-not. Instead, I believe it's something that can be developed, something that's practical and real, something that can be embraced by anyone willing to invest time into it. It's a lot like playing golf or tennis: We can all learn how to play these sports. Sure, some of us are better than others as a result of practice combined with perseverance and some natural ability. But practice and perseverance can take you a long way.

I believe the best thing you can give your followers is inspiration and purpose. It's my intention with this book to coach you on this journey. You can become a leader who provides authentic inspiration, fueled with energy, passion, and meaning. In other words, you can become a leader who understands and harnesses the art of looking ahead and who seizes the real power of the Vision Thing.

CONTEXT SENSITIVITY

Let's bring some gravitas to the argument that vision is a critical element of leadership. In an impressive effort to understand the secrets of leadership success, Harvard's Anthony Mayo and Nitin Nohria conducted an exhaustive study of a thousand of the twentieth century's most influential business leaders.[5] The results are extensively documented in their book, *In Their Time*, which provides many insights about the Vision Thing that we will review throughout. But let's first look at some of their statistical findings.

To determine those influential leaders—those who shape the way we live, work, and interact even today—Mayo and Nohria asked 7,000 executives to rank a list of 1,000 individuals. In addition, they asked respondents for their definition of a "great business leader"—what are factors that make people great?

On the latter question, five factors (see Figure I-1) dominated the responses:

Number one was the ability to articulate and harness a strategy/vision for the company. Nearly a quarter of the respondents rated this quality highest, followed closely by "pioneering" and "impact on the industry at

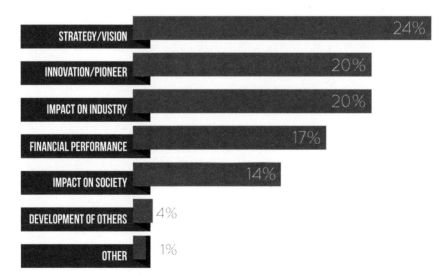

Figure I-1. Key factors for great business leaders.

large." Interestingly, the more internally oriented factor of financial performance is outweighed by externally oriented factors (vision, pioneering, and impact on industry).

Mayo and Nohria then identified and explored three executive archetypes: entrepreneurs, leaders, and managers. Yet even though representatives of each type enjoyed significant success for themselves and their organizations, the authors draw the following conclusion:

> [L]ong-term success is not derived from the sheer force of an individual's personality and character. Without a sensitivity to context, long-term success is unlikely and an individual risks being surpassed by competitors or falling victim to hubris. Companies do not succeed or fail in a vacuum.[6]

It's this pivotal factor that leadership guru Warren Bennis, whom we'll meet again later, calls *adaptive capacity*: the ability to be attuned to developments in the external environment and to act on these changes accordingly. It's this ability to anticipate and engage with these changing dynamics that make organizations—and their leaders—successful over the long run. Arie de Geus, the author of *The Living Company,* and a lifelong scholar in future-orientation and learning organizations, observed in a study he conducted during his years at Shell, that most commercial corporations have dramatic life expectancies. They die prematurely and rarely outlive the life expectancy of human beings, which is around seventy-five years.

But some do. A handful of companies on the planet have lived for hundreds of years.[7] And when de Geus studied those few companies that had been successful in navigating through the decades and centuries of change, he observed that they shared a strong sense of sensitivity to their environment. They always seemed to excel at anticipation, keeping their feelers out, tuned to whatever was going on around them. And they reacted timely to the changing conditions.[8]

So, context sensitivity and adaptive capacity are critical elements in developing visionary capacity. Hence, they are given a prominent role in our exploration, which includes practical approaches for nurturing these abilities.

SHORT-TERMISM

To enter this exploration of the Vision Thing with our eyes wide-open, we must understand its greatest enemy.

While the world is in many ways still dealing with the consequences of the worldwide financial crisis that has dominated the news since 2008, the "whodunit" question continues to surface in discussions. Yet the complex and systemic nature of the collapse makes the finger-pointing arbitrary. There were greedy bankers and hedge fund managers driven by the promise of fat bonuses; slacking regulators who turned a blind eye; central bankers who kept interest rates at irresponsibly low levels; ratings agencies that were unwilling to assess risks appropriately; unrealistic politicians who refused to tackle the tough issues; and reckless consumers who used credit to live beyond their means.

They all played a role. And they all suffered from the same disease called *short-termism*. They valued short-term gains above long-term, somewhat foreseeable, consequences—whether at personal, organizational, or societal levels. "Anyone who is willing to postpone the long-term strategy to make the short-term numbers is in route to going out of business," warned Bill George, Harvard Business School professor and former Medtronic CEO, in a plea to rethink capitalism.[9] He is very concerned about the effects of excessive Wall Street orientation and the aggressive influence of activist shareholders looking for short-term gains. As an advocate of the long-term perspective, his recommendation is that "it's extremely important for management of a company and the board of directors to get alignment over the long-term goals and objectives and strategy to get there, and then to shape its investor base to match that goal. Do not let your shareholders manage you; you have to manage them. You have to say what we're going to be."

Hence, he's not merely finger-pointing external forces, but he underlines the responsibility of developing a clear future-oriented perspective in order to fight the pressures that work against it. In itself, this is nothing new, and if anything, it should be one of the most important lessons learned from the crisis that hit us so hard.

Remarkably though, that research by McKinsey five years after the near meltdown of 2008 seems to suggest that little of that learning has actually taken root. Sixty-three percent of responding managers admitted that the pressure to make high short-term profits had increased since the start of the crisis, and nearly four out of five managers (79 percent) reported that maximizing profits for the next two years was still a priority.[10] Most (86 percent) declared that using a longer time horizon to make business decisions would positively affect corporate performance. The awareness seems to be there, but regrettably, despite the ice-cold shower of the financial crisis, the lessons are not learned or applied. Short-termism has not been overthrown; instead it seems to have increased. Today, bankers heading financial institutions that were bailed out by public money because of their recklessness have their confidence back and are arguing against intensified regulatory oversights.

We're supposed to learn from the past, but short-term success appears to shield our willingness to accept long-term implications.

LONG-TERM LANGUAGE

Fortunately, there are a few enlightened leaders who have learned from these mistakes. Sir David Walker, the chairman of Barclays Bank since 2012, publicly admitted that investment bankers' focus on short-term targets has caused enormous damages.[11] More concretely, Paul Polman, CEO of Unilever since 2009, doesn't just talk the talk. Polman decided short-term investor anxiety would hinder his plan for structural renewal of the company, designed to prepare it for the future and for long-term benefits. He set lofty and challenging transformational goals for the company (and himself), such as a 50 percent reduction of the greenhouse gas impact of Unilever products and 100 percent sustainable sourcing of raw materials, and pledged to help one billion people improve hygiene. He recognizes that such shifts require time and perseverance, and the road ahead is not a straight line. Short-term investors breathing down his neck would be unsuitable for this journey, so he did away with quarterly earnings reporting and told hedge funds they are no longer welcome as investors[12]—a huge and controversial step for a publicly listed multinational.

Leaders like Walker and Polman are up against a tough opponent. Short-termism has deep roots, and the influence of short-term-oriented investors continues to grow. But at the same time another study pointed out that blaming short-termism on external factors is too simplistic.[13] Francois

Brochet, George Serafeim, and Maria Loumioti analyzed the language used in over 70,000 earnings conference calls by more than 3,600 companies between 2002 and 2008. By counting the words and phrases that suggest both short- and long-term emphases, they found that businesses that leaned strongly toward short-term results, judged by the language they used, attracted short-term-oriented investors. Short-termism, then, is at least partially self-imposed and not just externally enforced by investors.

It's no surprise that family businesses, by and large, have weathered the financial crisis much better than those operating under markets mantras. Stijn Swinkels, currently the seventh-generation family member heading international brewery Bavaria Beer, likes to say that "we borrow the company from our children." A mindset defined by such values makes it far less likely to lose sight of the long term than a mindset that keeps thinking of "quarterly results" and "increasing shareholder value."

On the bright side, there is hope. Executives can influence the type of investors they attract, just as Paul Polman found, by adjusting the horizon they take when communicating about their business. The absence of a long-term view, or the inability to formulate and communicate one powerfully, not only draws like-minded investors but also reinforces short-term thinking and behavior. The presence of a powerful vision attracts a different type of investor.

THE BATTLE

Can a vision survive against this backdrop of intrinsic, hard-to-battle short-termism? It's a tough question. Short-termism is the biggest enemy of developing visionary capacity for both the organization and the individual leader. Compelling visions rarely have immediate monetary returns. In fact, the immediate consequences of a powerful vision might be detrimental to short-term results. The fear of affecting these short-term results often prevents leaders from making the kinds of organizational transformations they would want to make if they were faithful to their long-term view.

To return to Bill George's thoughts once more, he underscores this long-term responsibility in current leadership. "You cannot put a strategy in place today in the pharmaceutical industry, in the automobile industry, in the food industry with less than a seven- to ten-year time frame. That's how long it takes. Particularly [for] companies going through a cultural transformation it takes closer to ten years to get it done."[14] Witness the print industry: In December 2012, *Newsweek* published its last print issue after its subscriber base and advertising revenue had shrunk by 50 percent and 80 percent, respectively, over ten years. (In March 2014 *Newsweek* relaunched its print edition under new ownership and with a different business model that no longer relies on advertising income.)

This is the publishing industry's new reality. An aging subscriber base won't get replaced with new, younger subscribers that have grown used to free digital content. At the same time and as a result, advertisers are increasingly moving to digital platforms, depleting the second main income stream for the print industry. Publishers soon need to face the obvious choice: Follow *Newsweek*'s December 2012 decision and stop printing, or reinvent oneself to find a new, profitable model. (A third possibility is to mindlessly stick your head in the sand and hope it will all blow over, a strategy that, at the time of this writing, still has a remarkable popularity.)

Most executives lean toward the second option, transform, even though—as pointed out by Bill George—transformation tends to be slow and results in the immediate future are likely to be weak. From the long-term point of view, though, it's their only option. So, if you are leading a publishing house today, you better have a compelling vision for the future of your business. It won't be easy, but it should have the highest priority over anything else. And you better be prepared to fight a battle with short-termism. You will need shareholders with a long-term perspective who will allow you the time to transform. This is what Paul Polman understood so well when he led his organization forward: On this journey, there is no room for short-term-oriented hedge fund managers who enter only with an interim perspective to make a quick win (even though they would never admit that).

To conclude, a powerful vision isn't just *nice to have*. It's the most important tool in the transformational leader's toolbox. "Where there is no vision, there is no hope," is how George Washington Carver dramatically put it. You need a compelling story to inspire people to join the transformational journey and persuade them to stick around for the long run. But how do you do that? That's the real question. And that's where we are heading.

PART 1

1 VISIONARY CONTENT 2 VISIONARY PRACTICES 3 VISIONARY SELF 4 VISIONARY COMMUNICATION

1

The Groundwork

Mostly, however, it is the future that has attracted man's dreams, hopes, and fears. The future rather than the past is seen as holding the key to the riddle of his existence.

—FRED POLAK

YOUR PERSONAL VISION

I've been toying with the word *vision* for a long time. In two decades of work with arrived and aspiring leaders, from executive boardrooms to business school classrooms, I've noticed that the word instantly stirs up passionate debate. Debate about our company vision, debate about whether or not our leaders have one, debate on the current humdrum or unrealistic version that's on the company website, and debate about whether it is of any real value at all to have a vision. I've heard everything from "Finally, we're talking about what's really important," to "Oh please! Not another hazy discussion on that abstract notion that won't help me deliver results."

What I've learned from these debates is that the Vision Thing intrigues and frustrates at the same time. We look up to people and companies that seemed to have mastered it, but feel thwarted in achieving similar results. Most people agree that, when understood and practiced well, vision can be an extraordinarily powerful concept; a tool, in fact, that significantly bolsters your ability to influence. Highly respected scholars in the field of leadership even put vision at the center of it. Harvard Business School professor Abraham Zaleznik declared vision the hallmark of leadership,[1] and when Warren Bennis studied leaders he noticed that "of all the characteristics that distinguished the individuals, the most pivotal was a concern with a guiding purpose, an overarching vision."[2]

But when the idea of a vision isn't framed properly, it quickly becomes muddy and fuzzy, incomplete and unproductive, and loses the interest of those you wish to engage. A proper understanding and agreement of terms around the concept of *vision* is therefore essential, so I'll first clarify in this chapter what I do and don't mean when using the term before we start improving your ability to make it work for you.

Above all, I want to make a clear distinction between the *company* vision and your *personal* vision. In contrast to most strategy textbooks that usually allude to company vision, we will focus on your personal vision throughout this work. My aim is to increase your *personal visionary capacity* and bring out what a powerful vision can do for your personal leadership—whether or not you are hierarchically in a senior position.

After all, vision is not an exclusive for those in top-ranked positions. I have seen many people lower down the ranks galvanize their teams with a highly motivating and inspiring future-oriented perspective. Those team members took energy from the personal vision of the one leader that was most relevant for them: their immediate boss. That energy did not depend on the company vision; it was the boss's personalized version that made it work. It was the boss's attitude to look ahead and go beyond the immediate reality of today that provided meaning and direction.

Admittedly, in a corporate context, it often does imply that your *personal* vision as a leader needs to reasonably align and live within the constraints of the *company* vision. But to me that's in a way just an aside, just as your personal vision needs to live within ethical and legal boundaries. That's not what this is about. Your compelling story has everything to do with igniting excitement in those people who look to you for leadership. Your personal imagination and inspiration is what counts for them. It's *your* dedication and *your* authenticity that they are looking for; it's about the story that *you* bring to them, and much less about what is stated on the corporate website.

I'm not implying that a company vision statement is not useful or desirable. Crisp, empowering company statements can be extraordinary useful. Microsoft's original idea of "having a computer in every home running Microsoft software" is often rightfully cited as a showcase of excellent company vision statements. Less glamorous firms like Progressive Insurance have managed to arrive at a rich company vision statement. Progressive's vision is "to reduce the human trauma associated with automobile accidents," which has opened up new areas of servicing clients and outperforming peers by operating differently and offering "unusual" products and services. Or think of Ben and Jerry's mission: "Making the best possible ice cream, in the nicest possible way."

These are examples of very powerful company vision statements. Unfortunately, these great examples often seem to be the exception to the rule. With the rule being that in most companies the company vision is good stuff for the marketing department that—after lengthy debate—ends up pulling together a series of trendy buzzwords to dazzle the public. The statement usually lacks all the ingredients of a *powerful* vision—including something that inspires, such as unconventionality, meaning, and authenticity.

But all that is company vision terrain. The one I talk about throughout this book is your *personal* vision, the compelling future orientation you want to develop to ignite *your* followers. It is a leadership marker, something that reflects who you are as a leader and inspires others to enlist for action—regardless of whether that is three or 30,000 people.

VISION 101

Let's explore some basic themes first, before we move to a more foundational perspective later on in this chapter.

A vision is future-oriented. That probably sounds quite self-evident. Yet there is quite a bit more to this obvious observation. Since it is about the future, which is intrinsically uncertain, it is predominantly a product of imagination. You might have some beliefs, hunches, and past patterns to support your ideas, but it remains an opinion that cannot be backed up with factual experiences, research, and other quantifiable data. That simple reality already explains why people find it so difficult to imaginatively look ahead, since we have mostly evolved in a business reality where facts and figures are deemed very important. So unlocking your imagination is an important aspect of developing your ability to anticipate.

A vision is therefore a particular form of opinion. It's one that—when done right—evokes energy and inspiration. A well-developed vision stimulates our thinking and opens us up to new possibilities. This creativity aspect unleashes playfulness and curiosity, which produces positive energy. This makes it very different from opinions based purely on logic and reasoning, which quickly bog us down and impede our imagination.

Powerful visions have at least four fundamental purposes.

A Vision Shows the Path Forward

A vision provides guidance and direction about where an organization (or a country, a team, or any other group) is headed. In the traditional notion of strategy, the vision is the starting point. It helps everyone involved decide what to focus on, what horizon we aim for, what boundaries and constraints to be wary of, and subsequently how to set priorities, resolve conflicts, and overcome the inevitable challenges that arise as strategy rolls out.

Take, for example, the state of Dubai, which grew in just a few decades from a desert village into a glittering global financial hub and tourist destination. This development stemmed from the vision of one man, Sheikh Mohammed bin Rashid al-Maktoum. Realizing that the region's oil supply would one day run out, he transformed Dubai into a modern city that would be able to thrive in an oil-free future. The Sheikh's book, aptly titled *My Vision,* provided explicit directions, which have been followed diligently since the early 1990s, for achieving a high growth rate. Focusing on excellence in service and industry, he oversaw the development of Dubai with a vision that was clear, direction setting, and left little room for misinterpretation.

Without doubt the Sheikh's deep pockets of oil wealth have been instrumental in realizing this imagined future—it wasn't his innovative capacity that got him to accumulate this wealth. And from our contemporary view on management, we can have reservations about aspects of the aristocratic leadership style of the region. But those objections aside, it is evident that his ability to look well into the future and develop a clear and unconventional direction for Dubai stands out in the region. Neighboring countries such as Oman, Bahrain, Kuwait, and Qatar, which similarly accumulated tremendous wealth from their oil reserves, now look up to Dubai as they start to wake up to a reality in which their oil exports and income will begin to diminish in the foreseeable future. But they are twenty years behind Dubai, where the Sheikh saw this inevitable change much earlier and developed the emirate's post-oil-era direction.

Therefore, a vision is the essential starting point from which to develop a strategic agenda that ensures you get where you want to be and helps you tackle any barriers that might come up in the process. "Strategic planning is worthless unless there is first a strategic vision," the prominent futurist John Naisbitt once said.

A Vision Stretches the Imagination

A potent vision takes us beyond the obvious into the unknown and stretches the boundaries of what we conventionally think up to that point in time. President John F. Kennedy's 1961 speech to a joint session of Congress, announcing the goal of "put[ting] a man on the moon by the end of the decade," stretched the imagination of a nation. It became not only a source of patriotic pride, but also a driving force behind a tremendous amount of technological and educational innovation.

Admittedly, it was also fueled by Cold War tensions: The speech was delivered a month after the embarrassment of the Bay of Pigs invasion as well as the Soviet Union's achievement of manned space flight. After careful examination of their options, President Kennedy and a small group of high-ranking officials concluded that putting a man on the moon was the best way to beat the Soviets. But the challenge was a colossal one. Kennedy stressed, "No single space project . . . will be more impressive to mankind, or more important for the long-range exploration of space; and none will be so difficult or expensive to accomplish."

It was a powerful long-term perspective that surpassed the obvious, stretching the imagination into *unconventional* territory without becoming absurd—otherwise it would have quickly lost its power.

A Vision Challenges the Status Quo
and Breaks Through Existing Paradigms

In addition to stretching the imagination, a well-developed vision can provide new and previously "unseen" opportunities. Challenging our current way of thinking can help us break through existing paradigms to find fresh ways of working, thinking, and behaving. This is why unlocking your imagination, freeing yourself from the constraints of existing assumptions, beliefs, and dogmas, is vital to nurturing your visionary capacity. We'll explore this subject more extensively in the next chapter, but let's briefly look at the story of IKEA to illustrate the point.

Ingvar Kamprad, IKEA's Swedish founder, became one of the wealthiest people of our time by building an empire on his vision that "design furniture should not only be accessible to the happy few." He wanted to offer attractive, functional products in a low price range.

But this is where the vision ran into difficulties. It either had to overcome barriers—namely, the existing furniture industry model—or remain a dream. Kamprad needed to find a way to get to prices well below standard levels, breaking through the paradigms of traditional thinking (or, in this case, traditional ways of production, distribution, and sales). He challenged the entire model of the furniture industry by handing over the parts and assembly instructions to the end user. Kamprad created a highly efficient model that significantly cut back on production and distribution costs. IKEA's philosophy, "You do a little, we do a little, together we save a lot," succinctly captures the company's focus on customer involvement and cost savings.

Experimentation, challenging conventions, and willingness to embrace failure—all are required to successfully toy with reality, as Kamprad did. Also, at IKEA the path from concept to industry leader wasn't as smooth as it seems when the story gets retold decades later. The real story was one of trial and error, with some smart ideas and some crazy ones ("Manland," an area of the store dubbed "daycare for dudes," may be one of them). But fundamental to the journey was a recognition that the current belief system needed to be challenged in order to reach the "better future." That's what a powerful vision can provide.

A Vision Energizes and Mobilizes

Finally, a powerful vision provides something very few other leadership tools can: It has the potential to galvanize those you lead. A vision inspires people to put their best effort into the cause. It unites them around a shared purpose, gives meaning to the day job, and mobilizes them into action. Think of what Martin Luther King, Steve Jobs, and Richard Branson accomplished with their visions.

And it's not only these larger-than-life, charismatic leaders who benefit from a vision's energizing power. It also works for people with names such as Peter Kapitein, Scott Brusaw, Chanda Kochhar, Jørn Utzon, Taïg Khris, and Malcolm McLean. You might not have heard of them, but you'll meet them in this book. They are fairly "ordinary" people—probably much more like you and me—who also made the Vision Thing work for them by mobilizing people behind their endeavors and dreams, inspiring them with a direction-setting, imaginative, and often paradigm-breaking idea, and following through on them with passion and dedication.

TRANSFORMATIONAL LEADERSHIP

In 1977, Abraham Zaleznik of Harvard Business School threw a rock in the pond of management theory with his article "Managers and Leaders: Are They Different?" and invigorated a vivid debate among academics around the theme of leadership. The field hasn't been the same since. In his article, Zaleznik pointed out that management theory had missed half the picture thus far. The focus had been on rationality and control, with themes such as goals, organization structures, and resources. The view of the manager was that of a problem solver, succeeding through hard work, analytical abilities, and tough-mindedness. But "managerial leadership unfortunately does not necessarily ensure imagination, creativity, or ethical behavior in guiding the destinies of corporate enterprises,"[3] he pointed out.

He brought forward avant-garde themes such as inspiration, integrity, emotional commitment, drives, and motivation; themes we now commonly associate with leadership and that seem so obvious once expressed. In realizing this kind of leadership, he underlined the importance of vision:

Where managers act to limit choices, leaders develop fresh approaches to long-standing problems and open issues to new options. To be effective, leaders must project their ideas onto images that excite people and only then develop choices that give those images substance.[4]

That image is the vision. The four purposes of vision we just covered illustrate the key differences between leaders and managers once more. A manager's role is a very important one (let's not underestimate the inherent difficulties of being a good manager!), but it essentially boils down to keeping things on track. A leader's role is fundamentally different. It's about transformation, about motivating and inspiring people to move toward a new reality. Another eminent thinker we met before, John Kotter, continued the path broken open by Zaleznik. In his 1990 article "What Leaders Really Do," Kotter stated: "What leaders really do is prepare the organization for change and help them cope as they struggle through it."[5] To achieve this organizational change, a leader must stretch the imagination, challenge the status quo, show a way forward, break through existing paradigms, energize and mobilize people to follow . . . In other words, a leader needs all the elements a vision brings.

So how does a vision connect with contemporary views on *leadership?* The concept of leadership is a dynamic one, trending through strategic leadership, situational leadership, authentic leadership, charismatic leadership, team leadership, servant leadership, and vigilant leadership, to name a few. But ever since Zaleznik and Kotter paved the way for seeing leadership in the light of pressing for change, most attention in the arena of leadership research goes toward *transformational leadership,*[6] emphasizing intrinsic motivation, follower development, inspiration, and empowerment—all elements that are closely aligned with contemporary thinking about success in a turbulent, increasingly uncertain, and complex world.

In his standard work, *Leadership: Theory and Practice,* Peter Northouse, a professor at Western Michigan University, defines transformational leadership as:

[T]he process whereby a person engages with others and creates a connection that raises the level of motivation and morality in both the leader and the follower. This type of leadership is attentive to the needs and motives of followers and tries to help followers reach their fullest potential.[7]

The concept of transformational leadership is very rich; it includes moral standards, role modeling, ethics, and other important concepts. But central to this view on leadership is the role of a compelling vision. According to Northouse:

> The vision is a focal point for transformational leadership. It gives the leader and the organization a conceptual map for where the organization is headed; it gives meaning and clarifies the organization's identity. Furthermore, the vision gives followers a sense of identity within the organizations and also a sense of self-efficacy.[8]

So again, as stated in the introduction, a vision is more than a nice-to-have. It's not something we should get to once we have the luxury to think about it. It's the cornerstone in contemporary thinking on leadership and a critical aspect for everyone aspiring to lead.

THE ALPE D'HUZES

So far, I've relied on larger-than-life examples of leaders to demonstrate the points. While these leaders serve well as illustrations, since we all know them, they come with a risk of alienation. Visionary leadership isn't just for charismatic, legendary heroes who seemingly stepped down from heaven to personally do God's work on earth. It is just as useful to far less heroic and iconic people working in less glamorous roles under less obvious spotlights.

Take Peter Kapitein, an "ordinary" program manager at the Central Bank of the Netherlands. His story starts with a diagnosis of lymph node cancer in January 2005. With treatment, his cancer was brought under control, and he joined several other cancer patients and cycling fanatics to raise funds for cancer research. They started an event they call the Alpe d'HuZes, playfully morphing the name of the legendary French mountain Alpe d'Huez that is often the decisive leg in the Tour de France cycling race.

The *Zes* in the name means "six" in Dutch, because here's what the event entails: Kapitein and his group decided to scale the famous mountain not once, but *six times* in one day. To put that in perspective: the Alpe d'Huez has twenty-one hairpin turns that need to be navigated while climbing 13.8 kilometers at an average gradient of 7.9 percent. It's a serious climb with some daunting slopes that takes a professional cyclist about an hour to complete and a well-trained amateur about one and a half hours. That's one and a half hours of straight uphill climbing. It's bad enough to go up once. But Kapitein's group decided to do it six times in one day!

The event ran for the first time in 2006 with Kapitein and a handful of friends and supporters. Today, it's the largest cancer research fund-raising initiative in the Netherlands, with over 15,000 participants in 2012. From an original 400,000 euros raised in 2006, the Alpe d'HuZes now raises more than 20 million euros annually.

But despite its incredible success and glorious legacy, this community of cycling fanatics has faced—and continues to face—tragedy as well. Each year, several participants can no longer make the climb, losing or having lost their battle against cancer. One of them was Bas Mulder, an Alpe d'HuZes founder. He continued to participate despite the recurrence of his cancer, following his life's motto to never give up. His perseverance and positivism became a source of great inspiration to many. In 2010, he lost his battle and passed away at age 24.

At his close friend's funeral, Kapitein vowed to find out why cancer had spared him but not his friend Bas Mulder. He followed through on his promise by starting a new initiative, Inspire2Live (www.inspire2live.org), with the aim to bring together the world's leading researchers and institutions to accelerate the fight against cancer.

Supported by his employer, he spent several months traveling and meeting with some of the world's most renowned thought leaders on cancer treatment. On January 14, 2011, Kapitein hosted a conference called "Understanding Life" in Amsterdam. He invited all the people he had spoken with. On that day, eighty of the world's leading cancer experts, including several Nobel Prize winners, showed up.

But wait a second. Why would these highly successful and sought-after thought leaders from around the globe show up at a conference arranged by a banking manager? If you're among that selective breed of world-class doctors and researchers, you manage your time very carefully. There's no shortage of conferences and events around the world that want you as a speaker or guest. You could attend one every day if you wanted to. And although Kapitein had learned a lot about cancer over the years and clearly knew his way around the field, he didn't hold any significant academic credentials or remarkable research results—important factors for attracting top researchers to a conference. So why would they travel all the way to Amsterdam for his conference?

The answer is simple. Kapitein focused the invitation and discussion on one thing only: his vision that, by 2020, cancer would no longer be a deadly disease but a chronic one. Instead of seeking a cure, he sought ways to control it, much like what the medical community did with HIV two decades earlier. That's what convinced them to join and compelled them to contribute.

The world's leading scientists wholeheartedly embraced Kapitein's recasting of Kennedy's "man on the moon by the end of the decade" vision. They concluded the conference by declaring the vision feasible. It would neither be easy nor straightforward, and it might not apply to all types of cancer. But for the first time, the lack of cooperation and practice-sharing between the different cancer disciplines was addressed and discussed. A concerted effort between them would make it possible to significantly outperform the current pace of development. This was the story that mobilized them to go to Amsterdam and work toward this shared goal.

In this way, an "ordinary" person like Peter Kapitein—no larger-than-life leader—is getting the Vision Thing to work for him and making the adjective *ordinary* a misnomer. He provides direction, stretches the imagination, breaks through paradigms, and energizes and mobilizes a large group of people to join and work toward his vision.

CORE INGREDIENTS

So far, I've loosely described the components that constitute a vision, its four key purposes, and an idea of the power it could give you as a leader. Let's now dig deeper and identify the specific core ingredients that combine to create great results on the vision front.

We've seen that there are always elements of *guidance and direction setting*: A vision shows us a future ideal to strive for. The element of direction setting is critical, because followers use it to guide the decisions they make, the initiatives they start, and the priorities they set. "Since the function of leadership is to produce change, setting the direction of that change is fundamental to leadership,"[9] Harvard Business School's John Kotter affirms.

But that's only the rational, cerebral part; it needs something else, something more, to make it compelling and powerful. Followers need to *feel* something in order to really spark their enthusiasm. They need to be touched emotionally; they need to feel motivated and energized. When this emotional dimension comes together with the cognitive one, the inspirational level rises significantly. In Chapter 3—in the section titled Visionary Shoes—we'll explore some research into the *followers' effect* of a vision and discover that emotional engagement has even more impact on followers than the rational aspect does.

So how does this emotional layer become part of it? How can you make your future-oriented story touch your followers emotionally and reach their hearts rather than their heads? There are two elements that predominantly ignite this emotional factor:

- *Unconventionality.* Unconventionality triggers emotions such as curiosity, excitement, desire, optimism, and empowerment. President Kennedy's vision is one example I've already cited. Steve Jobs was a master at making this connection, grasping every opportunity to tell his people that "at Apple we are revolutionizing the world." Jobs consistently emphasized the unconventionality of whatever Apple was doing. Remember the "Think different" slogan? We also see this connection at play in Kamprad's unconventional furniture model at IKEA and Kapitein's unconventional view on the future of cancer research.

- *Connection to a Noble Cause.* This connection sparks emotions such as pride, belonging, willingness, passion, nobility, warmth, empathy, and trust. Just to be clear, the noble cause need not be something as hippy-ish and vague as peace on earth. "Revolutionizing the world at Apple" involves a noble cause: drastically improving the accessibility and usability of technology. Kamprad, while pursuing a less noble goal of making lots of money, hitched his vision to the unfairness that only the happy few could afford well-designed furniture.

At least one of these two emotional factors—unconventionality and noble cause—should be present in order to allow emotional attachment to a vision. Ideally, though, a vision should include both. Consider the case of Peter Kapitein: The idea of transforming cancer from a lethal to a chronic disease by 2020 is both unconventional *and* noble.

LOGOS, ETHOS, AND PATHOS

Are these elements of direction setting and emotional engagement the only key ingredients? Not quite. There is a third and final ingredient that's of crucial importance when creating a powerful vision. Nearly 2,500 years ago, the Greek philosopher Aristotle already described the art of persuasion, of getting people to follow a leader. In *On Rhetoric* (350 BCE) he wrote:

> Of the modes of persuasion furnished by the spoken word there are three kinds. [. . .] Persuasion is achieved by the speaker's personal character when the speech is so spoken as to make us think him credible. [...] Secondly, persuasion may come through the hearers, when the speech stirs their emotions. [. . .] Thirdly, persuasion is effected through the speech itself when we have proved a truth or an apparent truth by means of the persuasive arguments suitable to the case in question.[10]

According to Aristotle, in order to persuade followers, a leader needs (in reverse order) convincing arguments, the emotions they elicit, and credibility. Today we refer to his threefold description as *Logos*, *Pathos*, and *Ethos*—the cornerstones for creating engagement.

Logos means that the message needs to make sense and not crumble under scrutiny. Followers must be able to understand the rationale of what you are trying to do. In Aristotle's words, "persuasion is effected through the speech itself when we have proved a truth or apparent truth by means of persuasive arguments." If the argument isn't logically consistent, it's unlikely that followers will buy into it (or at least not with the intensity we'd like them to). Logos, in other words, aligns with the *setting direction* part of a vision: Followers need to understand clearly and coherently why you are taking them in a particular direction.

But that only covers the cognitive part. Without the help of a marketing department, Aristotle figured out that understanding alone would not suffice. Followers must be emotionally moved and touched by your words. In addition to a logically consistent argument, they need a more compelling reason to go the extra mile. As Aristotle wrote, "persuasion may come through the hearers, when the speech stirs their emotion." We refer to this quality as Pathos, which connects to the emotional engagement I spoke of. Think about the way unconventionality and a noble cause (ideally in combination) work to create a powerful vision: They allow for an emotional engagement that goes beyond the rational and make followers part of something more meaningful and enduring.

Aristotle's third element has been missing from our discussion so far. It refers to the integrity or character of the speaker. Aristotle called this Ethos: "Persuasion is achieved by the speaker's personal character when the speech is so spoken as to make us think him credible." If your behavior and integrity do not fully align with your vision, if your followers cannot associate your words with your character and your actions, the words will be considered empty and meaningless. Leaders need to exemplify the vision in everything they do, to connect it to personal values, motives, and deeper emotions. It's this famous *walk the talk* criterion that makes us trust or mistrust leaders. It is often also the first thing people look for when confronted with the leader's vision toward a new reality: Is the leader willing to personally change accordingly, or are these just hollow phrases?

Does the triad of Logos, Ethos, Pathos sound familiar? Remember Peter Northouse's definition of transformational leadership: "a conceptual map for where the organization is headed" (the Logos part of the vision), "it gives meaning and clarifies the organization's identity" (closely associated with Ethos, which is about values, identity, and integrity), and "the vision gives followers a sense of identity within the organizations and also a sense of self-efficacy" (the Pathos part, which is about a feeling of belonging and pride).

How to integrate Logos, Ethos, and Pathos into your vision and leadership behavior will be the focus of Chapters 6, 7, and 8. Let's leave them for now and focus on one final, essential piece to help us create a foundation for our understanding of the Vision Thing. For that, we will need to descend into the basement—or, actually, the graveyard.

THE DARK SIDE

By now, I hope you are convinced that a compelling vision commands unique leadership powers. Good. Now I'm going to put a damper on your enthusiasm for a minute, or at least inject some realism. Our subject has a flip side we can't ignore.

Because of its ability to energize and mobilize, a vision can be highly effective in mobilizing in toxic and undesirable ways. It can persuade people to engage in fraudulent behavior, as we saw at Enron, the infamous energy giant that went belly-up in 2001. Only a year before its demise, Enron was rated the most innovative large company in the United States in *Fortune* magazine's annual Most Admired Companies survey (for the sixth consecutive year). Enron stated on many occasions that it set out to revolutionize the U.S. energy market. Direction setting? Check. Unconventional? Check.

But that appealing goal also created a culture in which people became not only highly entrepreneurial, but also blind to fraud. They rationalized dubious business practices and justified nearly any action that would help them achieve their "lofty" goals. Extraordinary risk taking became commonplace for the senior leaders of Enron, whether in the boardroom or on team-building retreats. An obsession with increasingly extreme sports illustrated a culture that only rewarded those with the nerve to test their limits. The vision led to prison terms, the dissolution of one of the world's top-five accounting firms, and the largest corporate bankruptcy in U.S. history at the time.

Moreover, dictators throughout history have had their visions. Stalin, Hitler, and Bin Laden all painted a picture of a "better" world, which—technically—could be considered unconventional and paradigm shifting. They demonstrated their ability to energize and mobilize large numbers of people and easily connected their ideas to causes that, in their distorted worldviews, were deemed noble.

These are just the most obvious examples of how a vision can do tremendous harm. They often come together with narcissistic leadership styles. As pointed out by psychoanalyst and anthropologist Michael Maccoby, narcissistic leadership thrives in a world of tremendous change, where visionary leadership is called for. "Productive narcissists understand the vision thing particularly well, because they are by nature people who see the big picture,"[11] he says. "Narcissistic leaders are often skillful orators, and this is one of the talents that makes them so charismatic. Indeed, anyone who has seen narcissists perform can attest to their personal magnetism and their ability to stir enthusiasm among audiences."[12] So this style and the illusion of invulnerability that radiates from it, no matter how reassuring at moments of uncertainty, provide the perfect setup for toxic and tunneled versions of the aspired future.

But there is more to be concerned about—an even harder to catch "dark side" aspect. This happens when the vision isn't in the spotlight, when it does its damage under cover and over time. In 1662, the French physicist and Roman Catholic priest Edme Mariotte discovered that every eye has a blind spot.[13] At the point where the optic nerve exits the retina to the brain, there are no cells to detect light. So biologically, part of the field of vision is simply not observed. The brain makes up for it by filling in the gap, extrapolating from what it has perceived, and "guessing" what the missing information might be. For the brain, that guess becomes as much a fact as observed reality.

It can be the same for the Vision Thing. There are always things we don't perceive—and that's when two potentially dangerous things can happen. First, we might miss the signal altogether and get caught by our (metaphorical) blind spots. This is rooted in our psychology; we often don't see what we don't want to know. Worse, we are sometimes incentivized to *ignore* the signal, especially when our job, relationship with our boss, or mortgage payment depend on it. And this incentive works wonderfully well in having us ignore reality. (For a convincing read on this "quality" of incentives, check out Steven Levitt and Stephen Dubner's *Freakonomics*.)

Second, and equally as dangerous, our brain makes up for the missed signal—as with the biological blind spot—and fills the gap. We *convince* ourselves that we saw something we didn't actually see. It might be that the "observed" signal never existed, or that we morphed something we did see into something we wish we had seen. Again, psychology helps to explain these phenomena, and we will review them more extensively throughout this book. The point is that they blur our perception. The fact that they're so powerful and so easy to believe warrants us to be careful with what we base our conclusions on. That's especially important when we are dealing with the future, when facts and figures are still missing and all we have are weak signals, beliefs, assumptions, and our imaginations.

The more responsibility you have in your leadership position, the more powerfully a vision can affect the future of your organization and your followers, the more conscious you must be of these imperfections. We should never underestimate the power of a vision—a power that can be used for good as well as for ill.

Starting in Chapter 3, I'll focus on the how-tos of reaping the benefits while watching out for the inherent dangers. First, let's explore a subject central to developing our ability to look ahead and better anticipate the future—the productive use of your imagination.

2

Tapping into Your Imagination

Vision, the hallmark of leadership, is less a derivative of spreadsheets and more a product of the mind called imagi-nation.

—ABRAHAM ZALEZNIK

REJUVENATED RESTAURANTS

A San Francisco restaurant owner once asked creativity guru Edward de Bono for advice. The restaurant had been popular in the neighborhood for years. But as the area developed, several other restaurants opened their doors nearby. The increase in choices for his customers brought about a gradual decrease in revenue. Distressed with the downturn, the owner called on de Bono to help find a new edge.

When they met at the restaurant, de Bono asked for a tour. The owner showed him the seating area, the kitchen, the storage room, the cellar, and the office space above. They finished the tour at the bar, where de Bono thanked the owner for the tour and said, "It seems like a great place you're running here. Now I'm wondering, which part of the restaurant are you most proud of?" Without missing a beat, the owner replied, "The kitchen of course. You've seen the equipment—it's the best. And the workspace is perfect. Our kitchen produces amazing, high-quality food, which is the heart of our formula, and will always remain so. We just need to find a way to promote that again, and win our customers back."

After a moment's consideration, de Bono remarked, "Let's see—you want to revive your business. And you are most proud of the kitchen." He pondered for a while and suddenly said: "Let's get rid of the kitchen."

The restaurant owner was shocked; it wasn't the advice he'd expected—or wanted—to hear. Worse, this consult was costing him serious money. "What do you mean, get rid of the kitchen?" he replied, unable to hide his panic. "That's the heart of our business; that's what we stand for; that's who we are," he said, exasperated.

"Well," de Bono said calmly, "if you want to revive your business, you should get rid of the kitchen."

"But how can we run a restaurant without a kitchen?" the owner bemoaned.

Detecting early signs of a subtle shift in the owner's thinking—from denial to resistance laced with some curiosity—de Bono said, "Let's think about it. What would happen if you no longer had a kitchen? What would your restaurant look like? What would people come here to do? What would attract them? What would be some of the barriers for you to overcome?"

Although the restaurant owner still wasn't comfortable with the idea, the questions did make him think. "What if we weren't a restaurant at all, you mean?"

"No," de Bono said. "Stay focused on the concept of a restaurant. But without a kitchen."

The restaurant owner, albeit still unconvinced, started to play along. "Well, for one thing, we could use the kitchen space to double the size of the seating area."

"And how would that be attractive for your customers?" de Bono prompted.

"Well, our seating area hasn't changed in years; we might be able to remodel it to give it a more upscale, spacious look. Maybe we could even create various different atmospheres to match the moods of our customers." The restaurant owner, moving beyond his initial resistance, was starting to explore the seemingly impossible idea of a restaurant without a kitchen. "We could actually run it without chefs, which would be a relief, because it's not easy to find good ones in this area. But there is one big barrier we'd have to overcome: How would we get food on the table?"

"You're right," de Bono said. "That is a barrier. What could you do about that?"

The restaurant owner considered some possibilities: "Do we get people to bring it themselves? Should we do something with astronaut food? Should we provide a little kitchenette? Or some sort of oven at the tables so they could make their own food?" He continued to suggest ideas—some good ones, some ridiculous ones—and de Bono didn't interrupt, careful not to condemn any of them.

And then came the epiphany. "Wait a minute," the restaurant owner said. "We could get the food from other restaurants. There are Thai, Indian, Spanish, Portuguese, Ethiopian, Mexican, and Italian places nearby. We could become an extra outlet for them, as well as the restaurant with the widest menu choices. And offer that in a modern, upscale atmosphere that fits the type of people that have come to live in this neighborhood in recent years." He was getting excited, a new formula was born: a voguish restaurant that sourced its food offerings through a nifty logistical system and partnerships with its neighboring colleagues.

Six months later, the restaurant was again the neighborhood's hot spot. Trendy and intimate, it offered the most diverse menu in all of San Francisco—and probably beyond.[1]

N.N. LIVING IN A PERMANENT PRESENT

I've identified the word *imagination* several times already as the source of the "unconventionality" aspect of a vision. Harvard's Abraham Zaleznik, whom we met in the previous chapter and whose contributions to the field of leadership have been monumental, emphasized the pivotal role of imagination: "Vision is needed at least as much as strategy to succeed. Business leaders bring to bear a variety of imaginations on the growth of corporations. These imaginations—the marketing imagination, the manufacturing imagination, and others—originate in perceptual capacities."[2]

Without imagination, you are stating the obvious or holding on to the status quo; your vision falls flat. With it, however, your vision becomes intriguing, exciting, refreshing. Suddenly, it has the potential to energize and mobilize.

"But I'm not a very imaginative person," people quickly tell me. I hear the same lament from senior leadership teams and midlevel executives all over the world. They tend to confuse imagination with exotic, bohemian, artistic ways of thinking. And sure, that way of thinking is highly imaginative. But it's not what we're looking for here. Think of it like this: The very fact that you can plan a vacation proves that you're imaginative. The ability to look ahead into the future and anticipate events that might unfold is an act of imagination. There's nothing artistic or eccentric about it. It's a unique ability that we, as human beings, have developed and that sets us apart from all other species.

In 1981 a patient, known in the literature as N.N. to protect his privacy, suffered damage to his frontal lobe (the part of the brain associated with complicated cognitive functions such as planning) in a car accident. He was no longer able to think about or plan for the future. When researchers asked him what he experienced when told to think ahead, he responded, "It's like being in a room with nothing there and having a guy tell you to go find a chair, and then there's nothing there."[3] N.N. was perfectly able to have normal, intelligent conversations, reflect on his behavior, and access his knowledge. But he was unable to plan his day or imagine life going forward.

N.N. lived in a *permanent present,* which is believed to be the state of the human brain in its earliest stages of evolution. Only when our frontal lobes developed did we start to become aware of past, present, and future. Along with our ability to envision ourselves on a timeline, we acquired the ability to plan and imagine what tomorrow might look like. We moved from a state of permanent present to one that can anticipate the future. In other words, our ability to engage with the future is one of the things that make us human and that distinguishes us from other species like dogs and cats, who, as far as we know, live in a state of permanent present.

THE IMAGE OF THE FUTURE

In his landmark work *The Image of the Future*, early futurologist Fred Polak discovered the critical relationship between a society's image of its future and its vitality:

Any student of the rise and fall of cultures cannot fail to be impressed by the role played in this historical succession by the image of the future. The rise and fall of images precedes or accompanies the rise and fall of cultures. As long as a society's image is positive and flourishing, the flower of culture is in full bloom. Once the image begins to decay and lose its vitality, however, the culture does not long survive.[4]

Over half a century after Polak described this correlation, we can see it in action in several countries in the developing world today, such as India, Brazil, Mexico, and Indonesia. Propelled forward by their positive image of the future, a future in which they expect a rise in the standard of living, they are energized and entrepreneurial, vibrant and positive. By and large, they accept the current deficiencies of their society because they collectively envision and expect a positive future for themselves and their children.

It's quite a different picture in some Western societies, especially in southern Europe. Even though the standard of living is often much higher than that of emerging countries, people are depressed, society has stagnated, and vitality is evaporating. Their image of the future is negative and dark. As Polak predicts, without a credible and compelling image of the future put forward by their leaders—specifically political leaders—their cultures risk becoming more and more threatened and becoming a ghost of what they once were.

Polak was among the first to recognize the important role an image plays in society's vitality, as well as the need for leaders to create and communicate this image, engaging with their creative side. He said, "The spiritual overstepping of the boundaries of the unknown is the source of all human creativity. Crossing frontiers is both man's heritage and man's task, and the image of the future is his propelling power."[5]

A core leadership responsibility is to find, shape, and describe that inspiring, hope-giving image that stimulates people's idea of the future. We call it a vision, but, like Polak, we could also have called it an *image*.

ALICE IN WONDERLAND

Not coincidentally, image and imagination are etymologically related. In fact, imagination can be defined as the ability to create new mental images

with the mind's eye. Psychologists speak of "the creation of belief-like enti-
ties in the mind"[6] to describe the term *imagination*. It's that kind of vivid
imagination that prompted an Oxford mathematics professor, C. L. Dodg-
son, to write stories for a little girl named Alice. In 1865, working under the
pseudonym Lewis Carroll, he published *Alice in Wonderland*, which still
stands as a masterpiece of playfulness and creativity in literature today.
Alice embarks on adventures that bring her from one logically challenging
or inconsistent place to another, taking readers young and old along with
her on her imaginative journey.

> If I had a world of my own, everything would be nonsense.
> Nothing would be what it is because everything would be
> what it isn't. And contrary-wise; what it is it wouldn't be, and
> what it wouldn't be, it would. You see?
> —*ALICE IN WONDERLAND*, LEWIS CARROLL

Are you following?

Our ability to be playful and imaginative is the essence of learning.
Without imagination, development and evolution would cease. Progress
would halt. This holds true for both society as a whole as well as for us personally. Working with our imagination is critical for self-development and
uncovering those unconventional ideas and insights that can fuel our vision. In order to do that, though, we must engage with our creative rather
than our rational side. Even Albert Einstein noted that "imagination is
more important than knowledge."

But this is where it becomes difficult. It's easy to *say* we have to engage
with our imagination and our creative side, but for many that remains a
hollow phrase. How do you do it in real life? Put your feet up on the desk
and stare out the window for hours? We've got more urgent things to do
than "wasting our time" like that, right? Fast-forward to the section titled
Neural Networks in this chapter if you want to understand the neuroscientific answer to this question (or bear with me, since you will get there soon
enough).

Interestingly, as children we used to be highly imaginative—without
having to stare out the window or put our feet up. We were able to come up
with comprehensive stories and adventures using anything on hand, in any

setting. A garden could be a football stadium filled with thousands of fans one minute, and a jungle complete with lions and snakes (that we could vividly "see") the next. Judgmental thoughts did not hold us back; we could thoroughly enjoy and build on our fantasies.

As we mature, though, our rational abilities become more valued and developed while our creative ones grow dormant. Social norms command us to "act normal," "be real," and "grow up." By the time we reach adulthood, our imaginative, playful side has been put on the back burner. And when we do try to ignite our imagination as adults, we often come up empty.

The process of imagination for adults is poorly understood. We've made good progress in understanding what suppresses it, but little is known about what fires it up. James Adams's classic book on creativity, *Conceptual Blockbusting,* focuses on defining, categorizing, and acknowledging the various blocks that prevent us from "seeing things differently." Creativity techniques are therefore essentially aimed at attacking what's in the way so that our intrinsic imagination can blossom. When we are more aware of these blocks, when we can identify and tackle them, the hope rises that we are better able to reach and exploit our creative potential.

Let's try to encounter some of these conceptual blocks and see what we can learn from the experience. Here's a great method if you have young children: Take a cue from Lewis Carroll and create stories for your kids (or someone else's kids), starting tonight. Whether at bedtime or at the dinner table, try to suppress any judgmental thoughts and let the story you create wander into playful, unknown territories. The practice Story Pace actually helps you deliver it in a fun way that will grasp their attention and feed their imagination. And you'll loosen up some imaginative brain muscles that haven't been flexed for a while— plus your kids will love it.

Practice 2-1.
Story pace.

Once the kids are asleep, consciously reflect on how you did. Was it easy to come up with stories? What did you struggle with? What surprised you about your story and yourself as the storyteller? Did your kids like your creation? Why, or why not? As you identify the kinds of blocks that may have gotten in your way, this homegrown practice teaches you a lot about the barriers you need to address in order to ignite your visionary capacity.

SCHEMAS, ASSUMPTIONS, AND FRAMES

Why is it that most of us find it difficult to tap into our imagination? What stops us from seeing things differently and thinking outside that legendary box? Let's look at some of the psychological phenomena that work to suppress imagination.

Biochemists and cognitive scientists study how our amazing neural system called the brain orchestrates bodily functions, from pumping blood to smiling to serving a tennis ball—sometimes even simultaneously. Our brain organizes these functions largely unconsciously. At face value it all seems rather miraculous—and truly, it *is*. Fortunately, cognitive psychologists give us ways to describe the processes that take place. Here's a primer of this large body of research to better understand how our imagination works (or not).

Every day we're exposed to an incredible amount of information. We look around us, we hear, we read, we meet people, discuss, surf the Web, and so on. We expose ourselves to a multitude of sensory inputs. These stimuli are registered, but fortunately not all of them are considered—otherwise we'd quickly go mad.

In fact, by counting the receptor cells of the five senses and their associated nerve pathways, researchers estimate that we process about 11 million bits of sensory data every minute. Yet, by the most generous estimate, we consciously process only forty pieces of that sensory data at a time. The rest is dealt with unconsciously. Or, as James Adams memorably put it in *Conceptual Blockbusting,* "we have a one-watt mind in a megawatt world."[7]

This means our mind does a lot of filtering for us. Even while reading this sentence, you should be experiencing this process. Your senses are picking up other data, such as noises, that you probably didn't notice until now. It could be birds singing, the dishwasher running in the background, or a car driving down the street; your brain "knows" your reading should not be disturbed by processing these sounds.

Other sounds, however, do grab our attention. If the dishwasher starts to make a funny sound or the car comes to a sudden, screeching stop, your brain alarms you by interrupting your reading. There is a constant filtering of data that your mind performs automatically—a steady stream of decisions about what's worth processing and what isn't.

So, your brain decides what to pay attention to and what to make of those things. To do this successfully, the human brain relies on what psychologists call *frames* (also called schemas, structures, and stereotypes). These frames simplify and guide our understanding of a complex reality,[8] protecting us from information overload while helping us comprehend and retain what's valuable. They "frame" the information that we observe and label it with something we know. These frames have developed as a result of our upbringing, education, and experiences; they provide us with the foundation we need to understand what we experience. In other words, frames are pretty helpful. They help us identify a chair (or a ball, or a pen) in the split second we enter a room, even if we've never seen that particular design before. Our sense-making frames immediately categorize the stimuli we take in through our visual receptors because they recognize characteristics we've learned over time. As we take in information, the appropriate frame is "pulled from memory" to match the object we're trying to identify.

TWO-FACED FRIENDS

But as helpful and powerful as our frames are (remember, without them we'd go mad from information overload), they can also cause trouble.

Sometimes these mental friends lead us to make flawed perceptions, draw completely unjustified conclusions, and prevent us from reconsidering those conclusions. Think about how quickly the process works. Let's say we see someone dressed in a dark uniform with a shiny badge on a street corner. We'll probably conclude almost instantaneously that we're looking at a policeman. That's because for most of us the only frame we know that combines a dark uniform, shiny badge, and street corner is one that labels the object a police officer.

We don't consider the possibility that the figure might be a street artist, a woman rather than a man, an actor on his way to a performance, a bank robber dressed up as a policeman, or just someone who likes to dress up in a uniform. We quickly and easily draw a conclusion that's closed-minded, uncreative, and dogmatic. There's no playfulness or curiosity at work. And once we learn the truth—that the person is in fact a woman in a dark suit with a gold pin on it—we resort to an embarrassed chuckle, a blush, and a strong desire to move on to something else. We might even get defensive: "Usually I'm more open-minded ... " Right?

Think about this one. Fred Jones was visiting his hometown when he bumped into an old friend. "Hey, Fred, how have you been all this time? It must've been ten years since we last saw each other." "For sure," Fred replied. "I'm fine—what about you?" The friend answered, "I'm married now, but to someone you wouldn't know. And this is my daughter." Fred looked down at the little girl and asked her name. "It's the same as my mother's," said the little girl. "Then I bet your name is Susan," remarked Fred. How could he know?

You'll find the answer in this chapter's endnotes. Don't rush to find it, though. Give it some thought. And remember, we're discussing mental frames—how they can help us, and how they can cause harm by preventing us from seeing all of the options.[9]

ETERNAL TRUTHS

So how come we—sane and rational, smart and well-educated people—fall into these traps? There are a few factors at play, and we need to be aware of them as we cultivate our imaginative side.

First, we unconsciously prefer to seek confirmation of our existing beliefs. Our frames filter out conflicting data, key information that could help us update our thoughts and beliefs. Instead, we hold on to existing beliefs, even when conflicting evidence is right in front of us. Our frames help reshape our perception, sometimes complementing it with things that aren't even there, just to make sure that our perception fits with our preferred belief system. In psychology, this is called the *halo effect*. It boils down to our human desire to remain psychologically consistent, so information is interpreted in ways that is favorable to what we already believe or like to believe—for good or for bad.

Imagine you are an amateur tennis player and you're competing in a local tournament. Your first opponent is the spitting image of Roger Federer, one of the best tennis players ever. The fear you'll feel is disproportionate to what's justified, because you've assumed your opponent—who plays in your league—would be of similar strength. That belief becomes blurred by the frame you carry with you of that great tennis player who moves quickly, has a great forehand and backhand, and will most likely kill you with his serve. Your perception of your opponent is completed with totally unjustified associations; he might *look* like Roger Federer, but he isn't. He might actually be a lousy player. But albeit irrational, psychologically you are already one set behind.

The second reason that explains why we fall into framing traps is that our frames tend to be more obstinate than they should be. The more confirmation we receive of our current thinking, the more convinced we become that it's true. In other words, our frames grow stronger with time. Our assumptions of what is true become real *eternal truths* for us, and our convictions can grow so deep that we literally filter out anything that's inconsistent with a belief that we now consider a truth. It blinds us in a way and shields us from considering alternative perspectives. We'll dig deeper into this subject in Chapter 5, but to quote Arthur Schopenhauer, "Every man takes the limits of his own field of vision for the limits of the world."

To make matters worse, if we're offered an incentive to hold on to certain beliefs—such as a bonus, an attractive career path, or even just the expectation that our boss will like us—the problem increases. We like to think of ourselves as stable and objective people, but psychologists have repeatedly demonstrated this is not the case.[10] For most of us, incentives can create mindsets and behaviors we might not be proud of.[11] Think of some of the bankers who contributed to the worldwide financial crisis. It didn't matter that they knew housing prices could drop (assuming they had some minimal education in economics that explains how prices fluctuate in a free market). Incentives gave them a reason to engage in predatory lending and other unethical practices and to spin a convincing story to reassure their clients that real estate prices only go up. They modified their belief system, as well as their ethical stance, to fit with the practices they were rewarded for. Some with ill intentions, but undoubtedly many also truly "believed" that there was very little risk since house prices had been going up consistently. And undoubtedly, too, some expert (or some senior leader) explained why prices could be expected to continue to rise. It was the explanation they wanted to hear, so they echoed it. Since everyone around them "believed" it, even those with assumed authority and expertise, reality became interpreted this way to ensure their own psychological consistency (halo effect). All of which created the "perfect storm" conditions for a huge framing trap.

In terms of a vision, the inherent risk of inflexible frames is the phenomenon of *tunnel vision*. This occurs when someone is unwilling to consider alternative perspectives and dismisses any data or arguments—no matter how coherent—that counter the person's belief system. We already alluded to this dark side in Chapter 1, and we will explore and discuss it (and what to do about it) in much more detail in Chapter 5. But as it relates to imagination, it's important to have an awareness and understanding of the phenomenon here. After all, any tool intended to increase your creativity is essentially supporting you in constructively breaking through the limitations of your own mental frame set, and looking beyond your assumed "truths" in order to get you to see things that you might otherwise have missed.

So, the concept of frames and their inherent persistence helps you understand what stops you from exploiting your imagination. Tapping into your imagination is about being open-minded: It's about having a fundamental willingness to challenge your assumptions about what you consider to be true, and reframing those assumptions when it's called for.

THE GRAND ILLUSION

David Copperfield, the illusionist who cuts himself in half daily (and sometimes twice a day) and makes Learjets, the Statue of Liberty, and members of his audience disappear, refers to himself as a scientist of show business. He says:

> The stage is our laboratory, and through trial and error we've learned a lot about the mysterious inner workings of the brain. We've figured out that, with some skill and misdirection, we can get an audience to focus its attention in the right place and at the right time so that we can create the illusion of magic. In fact, these illusions are created not on stage but in the brain . . . The kind of perception I deal with chiefly, though, is based on biology and psychology. The human brain—the most complicated organ on the planet—is the theater where the magic I perform

really takes place. The hand is not quicker than the eye, but the hand is quicker than perception.[12]

Copperfield is actually describing frames here. Our desire for "sense making," and the way our brain categorizes what we perceive into things we know and understand, is incredibly powerful. We seek the truth and mistake our perception for it. And then we're baffled by Copperfield's ability to make a Learjet disappear onstage.

To see how this works, check out the checkerboard image (Figure 2-1), invented in 1995 by MIT's Professor of Vision Science Edward H. Adelson. You see a checkerboard-patterned square and a cylinder in its right-hand corner. The cylinder is casting a shadow over the checkerboard as a result of a light source outside the picture. There are also two squares, A (outside the shadow) and B (inside the shadow). How do A and B compare?

You probably thought B was lighter than A, right? As you can see in the second picture (Figure 2-2), though, both squares are the same color. In its attempt to make sense of the picture, your brain made a mistake. Your "experience frame" immediately recognized that B was a white square on the checkerboard and should therefore be lighter than the darker squares on the checkerboard.

Edward H. Adelson

Figure 2-1. Grand illusion.

Edward H. Adelson

Figure 2-2. Grand illusion revealed.

Even though you now know the answer, your mind is probably still struggling. Did you go back to the picture a few times to check? You did, didn't you? The fact that the "lighter" square is the same color as the "darker" one doesn't match what you already know. You are confused, and it takes a few times of checking and double-checking for your rational side, which was tricked by the experiment, to accept this fact.

Now ask yourself a tough question. What was it like to undergo this experiment? Check in with your feelings. You're probably experiencing some embarrassment about having fallen into the trap. Chances are you also have a feeling of irritation. You're looking for a rationalization for having missed this answer ("didn't take enough time," "couldn't see it clearly," "didn't understand the instruction"), yet in the absence of any good excuse, you are slowly coming to grips with the fact that your mind has been fooled. And it feels unpleasant. You're probably attributing this to the fact that my prediction of your "foolish" behavior was spot-on. Right? But what's really at work here is your mind struggling with the apparent inconsistency that a seemingly lighter square can be the same color as a darker one. This struggle is annoying, it plays with your mind, and you probably don't enjoy it.

That's what cognitive dissonance does to you, and that's why we prefer to steer clear from this state of confusion—and if that requires denying reality, so be it (sometimes).

COGNITIVE DISSONANCE

Alan Greenspan was chairman of the U.S. Federal Reserve from 1987 to 2006. Arguably one of the most influential men on earth during that time, he was known for his market-oriented stance. As former NBC correspondent Lisa Myers once put it, he was "an unabashed champion of deregulation and free market." His deeply rooted belief system was grounded in these principles, and it served him well for some forty years.

And then it didn't. Greenspan's belief that the market would self-correct led directly to the worst worldwide economic crash since the Great Depression. According to American political economist Robert Reich, "Greenspan's worst move was to contribute to the giant housing bubble. In 2004, he lowered interest rates to one percent, enabling banks to borrow money for free, adjusted for inflation. Naturally, the banks wanted to borrow as much as they possibly could, then lend it out, earning nice profits. The situation screamed for government oversight of lending institutions, lest the banks lend to unfit borrowers. He refused, trusting the market to weed out bad credit risks. It did not."[13]

Despite several attempts at rationalizing his actions, beliefs, and assumptions as the crisis unfolded in 2007 and 2008 (when he was no longer Fed chairman), Greenspan finally conceded on October 23, 2008. In response to questions from Congress, in publicly broadcast hearings, he finally admitted to his flaw in thinking that markets would regulate themselves. In his mea culpa he said, "I was shocked because I had been going for forty years or more with very considerable evidence that it was working exceptionally well."[14]

The concept of cognitive dissonance was first introduced by the psychologist Leon Festinger in 1957.[15] It describes the discomfort that occurs when our beliefs are challenged by contradictory information. As said, most people are driven by a desire to remain psychologically consistent and will go to great lengths to avoid conflict, holding on to their beliefs by rejecting or avoiding any contrary data. Sometimes the brain actually convinces itself that there's no real conflict, finding reasons to explain the supposed differences away (called *rationalizing*).

Greenspan's confusion and dramatic acceptance of his flawed assumptions illustrates the discomfort of cognitive dissonance. It explains why Greenspan ignored earlier evidence from a Fed colleague that the housing market was headed for a cliff. After the fact, he desperately defended his dismissal of these clear warning signs: "There are always people raising issues. And half the time they are wrong. The question is, what do you do?"

As reasonable as that line of thinking might sound, and notwithstanding Greenspan's great dedication to his job, the fact is that with big roles come big responsibilities. An unwillingness to consider perspectives that don't align with your deeply rooted belief system isn't one of them.

We can only hope people in similar positions have drawn lessons from Greenspan's dramatic error. In Greenspan's case, his inflexible belief system that mistakes its own assumptions for truths is one we are still paying the price for today.

Let's look at another example where an unwillingness to reframe assumptions caused tremendous damage. Eastman Kodak is often cited for having completely missed the boat on digital photography. Founded in 1888, and market leader throughout most of the twentieth century, Kodak was brought to its knees in January 2012, when it filed for Chapter 11 bankruptcy (from which it emerged in 2013). What is often forgotten is that Kodak was actually well aware of the promises and developments in digital photography. Company executives analyzed digital technology as far back as 1981 (when Sony introduced the first commercial digital camera, the Mavica). So it wasn't as if Kodak woke up one day and, out of nowhere, digital cameras had emerged, taking the company by surprise. Instead, Kodak knew all too well how the technology progressed. But *still* the company did not act on it.

That's what cognitive dissonance is capable of. Kodak executives fooled themselves for too long with a rock-solid belief in their existing business model. As Paul Carroll and Chunka Mui explain, "They could not fathom a world in which images were evanescent and never printed."[16] The desire to hold on to that worldview was strengthened by the fact that the margins on film were so much better than on digital products (60 percent vs. 15 percent). To change course would have kicked a serious dent into their financial outlooks for a few years, so they were wary to enter that transformation, and in the end postponed for too long. This reluctance was most likely strengthened by the incentives that were in place for executives—performance bonuses—which undoubtedly heavily factored in quarterly or annual results and encouraged executives to hold on to a worldview that would pay their mortgage, not one that would challenge that worldview and that would have them consider the "unpleasant" implications of a more digital future.

So cognitive dissonance, and an unwillingness to challenge your own assumptions, can lead to disaster; artfully breaking through your inherent mental frames is therefore required to use the power of your imagination. But that doesn't happen automatically; it requires an understanding of what it takes to unlock the imagination. Let's look at two approaches to help us understand what fires up imagination: a neuroscientific suggestion and a psychological take on it.

NEURAL NETWORKS

Gradually, we are making progress in understanding what happens in our brain, at a neuroscientific level, that explains things like imagination. There is still a lot we do not know. Albeit popular, many of the claims about the relationship between brain activation regions and certain functions and emotions are still speculative (something scientist call "brain porn"). But some things about the brain we do know with considerable certainty. Adam Waytz and Malia Mason, scholars at the Kellogg School of Management and Columbia Business School, respectively, list four neural networks that have been identified: the default, reward, affect, and control networks.

The default network and control network are what interest us the most here. Let's start with the *default network*. That's the one at work when we aren't actively focusing on anything particular—it's kind of the standby light on your television set. This is by itself a very interesting finding; Waytz and Mason write that "one of the most exciting discoveries in neuroscience in the past decade is that the brain is never truly at rest."[17] That means that when it is in a "task-negative" state (doing nothing in particular) the brain spends considerable time processing internalized existing knowledge. In this state, the brain detaches itself from the external environment and allows us to imagine: what it would be like to be in a different place, a different time, a different reality.

This explains why it is difficult to actively engage with your imagination when there is too much distraction. Your brain simply doesn't go wandering off, since it is captivated by the state that requires it to process external stimuli. When you are very focused and "in control," it is predominantly your *control network* that is at work. In a sense, the default and the control network are therefore each other's countervailing forces.

It is important to realize that breakthrough ideas are unlikely to occur when you are very focused—your control network dominates and overshadows your default network. Most people recognize that solutions to problems they have been working on can come "out of nowhere" when they are not deliberately thinking about it. For instance, when taking a shower, a walk, or just zoning out. Some people actively seek these idle states through activities like meditation, running, or listening to classical music. And to answer an earlier question we asked about how we could possibly engage with our imagination (caricatured as "putting our feet on the desk and staring out of the window"), neuroscience seems to indicate that experimenting with total detachment would be a good strategy to boost your imagination.

BREAKING THE FRAME

Psychologists use a higher-level description to explain what it takes to unlock your imagination. Theirs builds on the concept of mental frames. Let's illustrate with a famous anecdote.

In 1983, Steve Jobs was asked to look for his successor as CEO of Apple. The company's board of directors felt that in order to take Apple to the next level, they needed a more seasoned leader. Although Jobs disagreed with this assessment, he found his ideal candidate in John Sculley. Sculley's conventional business background and considerable marketing successes at Pepsi appealed to Apple. He was the creator of the famous Pepsi Challenge (a highly successful marketing campaign that showed lifelong Coke drinkers preferring Pepsi in a blind taste test) and seemed to have what it takes to sway consumer opinion. Apple needed someone who could do the same and move Apple computers into the mass consumer market.

But Sculley, who started at PepsiCo as a trainee in a bottling plant, was poised to take over as CEO of the company in the near future. Other than introducing Apple computers into PepsiCo's sales organization, Sculley had little affinity with the emerging technology industry. Being from the East Coast, he also knew little of the Silicon Valley culture. He was hesitant to trade in his successful career at the praised multinational for an uncertain job at a tech firm that was barely out of its infancy phase. Even so, Jobs approached Sculley, who was reluctantly intrigued by the offer.

After having had several conversations, they were nearing the decision point. Jobs, noticing Sculley's final doubts, realized that more arguments wouldn't win him over. He decided to make a final appeal with this now legendary quote: "John, do you want to sell sugar water for the rest of your life, or do you want to come with me and change the world?"

The question hit a home run, and Sculley conceded. It's a classic example of the power of reframing assumptions, the psychological direction in unlocking your imagination. The picture Jobs painted of what could be, together with the persuasive final punch line, broke through Sculley's deeply rooted belief system. Describing the product that was dear to him as "sugar water" was nasty but ultimately true. And Jobs didn't persuade Sculley with the CEO role, but instead offered him to come along to "change the world." Jobs's radical, frame-breaking pitch worked and Sculley conceded. (Sculley's time at the helm of Apple wasn't a success, but that's a different story).

Practice 2-2.
Assumption
bowling.

THAT'S FUNNY

Jobs's successful pitch to win over Sculley worked much like a good joke does. Just as Sculley listened to some routine arguments for leaving his comfortable, well-paid position, we listen to an unfolding joke with our minds racing ahead in anticipation of an ending consistent with our beliefs. And then the punch line arrives, taking us by surprise. It's a "gotcha" moment—one that can generate a good laugh (or, as it turns out, a job contract).

Try following the pattern:

Two guys are on lunch break. As they open their lunch boxes, one says to the other: "Not again! I've got another peanut butter and jelly sandwich. I'm sick and tired of them!" Grumpily, he closes his lunch box. His friend asks: "Well, why don't you ask your wife to put something else on your sandwiches then?" To which the other guy replies, "My wife? I always make my own lunch."

Did you catch yourself framing the story that led up to the punch line? The joke may have lured you into a traditional gender-role frame, assuming the first worker's wife prepared his lunches. The punch line was unexpected, outside the frame you were lured into. That made it surprising and supposedly funny (although the fun factor in a joke rapidly degrades with explanation).

Humor, like imagination, has the power to change our frames—and our way of thinking. That's why the best salespeople are usually funny and entertaining—they get you to step over your initial reluctance or resistance. Their humor helps you flex your assumptive framework and opens up for the arguments they would like you to see or think about. Also, have you ever heard someone suggest that in order to create some breakthrough ideas you should hold creativity sessions in an unconventional, off-site location where you can really have a good laugh with each other? Now you know why.

Practice 2-3.
Business upside down.

LATERAL THINKING

> *Lateral thinking is closely related to insight, creativity, and humor. All four processes have the same basis. But whereas insight, creativity, and humor can only be prayed for, lateral thinking is a more deliberate process. It is as definite a way of using the mind as logical thinking—but in a very different way.*
> —EDWARD DE BONO, *LATERAL THINKING*

In 1967 Edward de Bono, the creativity guru introduced at the beginning of this chapter, invented the term "lateral thinking" and explored it in his book *The Use of Lateral Thinking*.[18] It has since become part of the vernacular and is even used as a synonym for creative thinking. Lateral thinking is a set of systemic, deliberate methods for challenging assumptions and opening up innovative ways of thinking and seeing.

One of those methods is the Random Entry Idea Generation Tool. It involves arbitrarily selecting a noun from a list (or the dictionary) and associating it with the issue you are working on. As random as the association appears at first, there's a good chance you will find some connections. If you're wondering how to improve the performance of your customer service department, for example, and you randomly select the word "pizza slicer," finding connections between the two could help you uncover new opportunities.

Practice 2-4.
Lateral thinking.

It might not be easy, and not all objects or nouns will yield instant success. But the process demands persistence. Because your assumptive framework will try to deny any connections, your mind won't immediately be willing to entertain associations between something as serious as your customer service performance and something as irrelevant as a pizza slicer. But by forcing yourself not to give up too quickly, possibilities will spring to mind. Thoughts of food, cutting, knives, and sharpness could lead to speedy delivery, frozen pizzas, and specialized utensils. Those might trigger thoughts about the importance of follow-through, delivery of fully prepared spare parts, and the development of a special "utensil" to deal with a common customer complaint—one that could delight customers who report a problem. That which at first glance appears unhelpful and silly can trigger a useful thought you might never have considered if you had looked at the issue within the usual frames.

Another de Bono method, provocation, involves generating provocative statements about the issue you're focusing on. In the case of increasing customer service performance, we might say: Move agents closer to the customer, reward self-service, get customers to help each other, or market it as a new product. Some ideas will be too impractical, too costly, or just too crazy. The value of provocation, though, lies in taking your thinking from static to dynamic. Considering the customer service examples could lead you to the idea of rewarding customers who help other customers, possibly in a virtual community environment. It's an idea that might never have surfaced if you maintained a strict focus on your own performance improvement.

Using creativity techniques like provocation might feel somewhat gimmicky at first, but they're very effective at challenging the strong preferences we hold because of our current beliefs and ways of thinking. Let's try a few more techniques.

WWGD

WWGD is a method that never fails to surprise me with its productivity. The abbreviation stands for What Would Google Do, a name inspired by Jeff Jarvis's 2009 bestseller.[19] To use this method, ask yourself (or preferably your team, because most of these techniques work much better when applied in a group) how Google—or some other remarkable organization—would solve the issue at hand.

Start by selecting a number of iconic companies that everyone has strong brand associations with: Think IKEA, McDonald's, Southwest Airlines, Zara, Nespresso, Singapore Airlines, Harley-Davidson, Toyota, Expedia, and Amazon.[20] It's good to have a variety, from self-service (IKEA) and streamlined production (McDonald's, Toyota) to customer centricity (Southwest, Singapore Airlines) and design (Nespresso). It's also important to focus on companies outside your industry, even though their products, culture, and ways of working might seem miles apart from yours.

Practice 2-5.
WWGD.

As you think about how one of these companies would tackle the problem at hand, you're reframing; you're reassessing your assumptions and moving from an intrinsic, static view of the situation to a more liberated, open-minded exploration of options. WWGD will very quickly generate a lot of ideas. Some of them will be completely useless, but you only need one good idea to get a return on the one-hour investment you're making with your team.

BLUE OCEAN

In a slightly different form, the WWGD method was promoted in the 2005 innovation classic Blue Ocean Strategy,[21] written by two strategy professors from the leading European business school INSEAD. The metaphorical title distinguishes between growing, uncontested marketplaces (blue oceans) and crowded, mature, competitive ones (red oceans). The authors aim to help organizations find the former, using two tools: the value curve and the four-action framework.[22] The value curve represents the attributes the existing industry is competing on, through the eyes of the customer. For example, the hotel industry competes on factors such as location, service level, facilities, room size, price, and a number of others. In order to find a blue ocean proposition—something that no one has offered yet and that represents a fully untapped market—you can brainstorm new attributes to complement a company's value curve.

But where would you get new, refreshing attributes from—ideas that nobody has considered yet in their value curve? Inspiration could come from other industries, much like the WWGD method suggests, or other alternatives to a hotel night, such as a caravan park, a friend's apartment, or even the ordinary night at home. Why look at other industries and alternatives? If you don't, you'll only see the factors everybody's already looking at. Your direct competitors may do a little more (bigger room, later operating hours for the restaurant, larger swimming pool) or a little less (lower price) to differentiate, but essentially they remain focused on the same things, creating a cut-throat red ocean.

Imagine you travel often, with a wallet filled with frequent-flier cards. You regularly stay in hotels, which, thanks to your generous boss, are four- or five-star rated. Yet they can't compete with home. Why? Because after a hard day at work you check into a hotel that—regardless of its promises—gives you a pretty similar experience: You dine on your own, at an annoyingly slow pace; you kill time getting some work done, having a drink in yet another anonymous hotel bar, or mindlessly watching TV for a while; and then it's time to sleep.

And here comes CitizenM, a hotel concept designed to meet the needs of a "smart new breed of international traveler, the type who crosses continents the way others cross streets."[23] Understanding this traveler's boring evening experience, CitizenM has overamplified the lobby space in its hotel. The lobby offers various areas with different atmospheres to suit your evening mood. According to the company's promotion, the lobby is "designed to function as your living room, whether you want to be alone or connect with some fellow mobile citizens, whether you want to relax or do some work."

CitizenM recognizes that, for those who spend a large part of their lives on the road, there's little glamour in killing yet another night in a hotel—no matter how many stars it has—and it extended the traditional hotel value curve with attributes that are more closely associated with home, strongly appealing to a specific market segment. It's a unique entry in an industry that seemed to have seen it all, where traditional chains fight in a red ocean of high competition.

Tapping into your imagination—something you were undoubtedly good at as a child—requires unlearning some of your grown-up beliefs and embracing playfulness and curiosity. It also requires a willingness to challenge your assumptions and suppress the defensive reflex that comes up when some of the things you strongly believe get challenged. As you now know, those beliefs, or sense-making frames, can't be stopped. They are going to keep making sense of what you experience, which can both help you and get in your way.

Whenever you need to get imaginative, remember the latter. Practice creativity techniques such as lateral thinking, WWGD, blue ocean, or one of the many others that have gained popularity over the years. Learn to appreciate these techniques, even if they don't instantly lead to breakthrough ideas. By frequently challenging and reassessing your beliefs and assumptions, you'll get better at tapping into your imagination. You'll get better at finding the kinds of unconventional, intriguing, creative ideas that can fuel your vision.

PART 2

1 VISIONARY CONTENT

2 VISIONARY PRACTICES

3 VISIONARY SELF

4 VISIONARY COMMUNICATION

3

Developing Your Visionary Capacity

What we see is often determined by what we are prepared to see.

—PAUL SCHOEMAKER AND GEORGE DAY

VISIONARY SHOES

Researchers Sooksan Kantabutra and Gayle Avery had a practical question regarding the Vision Thing. Ample anecdotal evidence demonstrates that a powerful vision inspires, but does this translate into real business value? Specifically, they wanted to know how the presence, or absence, of a vision affects and motivates followers—the so-called followers effect.[1] Can a vision provide greater job satisfaction, happier customers, and overall increased business success?

For their study they chose an unlikely setting: retail stores, including shoe shops, furniture outlets, and boutiques. This was a very interesting choice, as we are more likely to think of vision in terms of the corporate world and iconic companies like Apple, Google, and Amazon. Would a vision also be important in a sporting-goods chain, a supermarket, or a pet store?

Using a scale of one to nine, Kantabutra and Avery interviewed employees about the extent to which they considered their leaders or bosses to have a vision for the business. They also asked whether the vision provided guidance and direction in the choices the employees needed to make in the store on a day-to-day basis. And their third question was whether it motivated and energized them to operate at their best. Remember, this was at a bookstore or a deli, not a corporation led by Richard Branson! What they found was quite remarkable: Even in this unassuming setting, there was a positive correlation between the level of visionary leadership and the level of motivation of the employees. The presence of a vision also positively correlated with the perception of a helpful sense of direction. It turns out that even in such down-to-earth places, the Vision Thing is useful.

But there's more. The study also set out to determine whether the presence of a compelling vision had a monetary effect: Did it result in more and better business and improve overall business results? Tying the collected data on the impact of visionary leadership to a financial outcome was a challenge. After all, results are the sum of many factors, including location, economic conditions, aggressive competition, and marketing strategies. So, how could Kantabutra and Avery single out vision to see if, and how, it affects the bottom line? They decided to gather two more data points, both strong indicators of business performance and success.

The first was the level of *employee satisfaction*. Happy employees typically enjoy working for the company, provide good service, spread the word, and go the extra mile for their employers. Higher levels of employee satisfaction are therefore widely considered to have a positive effect on business performance. The second was *customer satisfaction*. High scores would indicate happy customers, who are known to provide word-of-mouth advertising, repeat sales, and other positive business effects. To get this data, the researchers expanded the scope of their interviews to include shoppers.

Guess what they found? Perhaps unsurprisingly, their results indicated a positive relationship between the presence of a vision and *employee* satisfaction. But, more interestingly, shops that had scored high on the assessment of the leader's visionary side also showed higher levels of *customer* satisfaction. Think about that: Shoppers probably have no particular awareness that the store is led by a more visionary leader. They're just shopping. Yet they still reported higher customer satisfaction scores at such stores. Apparently, the guidance and inspiration that a vision provides doesn't just affect people directly (followers who are aware of the vision), but also indirectly affects people (customers who are unaware of the presence of a particular leadership vision).

The results seem to indicate that the Vision Thing—when done right—leads to happier employees *and* happier customers, and thereby undoubtedly has a positive effect on the bottom line.

MADE, NOT BORN

Sometimes you are told a compelling future-oriented story, one that includes exciting descriptions of the changes the speaker envisions, spiced up with fascinating trends, intriguing future trigger events, and great clarity on how it all fits together. If the speaker does a good job, you are probably impressed and likely to conclude that the story is inspiring and the speaker is very gifted. It's easy (and all too common) to conclude that this ability to connect so powerfully, to provide such clear insights and voice them with such confidence and conviction, is a God-given talent. Some of us have it, and others don't. Great communicators such as Jack Welch, Larry Ellison, and Sam Walton are some of the people that fit this category.

If you are not in that category—and, honestly, most of us aren't—becoming more visionary and inspiring seems a daunting task. As a result, we might alienate ourselves from the Vision Thing, file it away in the "too hard" box because we believe it is not for us mortal souls. Steven Johnson, the author of *Where Good Ideas Come From,* explores a similar phenomenon of misconception: the generation of innovative ideas. We tend to believe that great ideas come as epiphanies, in breakthrough eureka moments when a lightbulb switches on within the mind of these rare, unique, and remarkable characters. That belief is probably strengthened by story—it's much more engaging to recount an epiphany as the tale of lightning striking and brilliance flashing before someone's eyes than to describe hours, days, and weeks of deliberate thought and research, writing and rewriting, bouncing half-baked ideas around, and many moments of getting it wrong before finally getting it right. We enjoy the illusion of a brilliant mind suddenly producing brilliant insights.

Reality is almost always quite different. To quote Johnson, "good ideas are not conjured out of thin air; they are built out of a collection of existing parts, the composition of which expands (and occasionally, contracts) over time."[2] This is akin to the process of visioning: Most visions emerge gradually. They demand soaking time. They start with an insight that's not typically as profound or lucid as it will become. And then they require time to form, bounce back and forth a few times, and become what they are eventually remembered for. Thomas Edison famously created thousands of lightbulbs before inventing one that worked.

Johnson calls this the *slow hunch*. He notes that virtually all innovative ideas start off as impressions rather than breakthroughs. The ensuing breakthrough idea is the product of perseverance and often a combination of hunches that collide and merge over time—not a flash of insight that instantly makes sense. A vision arises the same way. It's not a stroke of genius, but rather an emerging concept that requires work and time in combination with a perceptive and tolerant mindset.

CONTAINED EMERGENCE

Let's go back to 1937. Meet Malcolm McLean, a trucker who delivers cotton bales to Hoboken, New Jersey, from Fayetteville, North Carolina. Three years earlier, McLean saved enough money to buy a secondhand truck for $120. He now makes the monotonous 1,200-mile round trip up the East Coast and back a few times a week. After arriving at Hoboken with his goods, a long wait starts; it takes hours to get his truck unloaded. Staring out his window, he sees hundreds of longshoremen working hard to load and unload cargo from ships to trucks and vice versa. It strikes him that this is a great waste of time and money. One crate after another gets lifted off a truck, placed on the dock, tightened into a sling, and loaded into the hold of a ship. It happens piece by piece, one by one: a slow, endless, unrewarding, and even dangerous process. But it keeps a large crowd of people employed, and it's necessary work.

Contemplating the scene, McLean wonders if there's another way. "The thought occurred to me, as I waited around that day, that it would be easier to lift my trailer up and, without any of its content being touched, put it onto the ship,"[3] he later recalled.

It was the beginning of a vision that would transform the shipping industry and grow a multimillion-dollar company. Malcolm McLean became the inventor of the container, the same one that dominates the view of most ports worldwide today. His early insight also made him a very wealthy man. McLean's story is often told as an epiphany, a stroke of brilliance that came to him as he sat in his truck. It sounds heroic and satisfies the deeply rooted desire of the audience to be awed by the sudden, momentous birth of a groundbreaking idea.

But that's not how it went. It wasn't until the early fifties, some fifteen years later, that McLean fully realized the potential of his 1937 insight. After that particular trip to Hoboken, he continued to expand his trucking business, successfully building the largest trucking fleet in the South. McLean Trucking Company operated over 1,700 trucks and thirty-seven transport terminals along the Eastern Seaboard.[4] As he was amassing his trucking fleet, he wasn't spending time advancing his early business idea of "lifting his trailer up."

In fact, the original insight wasn't the container as we know it today, either. The seed of the idea needed soaking time—and a helping of external circumstances. It wasn't until some states adopted weight restrictions and levied taxes on interstate trucking that McLean revisited the idea, which must have been simmering in the back of his mind all that time. The dissonance between the state governments' restrictions made interstate transport by trucks a balancing act for truckers, who aimed to transport as many goods as possible while avoiding heavy taxes and fines.

McLean realized that efficient overseas transport of goods would avoid much of this frustration. As his 1937 insight began to take shape, he envisioned various seaport hubs that would work to transport large amounts of goods by ship, with trucks conducting the short, mostly intrastate, beginning or end leg of the journey. The new system would be cheaper (by avoiding taxes) and more effective.

He eventually redesigned his trailers into two parts: a base with wheels and an independent container. He also acquired a shipping company, which granted him shipping and docking rights to most important eastern ports, and he started to promote and develop the business. Not everyone bought into the vision immediately, though. McLean had to overcome strong resistance from unions, win over port authorities, and make significant upfront investments. His personal moment of truth came in 1955. With authorities unwilling to support him in expanding both businesses at the same time, he had to make a choice: his safe and established trucking business or his highly speculative shipping venture. He chose the latter, sold off his interests in McLean Trucking, and became the owner of Pan-Atlantic, which he renamed Sea-Land Industries. Containerization was born.

McLean's story is one of symbiosis between entrepreneurship and vision that transformed an industry that had remained virtually unchanged for centuries. He was a true innovator, among the most heralded business leaders of the twentieth century. But we must remember that his transformative vision *emerged* over a number of years; it didn't spring from his mind fully formed the way we like to think of brilliant ideas.

A DEVELOPMENT FRAMEWORK

McLean's story illustrates that, rather than a gift, the potential to come up with—and hold on to and cultivate—a brilliant idea or a vision is within all of us. Visionary leadership isn't a personality trait, although it is sometimes confused with concepts like charismatic leadership, which do have a strong personality-oriented element. This is the risk in using people like John F. Kennedy, Martin Luther King, and Steve Jobs as examples: They all seem to have had front-row tickets when the gift of charisma was handed out.

Visionary capacity is different. We all can work consciously and continuously to grow our ability to anticipate, improve our game of looking ahead, have more remarkable insights, and become more inspirational in how we speak about the future. We all can benefit from the effects of a compelling vision in the part of the world we influence. Being able to think, behave, act, and communicate in a more future-oriented fashion provides direction for the road ahead and guidance for decisions that will need to be made. It also inspires and fuels innovation and breakthrough thinking. And it energizes your followers with purpose and meaning.

The big question is *how*. How do you go about developing this crucial leadership competence? How and where do you start? How do you sustain it, and how do you integrate it into your daily life? As with learning a new sport, you will need to deliberately work on some specific abilities, getting the basics right, learning what to focus on first, transforming unproductive habits and routines, and making seemingly complicated things as simple as possible (but not one bit simpler, as Einstein famously said).

Naturally, as with all things in life, some of us will be better at this competence than others. But we all can improve our game. What we need is a developmental framework, something that simplifies this inherently complex learning curve and guides us with a process. That's what you'll find in the rest of this chapter.

Based on my observations (and testing done with hundreds of senior leaders, whom I work with on vision, strategy, and leadership), there are two critical developmental dimensions for growing your visionary capacity:

1. Your ability *to see things early.* The first signs of change often manifest as random noise or faint warning signals, often at the periphery of our attention and far less explicit in their game-changing nature than they are later. Growing your ability to notice these signals early, and recognize their potential impact, is an essential part of raising your visionary capacity.

2. Your ability *to connect the dots,* to create coherence in the future you face and turn it into a "bigger picture" story. This implies constructively and intelligently working through the complexity of the multifaceted and multidimensional future.

We'll explore both concepts briefly here, but since they are both vital dimensions in your development, I devoted a full chapter to each of them, to explain what they are about and how you go about nurturing both abilities (see Chapters 4 and 5).

SEEING THINGS EARLY

The first developmental dimension for your visionary capacity is the ability to see things early. In Chapter 2 we explored the brain's ability to tune out the noise, allowing you to focus on what seems most important. When the noise—let's say it's street traffic—becomes something else—squealing tires—your attention shifts to it. Also in our day-to-day information overload, most of what we hear is noise in terms of future change—but some of it is something else. It could be an early signal of change that could, potentially, create a substantial opportunity, and you would want to be among the first to recognize it. Improving your ability to detect, acknowledge, and understand such signals before others do is a key to developing visionary capacity. That's what Malcolm McLean did as he looked out his windshield in 1937. He picked up the signal and had a sufficient understanding of its potential impact as he realized that the process of docking could be redesigned and made much more efficient. It's what Ingvar Kamprad, the founder of IKEA, did when he realized the furniture industry did not address the needs of a large group of consumers.

This ability to anticipate and notice things early was one of the first things Alan Mulally pursued at Ford, after he took the wheel as CEO in 2006 and turned around the company from bankruptcy. "The first thing a leader does is facilitate connections between the organization and the outside world,"[5] he asserts. To institutionalize this practice of context scanning, he made it an intense part of the regular senior leadership rhythm:

> Every week we have a Business Plan Review meeting. Our entire global leadership team, every business leader, every functional leader, attends either remotely or in person. We talk about the worldwide business environment at that moment—things like the economy, the energy and technology sectors, global labor, government relationships, demographic trends, what our competitors are doing, what is going on with our customer. [. . .] Then we take it a step further and discuss how these trends are likely to evolve. Looking ahead is critical. We talk about more than what our customers value right now. We talk about the forces in the world that are going to shape what they will value in the future.[6]

The possibilities inherent in early signals deviate from conventional wisdom and only get picked up by those whose antennas are tuned to them. Luck occasionally plays a part, but getting this critical information early depends more reliably on being receptive to it, being mentally ready to understand what it could mean and to turn it into an opportunity for yourself and your organization. You might also decide that the time isn't right and choose not to take the opportunity. But that choice can only be present if you see things early; those who don't aren't even aware of the potential.

To take some of the pressure off, don't mistake *early* for *first*. You want to be among the early group to identify the signal of change, make use of it productively, integrate it into your vision, and possibly create opportunities with it. Neither Jeff Bezos (Amazon.com), nor Michael Dell (Dell Computers), nor Larry Page (Google) invented the Internet, or retailing, or distance sales, or search engines. However, they *were* in the early group that recognized the potential. That was more than just good luck (which is surely also always part of it); there was an open-mindedness that allowed them to embrace uncertainty and take advantage of an opportunity.

In fact, Malcolm McLean's early insight on containerization was not completely new, either. As early as 1929, a similar system of shipping containers was in operation between New York and Cuba. Railroad boxcars were used to drive cargo onto sea vessels and were, upon arrival, collected by a locomotive to continue the journey. It was also not uncommon for shipping companies to stack large, similar-size boxes on board. It just took someone like McLean to see it and to connect the dots properly.

CONNECTING THE DOTS

A powerful vision is never merely the early identification of a changing reality. Like McLean, you need to connect the dots, combining imagination and foresight into a comprehensive, coherent, and robust story about the future of your industry, organization, or the part of it that you are responsible for. The coherence factor is critical because visions do not exist in a vacuum. The ever-evolving world and the ever-changing future shape the context in which the vision needs to thrive.

Advances in technology, the results of legislation and government policies, shifting geopolitical powers, or "simply" the (future) readiness of society to conceive of a different future are examples of factors outside the control of the visionary that influence the context and therefore the conditions for success of the vision. Consequently, the story needs to be more than one or a few remarkable insights into what might be changing: It needs to connect and integrate with a larger context of future developments. The coherence factor makes it a holistic story that is rounded and complete and doesn't suffer from "flavor of the month-ism." This is where it becomes difficult to play the remarkable and unconventional card, as the coherence factor pushes the story from wild and radical (inspired by the *seeing things early* dimension) back into the realm of a responsible, don't-bet-the-house kind of perspective.

This might make the vision less tantalizing, but presumably more legitimate. Research conducted by Jerker Denrell, a professor of behavioral science at the Warwick Business School, exposed this catch in our fascination with the unusual. His finding: People who successfully foresee an unusual event tend to be wrong about the future over the long run. By analyzing years of experts' quarterly forecasts for interest rates and inflation, he observed that the analyst who successfully predicted the highest number of rogue events (six) had the worst forecasting record by far. Yet out-of-the-ordinary predictions that turn out to be right draw attention. Denrell says, "We tend to admire these people because we remember that they hit and no one else did—they separated themselves from the pack." But he continues, "If you rely heavily on the person who had that hit, you probably won't come out ahead."[7] Balancing exciting, out-of-the-ordinary perspectives with an appropriate—but not dampening—sense of realism is a more responsible way of working.

The art form of connecting the dots is therefore about maintaining the sense of excitement around the changes the future might hold *without* losing sight of the bigger picture of context and time. The coherence factor is pivotal in your visionary capacity since it stops you from becoming delusional. Often *timing* is everything. Visions that come too early die prematurely (e.g., Microsoft's Tablet PC introduced in 2000), and visions that come too late are nothing but me-too ideas.

McLean's vision of containerization illustrates these points clearly. He saw the potential for change in his industry earlier than most others did (as far as we know), envisioning a very different way of working. However, he didn't bring it together until external conditions, such as increased interstate taxes, levies, and weight restrictions, provided the right context to shape his insight into a grand vision of containerized cargo traveling between seaport hubs. With great sensitivity to context—something we'll look at in depth later—McLean was able to connect various dots into a larger scheme, which in combination with his early insight made him the great visionary he deserves to be remembered as.

2 x 2

At this point you may be thinking, "Okay, but how can I see things early and how can I connect the dots? It sounds good, but I don't know how to do it." Your mind is racing ahead; rest assured, we will turn to some powerful and proven techniques in the chapters dedicated to each ability. For now, let's explore this developmental framework further so that you'll get a better idea of its intention and its use.

The two dimensions are key. They are also independent of one another. Seeing change early is about spotting isolated signals of change on the horizon while connecting the dots is about integrating the larger context, the so-called big picture. In more colloquial terms, the first one is about your eye for detail whereas the second is about your helicopter view. So, you might be good at one, but that does not imply you are good at the other. For our visionary capacity to grow, we want to become good at both. Therefore, each dimension warrants its own practices.

The fact that they are so different and independent allows us to portray them in a two-by-two (2x2) matrix,[8] as shown in Figure 3-1. Each axis differentiates a low and high skill level of both dimensions. The four cells that emerge distinguish four different archetypes of visionary capacity, and even of visionary leadership.

Practice 3-1. Your current visionary self.

Now that you have developed a good understanding of the framework, it's worthwhile to take a moment to reflect on where you currently stand. Try out the practice, and establish for yourself how you do on both dimensions.

FOLLOWERS

In the lower left quadrant of Figure 3-1, we find the Follower: someone neither very good at early noticing nor skilled in creating and communicating a coherent story from the various insights he or she has about what the future might bring.

This is not to say that Followers don't have any idea of what the future might bring for their part of the organization or industry. They just don't have a compelling story or image ready to share when provided an opportunity to ignite others. It's either absent, poorly developed and unformu-

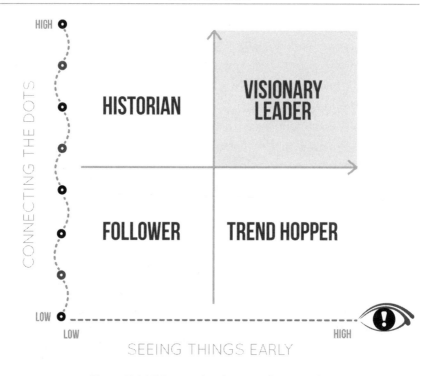

Figure 3-1. Visionary development framework.

lated, or all over the place and lacking coherence. The Follower may well be a wonderful person and an excellent manager, but don't expect this person to be a rich source of inspiration, to drive innovation, fuel fresh break-through ideas, or help others overcome mental barriers in order to go beyond today's reality.

Being a Follower isn't necessarily a bad thing (where would leaders be without them?) and can indeed be a fruitful strategy, particularly in risk-avoiding organizations. Healthy levels of carefulness, critical thinking, and apprehension can work for every leader, including the visionary one. But if you're a Follower *all the time,* don't expect any of the great benefits to emerge. You won't stretch the boundaries of your people's imagination, reap the fruits of new ways of doing business, or be seen as a source of inspiration and energy to your followers. It just won't happen. The upside, though, is that you will probably not experience the dark side of vision (tunnel or a fraud-inducing vision), either. In the short term, it's relatively safe ground and, especially in hindsight, sometimes even the wisest position to take. But in the long run it could severely hurt your organization or your team, since your preoccupation with today keeps you from anticipating what comes next, and over time your role, business, or skill set might lose its relevance.

This safe ground might also stop you from reaching your full potential. Business consultant Paul Smith points out that "most businesspeople will go an entire career and never have the opportunity to impact the future of the business beyond the next fiscal year."[9] Nurturing your visionary capacity puts you in a position to potentially impact the next decade of the organization. Rethinking the future, challenging conventional wisdom, imagining a better tomorrow should not only be exciting and inspiring, but they are also a great way to explore all of your talents. Ellen Langer, professor of psychology at Harvard, clarifies that "continually re-experiencing life from a fresh vantage point is part of being truly alive."[10]

TREND HOPPERS

In her fascinating work *Fad Surfing in the Boardroom: Managing in the Age of Instant Answers*, Eileen Shapiro defines fad surfing as "the practice of riding the crest of the latest management panacea and then paddling out again just in time to ride the next one; always absorbing for managers and lucrative for consultants; frequently disastrous for organizations."[11]

This is a perfect description of the Trend Hopper, the person who has a well-developed ability to see things early, is very much in tune with what's on the edge, and is existentially willing to embrace changing realities. The Trend Hopper is often an early adopter of new technology and among the first to fantasize about how things can become different— most always *radically* different in their view—soon. Trend Hoppers are usually inspiring to engage with and have plenty of compelling stories to share about what's happening on the cutting-edge of the business.

But the Trend Hopper isn't very good at turning early-stage insights into a coherent story that justifies an active strategic pursuit. It's not in this person's nature to find an appropriate balance between what could become radically different and what remains essentially the same, in the foreseeable future at least. The Trend Hopper runs the risk of becoming dogmatic,

embracing radical views, and losing traction with the rest of the organization.

Those in this category (lower right quadrant of Figure 3-1) are less
likely to develop true leadership profiles or to acquire a critical mass of
dedicated followers. After chasing several flavor-of-the-month ideas,
many people mentally tune out with the Trend Hopper and become reluctant to chase yet another "groundbreaking" idea or development. Trend
Hoppers, or Fad Surfers, are therefore ineffective in the long run in engaging the organization, mostly because they do not successfully integrate
their early insights into a larger context that provides coherence. They are
the kind of people we like to listen to on Friday afternoon, but not on
Monday morning.

HISTORIANS, OR CYNICS

Which brings us to the upper left quadrant of Figure 3-1, the leaders adept
at connecting the dots and spinning a story that makes sense. They like to
cite patterns, facts, and figures—ideally in PowerPoint—and marvel at
making the road traveled so far look very coherent and intentional. When
you listen to them, it all makes sense. But they have their eye trained on the
factually true past, not on the imaginative uncertain future. They're not
very good at spotting where the early signals are coming from and how
these could become potential game changers. I call them the Historians.
They have a strong thinking preference for consistency and logic, and are
therefore less interested in what breaks with coherence (unlike Trend Hoppers). Their focus is on making everyone understand why we are where we
are today by integrating past events into a logically consistent perspective.

I first spotted this archetype several years ago when I was hosting a series of three-day interventions with senior and future leaders of a very large
organization. Midway through these repetitive events, one of the leaders of
the company's executive team would be invited and engaged in a two-hour
open dialogue with the group. Soon enough, someone would ask this leader
for a clarification of the corporate strategy or some other strategic project.
To me, this was always the moment of truth: Would the senior leader provide a compelling story of what the future might look like, where this strat-

egy might bring us or how this strategic project will help prepare us for a promising future?

Sadly, I have found that these rare moments to demonstrate such forward-oriented leadership often get passed on. And I've been noticing this phenomenon ever since—with business leaders as well as political leaders. It seems that most of them, when given a unique opportunity to show their leadership, recite the past instead of envisioning the future. They start off saying something like, "Let me explain where we came from. Three years ago, we started with the new change program ONE that brought our focus back to the customer. As you'll remember, we started with three key initiatives. . . . " What follows is a careful reconstruction of history that explains why we are where we are today and justifies the chosen strategy. By the time the story ends, we have a historic, factually accurate recount of recent history that fails to inspire or energize anyone (but every head nods in agreement—or drowsiness). If you are really unlucky, the leader might say, "Glad you asked," and launch into a fifteen-page PowerPoint slide set that he has conveniently brought along in order to nicely explain where we came from—and you get to sit politely through this "exciting" recount.

Once they've covered this past ground, if anyone is still listening, they often treat the future as a reverse image of the past, emphasizing that a desired outcome will be reached if "we stay on course." It's an extrapolative trap, one that describes the past as somehow ordained and assumes the future is more certain than it actually is.

I'll let you think about how a visionary leader would have taken this question for clarification on the strategy or a strategic project—and give you some idea when we get to our final quadrant.

But let's explore this archetype a bit more, since the Historian doesn't just miss opportunities to demonstrate leadership. There are some real dangers to this overreliance on the past. For one, Historians are susceptible to tunnel vision. Their stories are so convincing that they rarely reconsider their assumptions, holding on to belief systems that have become fixated by past experiences. But we all know that the future is unlikely to be a copy of the past. Yet, not for Historians; they hold on to patterns of the past.

Moreover, Historians also quickly become, or are perceived as, *cynics*. And in the words of the remarkable Irish writer and philosopher Charles

Handy, "There are two kinds of people. Drains and Radiators. And I have chosen to spent my life with the latter." Cynics fall into Handy's first category: the people who sap your energy as they explain one more time why things are the way they are, and why your unconventional idea is *not* going to work. Sometimes it's reassuring to listen to a cynic, or even to be cynical yourself, but you'll never get a powerful vision from one.

I've come to believe that cynicism tops the list of unhelpful attitudes in leadership and organizational life. Cynics don't reframe, ignite, or energize—they drain.

Marketing guru Seth Godin is even more explicit on the destructive value of cynics. Under the title *The Selfish Cynic*, he writes on his blog: "Someone betting on the worst outcomes is going to be correct now and then, but that doesn't mean we need to have him on our team. I'd rather work with people brave enough to embrace possible futures at the expense of being disappointed now and then. Don't expect kudos or respect for being a cynic. It's selfish."[12]

That said, there is of course value in some historical perspective. It's important to understand your heritage, the roots of the organization, and what it stands for. It's important to have historical context, like the founder's story, the collective wisdom about the successes and failures of the organization, and a good awareness of the values the company authentically carries. What is important is to not let history cripple your ability to engage constructively with the future.

THE VISIONARY

A quote attributed to Albert Schweitzer says that "an optimist is a person who sees a green light everywhere, while a pessimist sees only the red stoplight. . . . The truly wise person is color-blind." I'd like to extend the metaphor and let our visionary be color-blind. The visionary would not overoptimistically jump on every fad that passes by, as our Trend Hopper risks. Nor would he become a naysayer and launch into the Historian mode. The visionary takes a mindful, future-oriented perspective, balancing the need for a compelling future with the awareness of the inherent dangers of becoming dogmatic and overoptimistic.

How would a visionary leader have dealt with the opportunity described in the previous paragraphs? Visionary leaders would seize the opportunity to energize, inspire, and mobilize followers by starting their explanation of the chosen strategy *in the future*: "Let me explain where we're heading. Three years from now, our company equals what FC Barcelona is in today's soccer: a globally recognized power brand that stands for intimacy with our fans, beautiful products, and a keen eye for continuous renewal." Or something similar: a fad-free, optimistic, hope-giving, and energizing perspective on the future (unless your company is based in Madrid, of course).

Such a response unleashes energy and engages people's imagination, allowing them to freely associate with the vision and derive purpose and meaning from it. That's what a vision foremost needs to do: allow others to "see" and embrace it. The future therefore concerns an aspirational image; it is something that we see, feel, and smell rather than something we need to process intellectually by a series of jammed PowerPoint slides or dreary bullet points.

Regrettably, I don't see many leaders who operate at this aspirational level and are able to convincingly share a compelling future-oriented perspective that fills people with meaning and energy. Maybe it's because they don't have a story ready to tell at such leadership moments of truth. Or maybe it's because it is much safer to stay within the historical context of demonstrable facts than to tap into your own and your followers' imaginations. It might also be because they don't understand the critical value of inspiration in engaging people in a desired transformation. Whatever the cause, it's a missed opportunity to guide, influence, and persuade those that matter most in your leadership, and who are pivotal in helping you achieve the goals and transformation you are aiming for.

The Follower, the Trend Hopper, and the Historian are archetypes. And while their descriptions are pretty extreme, you've probably met all of them (perhaps in a watered-down version) in your organizational life. You probably have firsthand knowledge of how each one falls short in the vision department. If they're good at seeing things early, they're not always good at connecting the dots. Or if they connect the dots, they fall short when it comes to picking up early signals.

To become a visionary leader, you will need to develop both of these essential dimensions. They're the topics of our next two chapters, in which I take you through the practical side of growing both abilities. In the two final sections of this chapter, let's dive deeper into the differences between the two dimensions, and discover how we differentiate proclaimed larger-than-life visionaries from *true* visionaries.

DEEPENING THE FRAMEWORK

The two dimensions—seeing things early and connecting the dots—have a number of things in common. Both are future-oriented; built around imagination; exploratory; anticipatory; potentially frame-breaking; and engage positively with uncertainty. On the developmental front, these similarities imply that there are a number of conditional factors essential for both. Behaviors and mindset factors such as curiosity, open-mindedness, and playfulness are important to the development of both dimensions. We will explore these human aspects, attitudes, and productive behaviors in more depth in Chapters 6 and 7.

But there are also key differences, ones that mean we need separate approaches for sharpening and growing those abilities. Let's lay out those differences.

Difference 1: Relevance vs. Implication

Research suggests that the average person consumes about 34 gigabytes of content and 100,000 words of information in a single day.[13] Because we're operating on constant information overload, it's vital that we filter out what's important and what's not. The ability to see change early depends on judging weak signals according to the relevance they represent. Without specific effort, you will only be able to identify events that were early manifestations of change in retrospect. But that's usually when it's too late. You want to identify them as they unfold or even before they unfold. So it becomes important to establish the relevance of certain early-warning signals to the future of the industry, country, organization, or whatever future you're interested in.

The ability to *connect the dots,* though, is focused on *implications* of changing realities. It takes the ideas generated from the early noticing ability and integrates them with other important factors, putting the early signals of a changing reality into perspective and making them logically consistent. The resulting story is then complete to potentially serve as a powerful vision.

Difference 2: Data Point vs. Model

In a parliamentary hearing broadcast on national television in the Netherlands, one of the key planners of the Dutch Planning Bureau defended the organization for not having foreseen the financial crisis of 2008. He sounded like a lot of other planners that year: "Our models just did not cater to the eventuality that banks would no longer be willing to lend each other money." For the Netherlands, the financial crisis resulted in nationalization of one of its three main banks (ABN AMRO Bank) and massive financial support to other banks of Dutch descent, such as ING. Naturally, there was no shortage of questions about how they'd gotten there and who was to blame.

At first glance, the planner's statement about their models seems reasonable. After all, the financial crisis was unprecedented. Maybe it was unrealistic to expect the planning bureau to consider such extreme possibilities in its models.

Or was it? Let's go back a year before the crisis fully unfolded, before the fall of Lehman Brothers. It was on September 12, 2007, that the interbank lending market locked up overnight fully unexpectedly. Suddenly, banks refused to lend money to one other to cover short-term liquidity needs, a practice otherwise all too common in the banking industry. Trust in each other's ability to repay abruptly disappeared. To keep the system afloat and prevent banks from going under, the European Bank, the U.K. National Bank, and the U.S. Federal Reserve pumped billions of euros into the interbank lending market, an unprecedented move.

Soon it became clear that the sudden banking panic was due to a rumor. British bank Northern Rock had just borrowed funds from the government to avoid a liquidity crisis, and the move sparked fears that it would go bankrupt. When word got out, depositors stormed in to withdraw their savings. It was the first run on a British bank in 150 years. The rumor was felt internationally as the wholesale markets froze, shutting down a system that had operated successfully for years. Once the culprit was identified, banks gradually eased their reluctance and started lending each other money again.

So let's get back to the Dutch Planning Bureau. It knew—or for sure could have known—that a sudden lockup of the wholesale markets was possible; it had already happened because of the fear that just *one* bank would fail. Twelve months before the fall of Lehman Brothers, the bureau's planners should have absorbed this data and made their models more robust for such (no-longer-obscure) eventualities, if they had had their eye sharpened to seeing things early. Regrettably, however, planning bureaus tend to focus more on connecting the dots, looking for the fairly coherent relationships between parameters instead of looking for rogue events.

Nassim Taleb's classic *The Black Swan: The Impact of the Highly Improbable* was, improbably, published a few months before the run on Northern Rock. The former trader's story and philosophy was written up by Malcolm Gladwell and published in *The New Yorker* in 2002.[14] As Gladwell describes him, Taleb runs an investment fund with a very unconventional approach. While nearly all fund managers pride themselves on their (often illusionary) ability to pick stocks, Taleb's fund is rather uniquely managed with the belief that rogue, unexpected events always appear in a market. Sooner or later the market will experience a big negative shock due to a rogue event such as 9/11 or Enron's collapse, or Lehman Brothers's demise, Dubai's insolvency announcement, Greece's fraud with its economic statistics, or Japan's tsunami. Therefore, the fund only invests in put options, investment instruments that materialize with falling prices. When that happens, as Taleb knows it will one day, his continuous day-to-day losses endured during uneventful periods are widely offset by the leveraged profits they make on that one day. It requires nerve to bear seemingly endless losses in normal periods of market growth, but since Taleb is convinced that rogue events are inevitable, he happily accepts these losses.

The Dutch Planning Bureau took—and probably still takes—a "connecting the dots" approach to engaging with the future. This bias creates an *illusion of control,* which we will recognize in Chapter 6 as one of the dangers leading to tunnel vision. Sometimes one data point can defy all the logic in the model. Even though it represents a different and often unwanted reality, it's the outlier that must be considered in serious planning. The ability to connect the dots isn't enough. A model, like a vision, requires an understanding of the relevance of single data points in addition to the model, even if these points are outliers. Especially if they happened just twelve months earlier.

Difference 3: Focus on Detail vs. Focus on Helicopter View

The third core difference between seeing things early and connecting the dots is a behavioral one. The ability to see things early requires astute attention to detail. You need to filter the signal from the noise, focusing on one or possibly a few weak signals that are undetected by most.

The ability to create a coherent story, however, takes a helicopter view. A generalist who isn't hampered by too much attention to detail can understand the implications of various developments and connect them in a logical, compelling story.

Developing both abilities requires the skills and focus of the specialist and the generalist. You must consider the relevance and potential consequences of rather vague, weak signals and then step into the helicopter and combine the signals with larger, possibly macroeconomic, trends and developments at play in the world and your industry. Collectively, these skills help us spot manifestations of changing realities earlier than others (e.g., competitors) and turn them into an overarching story that is both intriguing (through its early identifications) and logical (through its connections to other observable phenomena).

Difference 4: Risk Seeking vs. Risk Aversion

The fourth and last difference I want to bring to the surface—and which is perhaps the most pivotal in understanding visionary capacity as I promote it—relates to perceptions of risks. Your ability to identify change is about looking beyond the conventional and questioning the way things are as they are today. Hence, a challenging, risk-seeking stance. Your ability to connect the dots is more conservative and risk-averse, however, since it looks for a coherent bigger picture. In other words, it forces you to be mindful about the stance you take and not bet the house over attractive yet highly speculative views brought to you by your improved ability to identify early changes.

This fourth difference relates to a much larger theme in understanding visionary leadership—at least, the perspective I take on it. Let's zoom in on that in this chapter's next and final section.

NARCISSISTIC DISTRACTION

To round off our introduction to the framework of visionary development proposed here, it might be interesting to contemplate how well the model informs us about visionary leadership in real life. To paraphrase John Kotter's landmark article titled "What Leaders Really Do," let's ask ourselves the question: What do visionary leaders really do?

The problem with this question is that the colloquial use of the term *visionary* blurs with overlapping concepts such as charisma, entrepreneurship, and narcissism. Let's dig deeper, since it is important to understand the perspective we take here on the meaning of visionary, for it will guide our further exploration.

Many leadership challenges revolve around mediating dilemmas and trade-offs. Entrepreneurship is good, but too much of it might spin things out of control. Long-term focus is important, but without short-term gains it becomes hard to sustain. Incentives work well in aligning action, but too many might push people over ethical and legal boundaries. Growth is important, but so is sustainability. Persistence is a great leadership quality, but dogmatism is not. All such dilemmas call for finding an appropriate balance between forces deemed important in the strategy and leadership field. It is the leader's role to identify, confront, manage, and sometimes resolve these dilemmas, taking into account culture, legacy, aspiration, risk-profile, reputation, and other contextual themes.

Our visionary framework also represents such a dilemma. Stretching the boundaries by "seeing things early" and jumping on changing realities leans toward *risk seeking*: challenging the status quo, thinking differently, and exploring new opportunities early. On the other hand, seeking coherence by "connecting the dots" in a responsible way, and working from a richer position than one of mere faith and wishful thinking, leans toward *risk aversion*. We should be very mindful of our limited perspective and the risk of tunnel vision, so we must keep in mind that our version of connecting the dots is but one version of how the dots of the future can be connected.

Hence, the two axes are the yin and yang of visionary capacity: risk seeking vs. risk aversion. Balancing them is the *real* art of looking ahead. Therefore, our exploration of what visionary leaders really do should not be confused with *anecdotal evidence* of leaders who predominantly had their eye on the changing realities (that is, in "seeing things early") and turned their early insight into a formidable success. Such stories of heroic leadership have great appeal, but it's *responsible* visionary leadership that we should aim to develop—not "leadership by gambling."

The real challenge we face, therefore, is the popular use of the word *visionary*. We're inclined to apply the term to mystical, larger-than-life personalities who make the cover of *Fortune* magazine and whose books about themselves and their successes are instant bestsellers. Think of Larry Ellison, Andy Grove, Jack Welch, but equally Napoléon Bonaparte, Charles de Gaulle, Winston Churchill, and Bill Clinton.

The most prominent example in recent times would be Steve Jobs, undoubtedly topping most people's list of contemporary visionary leaders. His remarkable and astonishing track record at Apple, in particular its evolution from near bankruptcy in the mid-nineties to being the most valuable company in the world just a little more than a decade later, is a recovery story beyond imagination. Anyone's intuitive reaction to the question of whether Steve Jobs was a visionary leader would likely be affirmative. But notwithstanding his amazing achievements at Apple, and his extraordinary re-creation of the much-adored company (I'm a big fan of Apple's products), I must disagree. Let's elaborate, since I know this position is controversial.

Visionary leaders are often mixed up with what really are *narcissistic* leaders. Narcissists who get to the point of being leaders are—seemingly—very good at the Vision Thing. They readily share "big picture" stories, speak eloquently, and are self-assured in their ideas. But you do not need to be a narcissist in order to become good at the Vision Thing. According to Freud, who conceptualized the term in the psychoanalytic field in his work *On Narcissism,* "people of this type impress others as being 'personalities.'" He praised them for their ability to "give a fresh stimulus to cultural development or damage the established state of affairs." But he also identified their dark side: "Achievement can feed feelings of grandiosity"[15] in such personalities.

In today's world, the term *narcissism* generally has a negative undertone; narcissists have strong egos, care mainly about themselves, like to be the center of attention, and consider their point of view to be the only valid one. They can radiate an abrasive level of self-confidence, are often shamelessly assertive, and can be very pretentious, to mention just a few negative associations. Some extreme personalities even think of themselves as "the chosen ones." An executive at Oracle once characterized his narcissistic CEO Larry Ellison by saying that the "only difference between God and Larry is that God doesn't believe he is Larry."

Anthropologist and psychotherapist Michael Maccoby favorably reinterpreted part of that negative image when he introduced the concept of *productive* narcissism. In his acclaimed article "Narcissistic Leaders,"[16] he acknowledges the dark side, but points out that this type of personality can be extraordinarily useful in times of change, when decisive leadership is called for. Under these circumstances, narcissistic leaders excel at rallying the troops through inspiration, motivation, and direction setting—the same qualities that contribute to a powerful vision. "They are gifted and creative strategists who see the big picture and find meaning in the risky challenge of changing the world and leaving behind a legacy," Maccoby says.[17] Narcissists have the capacity to incite massive change.

So where do the two concepts of narcissism and visionary disconnect? This is where we return to Steve Jobs, whose biography provided a clear peek into his character and personality.[18] Jobs possessed all the positive qualities Maccoby pointed out: He managed to inspire and lead Apple through its tremendous transformation. His passionate personality was a perfect fit for Apple—in that period of time. Jobs spotted the changes on the horizons of the music industry, the cell phone industry, and the tablet industry very early, and he mobilized his troops with energizing views and speeches: a clear ten out of ten on "seeing things early."

But how about the other axis?

Studying his biography, you don't need a Ph.D. in psychology to spot the dark sides of Jobs's personality. He had remarkably little empathy, was a poor listener, intolerant toward different perspectives, dogmatic, self-absorbed, stubborn, and a fanatical troublemaker (also when it was unproductive). All qualities we would normally consider harmful in *responsibly* developing your ability to better connect the dots of the future.

Jobs undeniably got the big picture right—which we know with the benefit of hindsight. But the ability to connect the dots is not about getting the big picture right: It's about understanding that you are operating under great uncertainty, and therefore prudence is required. It creates balance between the risk-seeking yin of seeing things early and the risk-averse yang of connecting the dots. Qualities such as open-mindedness, thoughtfulness, playfulness with other perspectives, and genuinely listening to others are very important for developing this coherence-seeking dimension in a responsible way.

Remember, our two axes are *developmental* axes. In hindsight everything might look clear and obvious, but looking forward, being narrow-sighted, overconfident, and dogmatic can (too) easily lead to irresponsible big bets. Thus, these should not be considered qualities to strive for in developing your visionary side.

Making big bets fits perfectly with the narcissistic leadership profile. Narcissists love gripping visions of radical change. However, as Maccoby warns, the "tendency toward grandiosity is the Achilles' heel of narcissists." History has taught us that over time, narcissists tend to alienate themselves from reality and start overestimating their abilities. Their successes feed this tendency, frequently leading to destruction. To quote Maccoby once more, "One of the greatest problems is that the narcissist's faults tend to become more pronounced as he becomes more successful."[19] So, while Steve Jobs—and many other seemingly larger-than-life leaders—fits the profile of the big-thinking productive narcissist, this doesn't necessarily mean he is also a visionary. Not in my definition of responsible visionary leadership, at least, which puts risk seeking and disruption in check with a dimension of risk aversion and coherence.

To avoid confusion, we should be careful in defining what "visionary" really means. I propose to define it by the two—opposing—dimensions of early noticing (risk seeking, disruption) and creating coherence (risk-averse). True visionaries develop unconventional and possibly game-changing perspectives, but they are equally sensitive to the risks involved and take action to prevent their dream from becoming a hallucination. They are less publicity-prone than the spotlight-seeking narcissist is, and their success stories are featured on the cover of *Fortune* far less often.

———

In this chapter we've established a developmental framework for learning how to responsibly anticipate the future and grow your visionary capacity. It boils down to increasing your abilities to see things early and to connect the dots.

Now, we'll discuss *how* to go about cultivating these abilities in real life. What can you do to train yourself and your team to see change before others do? And what can you do to turn these early signs into a coherent story that becomes a compelling and powerful vision? These are intriguing questions, and the answers are not all that obvious.

4

Seeing Things Early

A good hockey player plays where the puck is. A great hockey player plays where the puck is going to be.

—WAYNE GRETZKY

REDUCING THOUGHTLESSNESS

In 1967, eminent futurists Anthony J. Wiener and Herman Kahn wrote a 431-page magnum opus titled *The Year 2000: A Framework for Speculation on the Next Thirty-Three Years*. It's filled with predictions—mostly technical advances and innovations ranging from applications for new materials and technologies (laser technology, ground transportation) to improved surgical procedures for changing the sex of children and adults.

They also predicted the arrival of home computers that would manage households and communicate with the outside world, as well as the use of personal pagers (much like cell phones). With the advantage of hindsight, it's easy to dismiss their predictions as inevitable, foreseeable developments. But compare Wiener and Kahn's view of the future with that of Ken Olsen. In 1977, ten years further into the future than when Wiener and Kahn published their work, he famously said at a convention of the World Future Society, that "there is no reason for any individual to have a computer in his home."[1] More remarkably even, Olsen was head of one of the largest computer companies at the time, Digital Equipment Corporation.

As right as they were about computers, though, Wiener and Kahn missed the mark on a number of their predictions. Noiseless helicopters haven't replaced taxis, artificial moons don't illuminate the sky, and interplanetary travel has not become everyday occurrence. Our life spans haven't increased to 150 years, either. Unfortunately.

These inaccuracies did not matter to Wiener and Kahn, though. Why not? Because their actual reason for engaging with the future and exploring possible changes in the decades ahead was to, in their words, "reduce the role of thoughtlessness." They referred to their work as "a framework for speculation": *Clarification,* not prophecy, was their goal.

SIGNAL AND NOISE

Now let's get back to seeing things early, the first developmental dimension for our visionary capacity. Similar to Wiener and Kahn's intentions, we're not aiming to become accurate, or even good, predictors of the future. Instead, we're working to develop an increased awareness of changing realities, building antennas for the distant signals that might push the future in a different direction from the one we currently and conventionally foresee. We can then become better at recognizing those signals and their potential impact when they present themselves in some early form.

Your ability to see things early is at the heart of what leadership expert Warren Bennis calls adaptive capacity. "The one competence that I now realize is absolutely essential for leaders—the key competence—is adaptive capacity. Adaptive capacity is what allows leaders to respond quickly and intelligently to relentless change,"[2] he argues. He lists that quality, together with vision, voice, and integrity, as the four cornerstone competencies of leadership (we'll explore them further in Chapter 6). Together with Robert Thomas, Bennis studied over forty leaders, some young (ages 21 to 34) and others older (ages 70 to 82), for the book *Geeks and Geezers*. Despite a few differences between the groups, Bennis and Thomas discovered that all of their subjects possessed the quality of adaptive capacity—the ability to be flexible and adapt to new situations and contexts.[3] Those with the highest levels of adaptive capacity are what the authors called *first-class noticers*: They're able to build and sustain a strong level of *context intelligence*.

This sensitivity to context correlates closely with the development of seeing things early; both involve the ability to gather relevant insights that allow you to notice changes before others do. To put it in engineering terms, it strengthens your ability to distinguish the signal from the noise. The signal is the important information you want to pick up, the early-warning signals. The noise is just news, entertainment, or a "fun fact," not something to remember or be alarmed by.

THE THEORY OF THE CAR CRASH

The strategic relevance of this first-class noticing ability is best explained by understanding what happens in a car crash (the parallel might at first sound far-fetched, but stick with me). I owe gratitude to one of my mentors, Jim Keen, for his creation of this memorable metaphor that visualizes the art and essence of looking ahead.[4]

In a car crash there are *two* critical moments (illustrated in Figure 4-1). First, there is the *point of surprise*. It's the moment when you consciously realize something is not what you thought it would be. In a car crash it would be the shock moment—the moment when sweat breaks out and cursing is forgiven. In our context, it is the moment at which you become aware of a changing reality, as you've noticed information that requires you to reassess your assumptions. Alan Greenspan's point of surprise came when he realized his deeply held belief that banks were better off with self-regulation had lost its validity. It's the point of realization that things are no longer the way they used to be.

The second moment in a car crash is the *point of no return*. Impact is inevitable; whatever you do from this point onward is of little use. It's only in the period between the point of surprise and the point of no return that you can deal with the changed reality. To further our car crash metaphor, this is why you want the interval between the two moments to be as wide as possible: It gives you the most time to react and prevent the crash. Since the point of no return is outside your control, the only way to maximize this interval is by influencing your point of surprise. That means concentrating

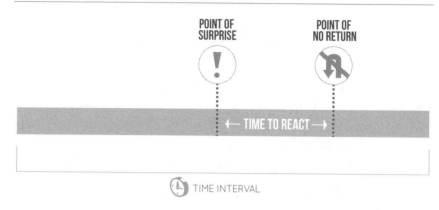

Figure 4-1. Two critical points.

on the road, avoiding distractions such as phone calls, and not driving under the influence. These factors can expand the length of time during which you can still respond to surprising changes.

In terms of visionary capacity, your goal is the same (see Figure 4-2). Seeing things earlier than others creates a distinct *strategic advantage*. By deliberately working on your ability to pick up early signals, by actively engaging with the future, by imagining changing realities, by making predictions (not for the sake of predicting, but for the sake of reducing your thoughtlessness), *you move your point of surprise forward*. This is what level 3 and level 4 future engagement (see preface) bring you: a significant strategic advantage through the extension of the interval in which you can successfully react to the change, either offensively or defensively.

If you and your organization are not actively engaging with the future and are not deliberately working on your ability to see things early, if you are rarely ahead of the curve, your conscious realization of changing realities most likely corresponds with that of others who equally lack this ability. You're only aware of something once it has become *conventional wisdom,* and by then the early adopters are well ahead of you. If you perceive the change earlier than others, however, you will find yourself with a tremendous head start. This is an invaluable lead in competitive environments since you have more time to understand, prepare options, decide, and react to the opportunities and their potential disruptive consequences. To use another popular metaphor, learning to do this systematically rather than inci-

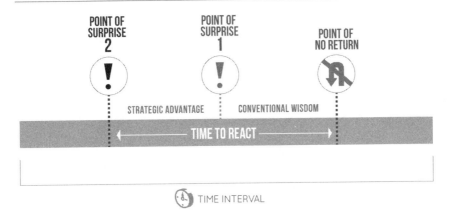

Figure 4-2. Strategic advantage.

dentally will position you for blue oceans, rather than battle in red oceans of equally ignorant competitors playing a catch-up game.[5]

Nolan Bushnell, the serial entrepreneur who founded Atari and is considered the father of electronic gaming, once remarked: "I try to get a vision of the future, and then try to figure out where the discontinuities are." That's how visionaries think: They deliberately stretch their imagination by deviating from conventional wisdom in order to gain a head start on the point of surprise. The sine qua non condition for successfully adopting this way of thinking is your willingness to be open-minded, because if you don't keep an open mind, you might find yourself in Greenspan's position, having your point of surprise fall at (or even after) the point of no return. That's severe enough in a car accident, but equally devastating in the leadership game.

MARKET TRANSITIONS

Let's put theory to practice and consider a company that consistently lives on the edge of the change game. Founded in 1984, Cisco Systems is the largest global provider of networking and communication equipment. It's part of a four-decade-old industry that has gone through tremendous changes, riding the wave of the stellar growth of the Internet and related networking applications, and known for a perpetual stream of groundbreaking innovations. Yet while related industries, such as the PC and cell phone markets, have experienced a revolving door of winners and losers, Cisco has remained a steady leader. This is as impressive as it is intriguing. How could this company stay ahead in an industry with such challenging dynamics, ever-present newcomers, technological breakthroughs, and big bets on new products and standards? How has it managed to stay on top for so long? What are the culture, processes, and systems that help Cisco repeatedly recognize early signals?

In a 2008 interview, CEO John Chambers shed light on the company's extraordinary performance, describing a strong focus on what he calls *market transitions*. These occur "when there is a subtle but clear disruptive shift. It could be social, economic, or technological and it begins many years before the market actually grasps its significance and adapts to it. A market transition gives you a glimpse of a new opportunity to take market share or move into new market adjacencies."[6]

Chambers elaborates:

> Market transitions are the precursors to market disruptions, and in many cases, transitions cause the disruptions. Transitions can be driven by the customer, by the industry, or by economic factors, and they usually occur well before the rest of the world realizes what's happening. Disruption occurs as the market responds to a transition with a game-changing innovation.
>
> I look for transitions that are way ahead of the current—or even impending—technology cycle. It takes us three to five years to reach $1 billion in revenue after a new product idea is launched. If you add to that a two- to three-year development cycle, plus the six to nine months it takes for the organization to grasp the transition opportunity before committing to the development cycle, you get an idea of how far out we must recognize a transition to really capitalize on it.

Sound familiar? This is what moving your point of surprise forward looks like in real life. It's why Cisco institutionalized the art of looking ahead by exploring market transitions, and why Alan Mulally institutionalized the global Business Plan Review meetings at Ford, in which the developments, changes, and disruptions in the outside world are discussed. They understand the value of contextual intelligence, early noticing, and "pre-perceiving" the future. But doing this takes more than a process or a strategy; it requires the right mindset and associated behaviors. It also means leadership: setting the standard and leading by example. At Cisco that translates to "closely listening to hints dropped by customers about new technologies on the horizon, shifts in the demographic or economic picture, and other trends," and applying a nondogmatic mindset receptive to exploring these hints and hunches. That's what future-oriented leadership looks like in practice.

TOYS IN THE BOARDROOM

The good news is that this kind of future-oriented behavior and mindset can be cultivated and nurtured within an organization. To understand how that works, let's first sidetrack to some fascinating research by Harvard's Sreedhari Desai and Francesca Gino. Their study shows that adults are less likely to cheat and more likely to engage in positive social behavior when primed with reminders from their childhood.[7] They demonstrated this behavior by having adults solve math puzzles in which they could easily cheat if they wanted to. Participants were told that the number of right answers mattered, so there was some incentive to reach a good score and therefore to cheat if they felt it would improve their results. And here comes their remarkable finding: The researchers discovered that their subjects were much less likely to cheat, by a factor of 20 percent, when they did these math puzzles in a room full of childhood cues, such as teddy bears, cartoons, and crayons, instead of in a neutral room. So, the sheer fact that they performed their exercises in a room that—unknown to them—was intentionally filled with reminders of children had a notable effect on the subjects' state of mind and their willingness to cheat.

Desai and Gino also found that people behaved much better around those cues, even when they weren't feeling particularly happy. They concluded that the better behavior was based on the idea of purity. Says Desai, "Child-related cues might unconsciously activate notions of goodness and drive us to get to a pure, nonpolluted state."[8]

These are fascinating outcomes, which, when you think about it, are actually not so radical. As parents, we behave differently around children—we mind our manners, we swear less, and we are much less tolerant of inappropriate conduct. Desai and Gino's study demonstrates that these behaviors can also be provoked in the absence of children by using childhood cues.

This intriguing research emphasizes that the thoughts we adopt, whether consciously or unconsciously, translate into how we behave. When primed with childhood cues, people become more honest and sociable. Imagine, then, what a boardroom filled with dolls could do for honest conversation. I'm guessing it would be more effective than a typical team-building cooking class, painting workshop, or off-site mountain biking trip. Try it!

THE PRIMING PHENOMENON

The childhood cues used by Desai and Gino are what psychologists Anthony Greenwald and Mahzarin Banaji refer to as primes,[9] prompts that activate particular associations and influence behavior. John Bargh, Mark Chen, and Lara Burrows revealed the profound effects of priming when they explored the influence of people's attitudes about aging on their actual physical state.[10] Participants aged 65 to 75 were randomly divided into two groups. They were then asked to solve anagrams, rearranging the letters of a word or phrase to produce a new word or phrase (for example, "schoolmaster" could become "the class room"). One group worked with words and phrases related to old age while the other group was given neutral, non-age-related anagrams.

When the exercise was finished, the subjects were thanked for their participation and told they could leave. And that's when the real experiment began. The researchers timed the subjects' short walk to the elevator in order to leave the building. Their findings were remarkable. Participants primed with words relating to old age walked more slowly to the elevator than those who had worked on neutral anagrams did. The study concluded that the words one group of participants was exposed to unconsciously primed their minds with negative associations about aging, which in turn affected their physical behavior.

Both studies show that priming can unconsciously influence subsequent thoughts and behaviors. How can we deliberately, consciously, prime our minds, then, to see things early? That's where *FuturePriming* comes in.

FUTUREPRIMING

I developed FuturePriming to help executives improve their ability to see things early. It's deceptively easy, very practical to integrate into the busy executive life, and proven to be very successful. Essentially, it's doing what we discussed previously: priming your mind to be susceptible to early-warning signals of change. It originates from an exercise called MindPriming, which I often use in my work with teams and groups. I ask them to take a look around the room and try to absorb and remember as much information about it as possible. I give them a minute or so to look at the objects, decorations, people, and all other things in the room. When they feel ready, I show nine different colors on a screen and ask them to select one at random. Then I ask them to look around the room again, but now only for things that match their color.

Inevitably, people start to notice "new" things: a jacket folded over a chair, a vase of flowers in the corner of the room, the emergency exit sign above the door, the color Post-it notes on their table. When their minds are primed to seek out one color, previously unnoticed details emerge. Even when they start with a conscious effort to notice as much as possible, people miss a lot. The truth is that our perception and memory are limited—we can't pay attention to and recall everything—so we're not interested in elements that seem to have no relevance to our purposes.

That's what happens to us as we process the daily onslaught of news and other information. As with the MindPriming participants, we can't remember or even give attention to all of it. We don't take notice to the jacket, the vase, and the emergency sign—these things seem irrelevant. But what if, amid all the noise, there are the first signs of change? Obviously we'd want to appreciate and remember those things!

FuturePriming helps to increase the chances of picking up these seemingly hidden, peripheral signals. It significantly raises the odds that you will recognize them and judge them on their potential impact. This "first-class noticing" process begins with awakening our imagination. Just like Wiener and Kahn suggested, we need to (learn to) tap into this powerful resource in order to become more thoughtful about the future. We can do so by envisioning future events that might be early indicators of a changing reality, which is essentially what FuturePriming is about. But with some conditions in place.

So how does FuturePriming work, and how can you make it work for you, too? It's very simple, but to explain it, I must first introduce the concept of FutureFacts.[11] (Although, in full disclosure, there's nothing factual about them. Just stick with me.)

FUTUREFACTS

Here's how I define this concept:

A FutureFact is a manifestation of a possible changing reality.

Each word in this definition has been chosen with care, so allow me to explain.

Change is often described in generic, broad terms. For example, a typical strategy paper starts with a list of a whole lot of trends and developments. It speaks of "increased urbanization," "further proliferation of technology," "decreasing welfare support," "growing influence of emerging economies," and so on. Effectively, this language describes trend lines, or at least prompts our mind to paint a picture of a gradual change, described in abstract language. We create illusions like "tomorrow the world will be a little bit more urbanized" or "proliferated with technology" than it is today.

The trend description doesn't really hit us in the face, so we tend to agree with it. Or disagree. But it doesn't update our thinking because we weren't provoked. We haven't really relayed any of the neural pathways in our brain. A sense of urgency and immediacy is missing, and although we might be inclined to believe the trend statement, it really doesn't do much for us in terms of awakening our imagination and challenging our current way of thinking.

Now check out what happens to your mind if I describe the following changing reality, to possibly take place three years from now: "Candy industry banned from advertising." This is not an abstract description of a trend, such as "increasing pressure on unhealthy food" or "tightening regulations to combat rising health care costs." The change has become manifest by imagining a concrete event that largely tells the story. Your mind has now created a tangible, memorable hook about a possible changing reality. I'm not saying that this exact event will happen in three years' time, but I'm imagining a manifestation of how abstract change might concretely appear in the real world we live in. Instead of saying "increased urbanization," I say that four years from now, "50 percent of children only spent five days a year outside the city." I don't say "China's global role becomes more dominant" (which it undoubtedly is), but I say "Chinese language classes are made mandatory in 25 percent of U.S. high schools" in four years.

Now that the changes are manifest, you're probably pulling up Google to see if 50 percent of children growing up in cities isn't a bit too radical a thought. Or you are toying with the idea that some schools might start offering Chinese classes, but 25 percent? And would it really be mandatory?

You'll notice that the more specific statement has a much greater impact on your thinking than the generic phrase did. It triggers you, intrigues you, and possibly worries or upsets you. It might even make you defensive and resistant; all these emotions are fine, as they show that your thinking has been activated, your brain has become really engaged in how the future might look quite different from today. Even resistance can be well explained using the concept of cognitive dissonance, which I spoke of previously (see Chapter 2).

Let's complement this explanation with a real-life example. In early 2014, I was invited to run a session in Abu Dhabi, one of the United Arab Emirates, with approximately forty leaders from a global oil company. It's an industry all too familiar with the fact that our natural resources are not endless. They invest in alternative sources, provide venture capital to innovators, and do other things to prepare themselves for a different future, but by and large, they are still very much oil-oriented. They intellectually know oil is running out, but since that's still too far ahead, they can afford not to think too deeply about it yet.

The night before I arrived, an industry analyst from a renowned investment bank had made a presentation. The analyst had asserted that by 2025 (roughly a decade ahead), Saudi Arabia would no longer export oil, but would keep what remained for itself.

It was a game changer that dominated the discussion the next day. Interestingly, they could see the trend—they knew for decades that oil reserves would be running dry one day—but it was *the event,* the manifestation of the change, illustrated by Saudi Arabia's expected policy change, that really did something with their thinking.

So it is the manifestation of the envisioned change that helps us work with the future and productively sets our imagination free. Capturing the envisioned change in a telling, noticeable, imagined milestone or event brings the change to the surface. Additionally, when it comes to communicating our vision, these concrete manifestations are essential in creating sticky and memorable stories (as we will see in Chapter 8).

Although the exact statement in the FutureFact might turn out to be incorrect, the mind is now much more concretely primed to those early indicators of change that we pick up in the news, even if they just closely or even remotely resemble it. Remember Wiener and Kahn? Clarification, not prophecy is what matters.

MORE MANIFESTATIONS

Let's look at some more examples of imagined FutureFacts, but now in the more appropriate form in which we like to capture them, which includes a catchy, telling title, a brief explanation, and a suggested year (ordinarily, we set real years in FutureFacts, such as 2018 or 2022, but refrained here to avoid confusion when this work is read in the years following its original publication).

The FutureFact shown in Figure 4-3 looks like the summary of an intriguing article you might find in your favorite newspaper or website. But it is fictional (or at least it was at the time of writing). It describes an invented future "event" that imagines public policy influencing and changing consumers' behavior to reduce their carbon footprints. The idea—which, by the way, originates from a participant in one of my sessions who was a member of the Club of Rome—alludes to the changes needed for a more sustainable future.[12] But an abstract description such as "intensified regulations to enforce sustainability" does not create the memorable mental hook

DENMARK INTRODUCES CARBON EMISSION RIGHTS FOR CONSUMERS

Denmark is the first country to apply the emission controls that exist in the business world to the consumer space. Individual consumers are provided allowances that represent their right to emit a specific amount of pollutants, such as greenhouse gases. To increase that amount, the consumer must buy additional rights from others. The results have caused many other countries to contemplate this system.

3 YEARS FROM NOW

Figure 4-3. A FutureFact.

that this FutureFact does—regardless of whether this particular event will become true.

In creating FutureFacts, it's important not to go into judgment mode. Worrying about whether you personally believe the FutureFact puts you in a binary yes or no position and it eludes the point of the exercise. There are reasons to believe this FutureFact might happen, just as there are good reasons to believe that it won't.

The point isn't that you accurately predict a future event as described. Denmark in this exercise is a proxy: It could easily have been Switzerland, the Netherlands, or some progressive U.S. state such as Vermont, California, or New York. What's important is entertaining the overarching idea that in order to combat greenhouse gas pollution, more significant and confrontational measures are needed, and these might be implemented in the future. Whether it will be a CO2 trading scheme is beside the point; what's relevant is that simply contemplating an idea that highlights the change we are interested in opens your eyes to something real you might read about in the next few months.

Before the exercise, you might not have noticed that article. Now, you're more likely to pay attention because you've primed yourself to early-warning signals. If this were a relevant, disruptive development for your industry, you would want to notice it as early as possible. But if you haven't engaged your imagination with what could be, even if it's just a half-baked prediction, you are likely to miss the very early signs of change.

Figure 4-4 shows a few more examples of FutureFacts that similarly prime you mind.

Again, it's easy to come up with valid objections to these examples. But being the eternal naysayer, no matter how right you may turn out to be,

Figure 4-4. More FutureFacts.

means you could lose sight of early, potentially highly disruptive signals before they're fully matured (which is when everybody sees them). What matters in future thinking is to see and contemplate the impact of changes while you can still adapt and act, before the window of opportunity closes. Remember the theory of the car crash? You want to see it *before* others do, before it has become *conventional wisdom*. It's in that earlier zone where you can use foresight to develop strategic advantage.

THE FOUR GOLDEN RULES

FuturePriming is the process I created to continuously prime your mind to possible changing realities in a deceptively simple form. Essentially, FuturePriming is about writing your own FutureFacts. You engage your imagination by entertaining unconventional, possibly disruptive, future events. This way you are priming your mind to notice these first hints that initially only present themselves at the periphery of our attention.

Yet, just randomly imagining game changers is not going to yield results for you. You would want to imagine FutureFacts that are maximally geared to bringing you strategically relevant insights and strengthening your ability to become a first-class noticer. Therefore, some further direction is required to apply this process in a useful and effective manner.

I've found that four simple rules help you get the most from this practice. I'll present them in order of increasing difficulty.

Rule 1: Scope for Relevance and Time

Look for relevant changing realities in your business, industry, and geography. FutureFacts are designed to sharpen your sensory capacity, so you want to consider your role, your organization, your industry. These are boundaries you must set yourself. If you are a person working in the financial sector in the United Kingdom who is functionally involved with mergers and acquisitions, your scope is naturally different from that of a Brazilian product development manager in the pharmaceutical industry.

Still, you shouldn't limit yourself too much. Do not only look for changing realities with respect to mergers and acquisitions in the U.K. financial industry. After all, that domain might be influenced by wider developments. So, your scope should be wide enough to capture any relevant signals, but not so wide that you have too much information to consider. For example, the financial sector in the U.K. might be influenced by regulations from the European Union, growing financial power in the Middle East, and evaporating trust in business leadership and the capitalistic model. All transcend the boundaries of the U.K. financial industry but might have significant impact on the future of that industry.

Also, scope your timeline to a minimum of three and a maximum of seven years into the future. Thinking only a year or two ahead limits your thinking because you're too rooted in today's reality. On the other hand, thinking too far into the future can make you inclined to believe anything. A three- to seven-year scope works best: It's far enough out to be creative, and it is near enough to already be relevant to think about today.

Rule 2: Don't Make Your Own Company Part of Your FutureFact

FuturePriming is an outside-in approach. It intends to stimulate you to look out the window and playfully engage with possible changes in the future environment you might need to operate in. It's about sharpening your contextual intelligence. But I have noticed that, without this specific rule, the first ideas people are inclined to create are FutureFacts in which they themselves, or their organizations, play an active role. It's apparently quite difficult for some to take that outside-in perspective naturally.

Organizational developments, achievements, and direction are to a large extent (usually larger than most companies like to admit) affected by influences that are completely outside the company's control. Economic crises, changing customer preferences, the development of the oil price or the interest rate, the arrival of breakthrough technologies, the entrance of a rogue competitor, and new government policies—all are examples of such developments. Organizations can shape their reactions to these changes, but hardly ever the changes themselves.

If you are working at GreatBiz, FutureFacts such as "GreatBiz Merges with StrongBiz," "GreatBiz Voted Most Favorable Company to Work For," and "GreatBiz Introduces New P-Ray Technology First" won't be helpful if you want to improve your visionary capacity. You focus too much on internal choices, decisions, and directions. The point of FuturePriming is to be attuned with the outside world and what might be happening there. Your strategic reactions to those changes can shape in the additional time you bought yourself by pulling your point of surprise forward.

So, after seeing too many of these internally oriented FutureFacts come up when people practice with FuturePriming, I introduced the company, division, and team exclusion rule to avoid that trap.

Rule 3: Explore the Area Between the Conventional and the Absurd

Now it becomes more challenging. It's quite common when you first start with FuturePriming that your thoughts and ideas about the future are pretty conventional. You probably bring up ideas you've already considered, that confirm current trends, or that are (politically) correct to agree with at this point in time. These ideas are part of your existing conventional wisdom and therefore neither add to your learning about the future nor challenge your assumptions.

When people realize that their first ideas are too conventional, they typically veer toward the absurd. (A few that I've seen: "The Law of Gravity Reverses," "First Spaceship Reaches the Sun," and "50 percent of Babies Now Have Phones.") Although they're funny, they're too far-fetched to be taken seriously. And while I'm a big advocate of humor (and humor has the potential to generate unconventional thoughts), these highly unrealistic FutureFacts are not going to help you grow your visionary capacity, either.

Therefore, the fertile ground for useful FutureFacts is the area between the conventional, on the one end, and the absurd, on the other (see Figure 4-5). You should stretch what you—and those around you—currently already believe. Without going overboard.

Now, there's no hard-and-fast rule for where the boundaries between the different zones are. For example, what might seem absurd today might not seem so tomorrow. If before 2008 someone created a FutureFact describing the default of Lehman Brothers as an indication of a collapsing financial system, it would probably have been dismissed as absurd (which goes to show how difficult it is to expect the unexpected).

But as a general principle, effective FutureFacts provoke, challenge, and play in the mental space where you think, "Hmmm, maybe . . ."

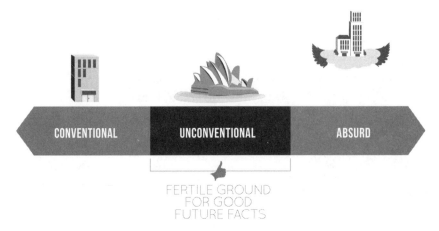

Figure 4-5. Unconventional zone.

Rule 4: Describe an Event, Not a Trend

Lastly, write your FutureFact as an event you might read about in the newspaper. Just as good journalists do, create a memorable hook that highlights something significant about the event. Descriptions such as "ever-growing need for clean water" and "dwindling interest in politics" won't cut it. These are descriptions of trends, not events. I've already made this point, but it's one of the things I've noticed people struggle with most. We easily engage in a conversation about generalities, but fantasizing how something might look in real life, in a remarkable event that tells us the rules of the game have changed, is clearly much more difficult. This is where your imagination comes in and your preference for abstract generalizations must take a backseat.

These four rules collectively provide the direction and boundaries for effective FuturePriming. The net result should be FutureFacts described in

remarkable, even visual, detail to help you remember them. Give your imagination full rein; invent research, statistics, company names, and country names in order to vividly capture the changing reality and get that kind of *aha!* effect you need to prime successfully. To reach this aha moment, research into this phenomenon suggests that your creation should bring up four effects:

Practice 4-1.
FuturePriming.

1. *Suddenness:* The experience is surprising; your created FutureFact should make something that has been abstract so far, tangible and evident.

2. *Ease:* The new insight is easy to grasp; the title should tell 80 percent of the story.

3. *Positive Effect:* The idea should spark interest and intrigue our desire to learn more about it and monitor its progression.

4. *The Feeling of Being Right:* The creation should be rightfully challenging, sufficiently plausible, and not too absurd.

These are the same effects we are after with effective FuturePriming.

FOOD FOR THOUGHT

With some people, ideas for FutureFacts pop up immediately. Other people can use some help. In his book *Wide Angle Vision*, business consultant Wayne Burkan provides three interesting suggestions on where to look for these disruptions from today's reality.[13]

1. Look at fringe competitors, and stop looking at what other mainstream players do. Look for the ones that appear on the horizon and are currently still out of sight for most others. They are the companies that have broken into a small niche, appear still somewhat irrelevant in terms of market share, but they are often a signal that the mainstream players have become complacent.

2. Look at lost customers. They are the ones that have abandoned the hope that you will satisfy them (different from complaining customers) and moved elsewhere with their needs. They could be an early indicator of changing customer needs, which always only surfaces at the edges at first.

3. Look at rogue employees, the mavericks that don't fit in, the ones that do not abide by the rules and always seem to stir up trouble. Often (but not always) their ideas are different from what everyone else has grown to believe, and if used productively, they could be great resources for unconventionality.

These are good and practical suggestions, particularly in business settings. In addition, I would encourage you to look even further than fringe competition, lost customers, and rogue employees. When I work with organizations on projects aimed at challenging their corporate mindset, I usually interview a number of their thought leaders before I start working with their teams. In my interviews, I aim to bring out the knowledge and insights they have themselves about what might be ahead of them and what could be disruptive changes. I have included the questions I use for such interviews in Appendix A: Strategic Questionnaire. They might stimulate your thinking and expand the issues to consider. But don't go there yet! Only use them when you hit writer's block. It is much more fun (and productive) to use your own imagination when FuturePriming than to run through my list of questions.

MISSING TRAFFIC SIGNS

Some years ago, I ran a FuturePriming session in Prague for a networking organization of local leaders. After explaining the task, I gave the participants twenty minutes to come up with three or four FutureFacts for their own industry. I stressed the importance of using the four Golden Rules and warned them that it might not be easy.

After some time I walked around to see how they were progressing. One participant seemed to be struggling. He looked at me with a somewhat desperate look in his eyes and I could see he was stuck. "Show me what you've created so far," I encouraged. The headline of his FutureFact was "Use of Traffic Signs Doubled," placed four years in the future (he was in the traffic sign business it turned out). It didn't sound very convincing to me or to him, apparently, so I pointed out that it sounded more like wishful thinking than a disruptive thought. I asked him, just for the sake of the exercise, "What if you said, 'Use of Traffic Signs Halved'?"

"But I'd be out of business!" he said defensively. Cognitive dissonance was clearly at work here. The thought was upsetting and didn't fit his mental model, so he was unwilling to entertain it. I reassured him this was just a mental exercise and encouraged him not to avoid unfavorable thoughts. It didn't seem to help him over the mental barrier of challenging his own assumptions. Then, for the interest of time, I had to move on to attend to other participants, feeling a bit uncomfortable for not having been able to help him.

A few weeks after the event I received an e-mail from my Prague participant. In the weeks following our session, he'd noticed some state-of-the-art research in telematics conducted at a university in Japan. The study involved the integration of traffic signs in GPS systems and dashboard displays. The report was short, hidden deep inside the industry journal. Normally he would have overlooked it, but now it grabbed his attention. If the study caught on, his traffic sign business would suffer significantly—perhaps even be reduced by half.

He contacted the research group and discovered they wanted to partner with experts in traffic signaling outside Japan. In his e-mail, he confided that he was now finalizing the details of their new partnership arrangements and would become the first company outside Japan to have access to this emerging technology. He thanked me for forcing him to think about a future in which half of his conventional traffic sign business disappeared. Without that mental exercise, however painful and unsatisfactory at first, he probably wouldn't have noticed the article, or at least wouldn't have recognized its potentially disruptive nature. He wouldn't have taken action and wouldn't have acquired ground-level access to new traffic sign technology. Now he had, because his mind had been primed to notice.

RUBBER HITS THE ROAD

So FuturePriming has the potential to radically change your mindset about the future, with the additional benefit of growing the perception of your leadership as a future-oriented, intriguing personality with interesting thoughts about what might be changing. It's also a practice that doesn't require an unmanageable amount of time. I would suggest aiming to create five to ten FutureFacts per quarter, which will ensure a digestible quantity of ideas; if you stick with the four Golden Rules, the FutureFacts will focus on what's relevant for you (rule 1), and they'll be externally oriented (rule 2), unconventional (rule 3), and mind hooking (rule 4). That's an impressive return for something that will take you only thirty minutes in the next three months.

To let the rubber hit the road, though, let's highlight a few practical considerations and suggestions to make this practice work for you:

- First, use the simple form of our examples: a catchy, self-explanatory title, a brief rationale, and a time set between three and seven years into the future. Together these elements form a small article that grabs attention and creates a hook that helps you memorize it and allows you to easily integrate it into your communication (which we'll dig into in Chapter 8).

- Second, focus on signals that would indicate the start of a changing reality, not the end. For example, "Amazon.com Sells Final Paper Book" (expressing the idea that digital books redefine the market) or "Bank of America Dismantles Its Last ATM Machine" (expressing the idea that cash payments have become a rarity and are replaced by cards and digital payments) mark the late signals, not the early signals.

- Third, you need to create these ideas *yourself*. You can involve others in the process, tapping into their imagination, but you can't outsource your own strategic development. Remember that this is level 4 future engagement (see preface), which works to form strong neural pathways in your brain *only* when you do it yourself.

- Fourth, FuturePriming can't have its positive effect if you don't make a conscious effort to log your FutureFacts. It doesn't have to take too much time—your goal is to create three to five per month, which should take about ten minutes. The thoughts will come to you at random moments; the logging discipline takes a minute or two per FutureFact. A good use of your time? Give it a three-month trial run. Does it seem worthwhile? If so, give it another three months and it will become second nature. My clients tell me it is well worth the return on investment.

- Fifth, I would encourage you to be quite demanding on yourself initially. Continuously review the four Golden Rules, improve your creation to live up to them, and if it is still not there after review, throw it away. Better ones will emerge, without doubt. If your FutureFacts don't adhere to the rules, your results will suffer. If they lack juice, they're probably too conventional. If they're too dubious, your credibility will suffer. They want the aha! factor. But getting to that provocative zone is not easy and needs work to perfect. Otherwise you'll eventually lose interest since you will lose sight of the value. With practice and a critical eye, though, you'll notice improvement and soon have a solid set of FutureFacts that intrigue and resonate, sharpen your sensory system, and boost your leadership perception.

- Finally, promote your ideas and make them visible. Put them up on your office wall. Talk about them with your team or other colleagues who can help sharpen your ideas. Claim a column in the company newsletter, or start a blog about your creations. Tweet about them. Make them the opening discussion of your (management) team meeting. This way you bring them to life, supporting both the development of your own sensory system as well as the perception of your future-oriented leadership with others.

I work with leaders and teams that have made FutureFacts part of their regular meetings. One of these teams assigns the role of writer to a different person each time they meet. At the start of their meetings, the team conversation begins with a five-minute discussion about that person's FutureFact. After a few months, they had collected over twenty themes that could impact their future business. Imagine what the exercise does for the strategic dialogue among the team members, and people's involvement in and engagement with the company's future.

But they tell me something else has happened as well. By using Future-Facts this way, the spirit of these team meetings changed subtly. It set a future-oriented tone, and discussions of day-to-day issues became generally more constructive and forward thinking. That shouldn't sound surprising. You know why now, don't you? Remember the priming phenomenon, the toys in the boardroom? This team unconsciously primes itself to the future every time it meets, and it notices the impact on conversations about current challenges (which, with a more expansive mindset, can seem much easier to resolve).

CREATIVITY IGNITED

FuturePriming is a creative process that allows you to develop innovative, imaginative, disruptive thoughts and ideas. Like any other such process, it doesn't yield outstanding results every time. That's the nature of creativity. But you can set up conditions to maximize the chances. Here are some helpful ones:

1. *Set a target.* Alexander Graham Bell invented much more than just the telephone. His inventions spanned a wide range of interests and included an audiometer that detects minor hearing problems, a device to locate icebergs, investigations on how to separate salt from seawater, and work on finding alternative fuels. In addition to his creative genius, Bell's achievements were the result of specific targets he set himself: He worked to come up with ten innovative ideas per month, and one breakthrough idea per quarter. Setting a target forces you to consciously and continuously look for new ideas. Don't worry if each one isn't groundbreaking. Aim for at least three to five FutureFacts a month, with one really good one.

2. *Start creative conversations with others.* The creative process is not sequential, logical, and deductive. Creative ideas typically break the causal flow and, like the punch line in a good joke, often come out of left field. Since you never know where they might come from or what will inspire you, work to gather influences and stimuli from others. Exploring different thoughts and ideas will help you build up a database of creative ideas.

3. *Recast yourself as an imaginator.* We admire innovative souls with unconventional ideas. These people are often held up as the exception, holding the keys to some magical process the rest of us mere mortals can only dream about. But just as visionary leadership is possible for more than just a select few larger-than-life figures, everyone is capable of being imaginative. Often it's a narrow mindset and our self-limiting beliefs that stand in the way. Recasting yourself as an imaginator rather than a manager, engineer, or consultant (or whatever other conventional label has been imposed on you) will help you step out of these confining beliefs.

We've explored seeing things early, the first dimension in our developmental framework aimed at growing the art of looking ahead. It focuses on your ability to challenge the conventional in a constructive way so that early-warning signals of change become easier to detect. This way you are growing the first-class noticer in you. And we have made it very practical with the practice of FuturePriming, which will take just a minimum of your time.

In addition to improving our ability to look ahead, we also discussed how your primed mind helps you behaviorally in the leadership field. Our mindset—mostly unconsciously—transcends into our behavior. Your more future-conscious thoughts will radiate in how you communicate, how you respond to unconventional ideas, how you deal with challenges, and how you demonstrate your open-mindedness. In other words, your primed mind affects how you lead and how your leadership is perceived.

We'll now focus on the second dimension, your ability to connect the dots.

5

Connecting the Dots

Not to be absolutely certain is, I think, one of the essential things in rationality.

—BERTRAND RUSSELL

JUNE 12, 2005

It's the afternoon of June 12, 2005, in sun-drenched Palo Alto, California. Hundreds of graduating students at Stanford University are listening to what will later be considered one of the most inspiring speeches of our time. A year after being diagnosed with cancer, Apple CEO Steve Jobs delivers a commencement speech that forgoes the typical formality. He shares three intimate, meaningful, and eloquent stories from his life. "That's it. No big deal," he says. It becomes a YouTube classic long before his death a few years later.

In his legendary speech, Jobs speaks from the heart about experiences that profoundly affected his development, including dropping out of Reed College. He explains why he decided to hang around at the school for another year and a half, taking classes strictly for enjoyment:

If I had never dropped out, I would have never dropped in on this cal-
ligraphy class, and personal computers might not have the wonderful
typography that they do. Of course it was impossible to connect the dots
looking forward when I was in college. But it was very, very clear looking backward ten years later.

He reiterates the connecting the dots metaphor at the end of his story:

Again, you can't connect the dots looking forward; you can only connect them looking backward. So you have to trust that the dots will
somehow connect in your future. You have to trust in something—your
gut, destiny, life, karma, whatever. This approach has never let me
down, and it has made all the difference in my life.

Let's return to where we started: growing our visionary capacity. In addition to strengthening the ability to see things early, which we discussed in
the previous chapter, we must equally improve our ability to create a coherent story going forward. As noted by Miles White, the chairman and CEO
of Abbott Laboratories, "People scanning the horizon for signs of change
must somehow separate the important and enduring trends from those that
are short-lived and ultimately irrelevant."[1] It requires judgment and some
heightened understanding of the whole picture. Therefore, our ability to
identify possible changing realities early on is very important and should be
strengthened—as explained in the previous chapter—and it must be com-
plemented and harmonized with an equally important ability to create coherence.

This coherent story must consist of what we expect, foresee, envision,
and anticipate. It needs to resonate, make sense, and be the guiding light
into the future for our followers. I call this second developmental dimension of visionary capacity *the ability to connect the dots*. The metaphor alludes to the importance of creating coherence in your story and building an
inclusive, integrated picture of your vision that not only contains some
early, unconventional insights from our previous dimension, but also aligns
with the larger frame, the larger context of our future. Call it "the big picture," if you will.

But wait a second. Here we have the legendary Steve Jobs emphasizing that it's only possible to connect the dots by looking *backward*. You cannot do it looking *forward*, he argues convincingly. So here's our problem: It's a nice catchphrase to talk of connecting the dots since it aligns with our accepted view of a vision as a "big picture" story, but how do you do that reliably looking forward? There are many developments we can highlight, discontinuities we can emphasize, and changing realities we can work with. So how would you know if your "connected version" of the dots even closely resembles what might happen in the future?

Of course Steve Jobs is right: We can't connect the dots looking forward. Not with great certainty, anyway. The future is inherently *uncertain*. You can make future plans, but unexpected things will undoubtedly happen, changing and sometimes upsetting everything you had in mind. As John Lennon put it, "Life is what happens to you while you are busy making other plans"—a truism repeated more recently by Nassim Taleb in his bestseller *The Black Swan*. It reminds us that the real future path always includes unforeseeable, improbable, yet severely impactful events that might—and quite likely will—derail parts of what we envisioned.

Therefore, the irrefutable challenge posed by creating forward-looking accounts is that, by definition, these seemingly coherent stories suffer from inherent uncertainty. How do you deal with the fact that, without a doubt, the future will turn out different than you expected? Even worse, the further out we go (and at least three years out is what we're generally looking at for productive visions), the more certain we can be that it won't be what we hoped for or expected.

Just think of how our view of the future changed in a matter of months during 2007 and 2008. Or recall the Internet bubble less than a decade before that. Even today we have significant, somewhat foreseeable major changes ahead of us: the inflated housing prices in China (which, if they burst, would kill the most significant growth engine of today's global economy); instability in the Middle East; the vast cultural, fiscal, and economic differences in the monetarily integrated Europe; health care and pension challenges of our aging society; the planet's vastly growing population; depletion of natural resources such as oil and water; power shifts from traditional Western societies to emerging nations such as China, Brazil, India,

Russia, and Indonesia; doubts about the U.S. dollar's continued role of safe haven currency; the unmatched challenges in creating sustainable environments; and unforeseeable technological breakthroughs and paradigm shifts. And those are just a few of the more prominent changes at the global societal level; we could also mention the many black swan candidates that specific industries face in terms of shifting customer behavior, competition and newcomers, regulations, and changing business models.

So, the real question becomes: How can we *responsibly* connect the dots and become better at creating a comfortable level of coherence in our vision while working with such fundamental, ever-present uncertainties? That's what we are about to explore. We'll first turn to the leading story of this chapter, one in which the lead players could have benefited from the ideas set out here.

A BELGIAN TALE

Over a period of nearly two decades, a small group of local insurance companies grew to be a financial contender. Based primarily in the Benelux countries—that is Belgium, the Netherlands, and Luxembourg—they had a solid track record of successful acquisitions and integration of smaller banks, insurance companies, and other financial groups. Over time their reach extended from the Benelux into Turkey, the United States, and Asia.

The year is 2007 and the company is Fortis, headed by charismatic Belgian CEO Jean-Paul Votron, a corporate veteran whose life before Fortis included leadership positions at Unilever, Citibank, and the Dutch ABN AMRO Bank. Fortis is officially Dutch-Belgian, but by 2007 the company's decision power has migrated to Brussels, Belgium, with an executive team consisting of mostly Belgians. Its chairman, Maurice Lippens, is a member of the Belgian aristocracy—a factor not to be underestimated in the country's business environment, also predominantly rooted in Belgium.

The financial reality of 2006 and 2007 is one of tremendous growth. Opportunities seem endless, and the promise of an increasingly integrated Europe feeds speculation of mergers and takeovers in the industry. It's widely believed that the European banking landscape will consolidate to a handful of large, pan-European banks. The only question seems to be whether consolidation will be driven by powerful U.S. investment banks, rapidly emerging Chinese banks, or European strongholds themselves. Banking executives are on the alert: It's either hunt or be prey. And in the Fortis boardroom, they consider themselves prey.

In March of that year, the top 300 executives are enjoying their annual two-day leadership session at a grand hotel near the seaside of The Hague in the Netherlands. In one room, senior leaders are engaged in discussions and exercises aimed at strengthening their cooperation and enacting the recently updated strategy, which called for aggressive expansion outside the Benelux region. In an adjacent smaller meeting room, Jean-Paul Votron is hosting Andrea Orcel, a Merrill Lynch investment banker who works for the mergers and acquisitions team.[2] Orcel requested the meeting, taking advantage of the senior executive gathering to fly over from London to present a proposal—one that will soon alter Fortis's destiny. And, tragically, the destinies of tens of thousands of families who have their life savings and pensions invested in Fortis.

It has been only a few weeks since the announcement of a merger between Dutch ABN AMRO and Barclays, now forming the first pan-European supersize bank. For ABN AMRO, it's a move designed to defend the organization from activist shareholders intent on breaking up the bank and selling it off in pieces.

Orcel has come to Fortis to present an alternative scenario to ABN AMRO's future. "How would you feel about joining a consortium with two other banks to buy up ABN AMRO?" Orcel asks Votron and his trustees. Specifically, he wants to know if Fortis is interested in ABN AMRO's large retail banking network in the Netherlands.[3] Naturally, Votron needs to mull over this idea. Showing too much enthusiasm at this stage would hurt later negotiations. But even though the move would be totally counter to his announced strategic direction, which is being explored in the larger room next door (focused on growth *outside* the Benelux region), Votron wants in. The neighbor's house will only be for sale once, he thinks. Soon after the meeting, on April 13, Fortis publicly announces its participation in what would soon be called the Consortium.

A wild period starts. The Consortium needs to convince its shareholders, leaders, and employees, as well as the analysts, the unions, the regulators, and the public, that the unexpected combination will be a success. They also need to battle a fiercely defensive ABN AMRO, which strongly opposes a takeover and perseveres in its plan to merge with Barclays. Furthermore, there are doubts whether Fortis will be able to absorb ABN AMRO, both financially and culturally, because of the traditional rivalry between Belgium and the Netherlands. ABN AMRO exemplifies the proud Dutch culture and will resist any efforts of integration by the Belgian firm.

In the meantime, Votron and his executive team grasp at every opportunity to promote and demonstrate their ability to make this deal work. They dismiss or avoid counterarguments. In fact, they make it clear within the organization that a critical stance is not appreciated. After all, the essence of business is taking risks, and the leaders of Fortis radiate that they know what they're doing. Negativity won't help.

The Consortium's offer is significantly better than that of Barclays, and—despite pushback from ABN AMRO's executive team—it becomes obvious that the Consortium will win the battle. On October 9, 2007, a little over six months after Fortis announced its participation in the Consortium, the deal is done.

Fast-forward twelve months to the autumn of 2008. The financial world is heading for a perfect storm. The debt bubble, which had been expanding since U.S. Federal Reserve Chairman Alan Greenspan dramatically lowered interest rates in 2001, has burst. Lehman Brothers collapsed in September. Bailouts, rescue plans, and bankruptcies hit the front pages daily. Uncertainty is skyrocketing.

The storm reaches Fortis as well. After turmoil earlier in the spring of 2008, forcing Votron to step down, it's only been a downward spiral for the company. In the last weekend of September 2008, Belgian, Dutch, and Luxembourgian officials gather in Brussels to rescue the firm as dwindling faith in the company, largely caused by doubts about its ability to finance and integrate ABN AMRO, pushes the share price to approximately 4 euros—less than 20 percent of what it was the year before. Rumors fuel fears of bankruptcy; billions of euros are withdrawn in a matter of days. The bank faces an immediate liquidity crisis. After heated debate and nightlong negotiations, the government officials of Belgium, Luxembourg, and the Netherlands announce a rescue plan that will provide unprecedented amounts of capital to keep Fortis from failing. But even that appears not to reassure investors. Fortis's stock price continues to sink.

It's October 3, 2008. Early in the morning, Dutch Prime Minister Jan Peter Balkenende, Minister of Finance Wouter Bos, and Nout Wellink, chairman of the Dutch National Bank, line up for a historic press conference. They look exhausted, and their contrived calm exterior can't hide their panic. Just before the opening of the financial markets, they completed a marathon overnight negotiation. They are about to announce the biggest bailout in the country's history: ABN AMRO Bank (which kept its name under Fortis ownership) is now fully owned by the Dutch government—at a price of 25 billion euros. Exactly twelve months after it celebrated the ABN AMRO takeover, the Fortis empire has collapsed. It's an unprecedented drama in the Low Countries.

BLACK SWAN?

What happened between the glory days of Jean-Paul Votron, about a year before, and the dramatic collapse of the dream? Surely, Taleb's metaphorical black swan[4] (which stands for the highly improbable but highly impactful event) flew by, with the fall of Lehman Brothers and the entire financial system grinding to a halt. But is the company's collapse therefore a matter of unbelievably bad luck?

Or did Fortis connect the dots wrong?

But hold on a minute: Isn't it purely *hindsight bias* to grill Fortis for the decisions it had taken, operating under very different skies than anyone could have foreseen at the time the company took the decision? Didn't any financial analyst with half a brain predict the consolidation of the European financial sector in those days?

Indeed, that was the expected future at that time, and let me prove that. Remember the FutureFacts of Chapter 4? Through the work I do with leadership groups on foresight development, using FutureFacts as a method, I've been tracking the votes on hundreds of FutureFacts since 2004. Including one titled "European Banking Sector Consolidates to Ten Major Players in Three Years' Time."

The graph in Figure 5-1 shows the voting pattern on that FutureFact, starting in late 2005 and ending in early 2008. It's based on the votes from 462 groups of typically five to seven people (hence around 2,500 individuals). After some debate, they expressed their expectation of this future event

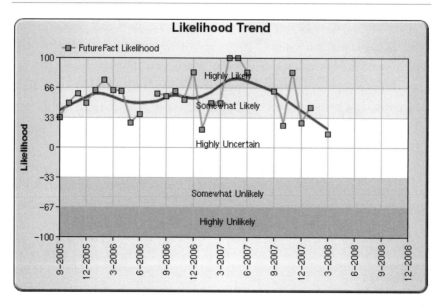

Figure 5-1. Likelihood voting for FutureFact "European banking market consolidates to ten major players."

by voting likely, neutral, or unlikely on the FutureFact. Brown dots in the graph show the monthly average of group votes; the blue line is the smoothing line.

It clearly shows that a consolidating European banking sector ranked likely to highly likely at that time as our collective wisdom about what the future would bring. And with a booming economy, justifying the growth perspective and strategy Fortis had adopted, weren't the leaders at Fortis merely acting on these *inevitable* realities? Should the CEO and the other decision makers at Fortis therefore be blamed for something as unpredictable, unimaginable, and unprecedented as this course of events? It sounds tempting to let them off the hook, given these circumstances.

But let's see. Since Fortis did not have the cash to take over ABN AMRO, it had to rely on the financial markets to fund its adventure. Access to capital became the Achilles' heel of the transaction, a reality the senior leadership at Fortis must have been well aware of. Under normal circumstances this inadequate funding need not be problematic, as healthy companies can access the capital markets for additional funding and pay off their obligations over time. But the dramatic financial system lockup following the crisis in 2008, and the disappearance of trust, made all players in the capital markets reluctant—to say the least—to lend each other money, which blocked Fortis's access to capital, at the time it needed so much of it. Now this sudden lockup, following the Lehman Brothers's demise, was not and could not have been anticipated, right?

THE TUNNEL VISION

Think again. Fortis's takeover scheme could well be described as the result of tunnel vision. In biological terms, this term refers to the loss of peripheral vision, literally resulting in very limited perception. In our context we use it metaphorically, but with the same implication: We tend to perceive only what is right in front of us—what we like to see, or are encouraged or incentivized to see—and miss anything on the periphery. Tunnel vision creates an illusionary view that screens out any early-warning signals unfavorable to the desired future.

How can this phenomenon be explained? How can rationally sane, well-educated, and extraordinary experienced people ignore reality and fixate only on one particular worldview that suits their needs? We'll dig deeper into it as we progress, but fundamentally it derives from a concept known as the Consistency Principle. Psychologist have long understood the power of this principle to direct human action; the earliest research and theory dates back to the 1940s and 1950s of the twentieth century.[5] A high degree of consistency in human interaction is generally a good thing. It signals intelligence, stability, rationality, integrity, and honesty—all things we value and appreciate. In fact, without a significant degree of consistency our lives would be chaotic and messy, and our credibility would be low. Therefore, the intent to be consistent is deeply rooted in our behavior. As a result, it triggers many *automatic behaviors*. More specifically, our consistency drive provides shortcuts for directing our behavior, since it frees us from the need to reconsider, reassess, and think deeply. As Robert Cialdini, an expert in persuasion and influence, notes: "Once we have made up our minds about issues, stubborn consistency allows us a very appealing luxury: We don't have to think hard about the issues anymore."[6]

Canadian psychologists Robert E. Knox and James A. Inkster demonstrated how that consistency grows on us. They discovered that, at the racetrack, people were much more confident of their horse's chances of winning just after placing their bets than they were immediately before laying down the bets. Even though nothing changed and the horse's chances of winning were exactly the same as before, they made a remarkable mind shift in confidence simply by placing the bet. The explanation for this somewhat bizarre mental change stems from our desire to be—and come across as—consistent with our actions. Cialdini explains: "We encounter personal and interpersonal pressures to behave consistently with that commitment—those pressures will cause us to respond in ways that justify our earlier decision."[7] We simply convince ourselves that we have made the right choice, feel better about our decision, and start acting accordingly with a greater amount of confidence of the rightness of our choice than objectively warranted.[8]

In the same vein, tunnel vision develops. A difficult decision needs to be made or a harsh reality needs to be faced, and once we have made up our mind and decide how to move forward, we have a strong, mostly unconscious, desire to remain consistent in our behavior, even if that becomes foolish consistency.

I know it's bold to accuse Fortis of tunnel vision at this point, in a case so highly complex. We will return to this case, digging deeper, toward the end of this chapter, once we've covered the art of connecting the dots. The real art: a way of working that takes tunnel vision into account and aims to prevent it. But as the Fortis case shows, just having a powerful story that relies on some "inevitable" trends is not good enough to support an actionable plan for the future. Remember, Fortis told itself and others a rock-solid story that included a consolidating European banking market, which was supported by nearly everyone in the market, with fairly foreseeable trends and data points going forward. And yet they blew up the company.

IRRATIONALITY RULES

Let's take a side step into some important psychological notions via an unconventional route: understanding capitalism. A large part of recent economic theory was built on the belief that human beings are (at least collectively) rational creatures—homo economicus—who are able to arrive at optimal decisions when provided with full and transparent information. The foundation of rationality supporting this theory stood tall for a long time, even as it incorporated more nuanced ideas about temporary irrationality over time, such as groupthink. The foundation is essentially three-fold:[9]

1. In principle, people use their brains, and therefore act wisely (are rational thinkers).
2. Those who deviate from rationally optimal positions are countered by those who do the opposite. In other words, people who irrationally operate at too high a level of risk aversion are matched with those who irrationally seek risk—statistically this evens out to a normal distribution around a rational optimal.
3. To the extent that larger groups deviate from the optimum, experts in the market (called "arbitrageurs" in the theory) quickly act to take advantage of the irrational glitch, thus restoring the rational balance.

In economic theory, this is known as the efficient market hypothesis. It's at the heart of the capitalistic worldview that promotes the idea that free markets are self-guiding and optimal under the condition that transparency is ensured. In other words, once transparency of information is in place, governments should take a hands-off approach and do nothing more than facilitating and possibly regulating this efficiency. Capitalism in a nutshell.

All this sounds logical and, well, rational. "There is no other proposition in economics which has more solid empirical evidence supporting it than the efficient market hypothesis,"[10] noted University of Chicago's Michael Jensen, who was involved in its invention. That was the rock-solid belief for about a century.

Until psychologist Daniel Kahneman demonstrated that the assumption of rationality is fundamentally wrong and shattered the validity of the theory and the concept of the human decision maker as rational agent. It got him the Nobel Prize in Economics in 2002 and spawned the disciplines of behavioral economics, behavioral finance, behavioral strategy, behavioral decision making, and other "behavioral" disciplines.

In essence, the behavioral disciplines start from the belief that we are inherently *irrational*. Irrationality, it argues, is a human trait, embedded in the way we think, perceive, and behave. Kahneman has demonstrated this "unpleasant" reality extensively; for the interested reader, his books, as well as those by Daniel Ariely, are great sources that explore the subject of irrationality in greater detail.[11]

For us, Kahneman's work describes what we face when we attempt to connect the dots—namely, our own irrationality. Tunnel vision isn't the result of bad luck or a leader who didn't do her homework. Understanding tunnel vision starts with a basic understanding of who we are and what we are made of: We are wired to think and behave irrationally. Somewhere in the back of your mind, you may be thinking that this holds true for others, but, as you are an intelligent, open-minded, and diligent person, it doesn't apply to you. But that would be irrational. It applies to you, too. And to me.

FRAME BLINDNESS

Therefore, before we can become better at connecting the dots, we need to understand some of these psychological challenges we'll inevitably face as we build our vision. Then we can move on to ways of working that help us handle our inherent flaws.

In their formidable book *Predictable Surprises,* Max Bazerman and Michael Watkins identify the sources of leadership blindspots:

> Individual recognition failures occur when organizational leaders remain oblivious to an emerging threat or problem. Positive illusions, self-serving biases, and the tendency to discount the future may prevent people from acknowledging that a problem is emerging. If their state of denial is strong enough, they may not even "see" the storm clouds gathering. Even if they do, they may downplay the likelihood and significance of ominous developments.[12]

This is what we're up against: We are hardwired to see what we want to see. It's this risk factor we must learn to deal with when we take on the highly responsible task of creating a vision for our team or organization. Our powerful vision can have such a profound impact on where we are headed that it would be foolhardy to ignore this aspect of our irrational selves.

Two culprits play a particularly damaging role: *frame blindness* and *overconfidence*.

In Chapter 2, I introduced the cognitive-psychological concept of frames: the mental constructs that help us make sense of a complex world.[13] While processing the signals we receive from our senses, our minds quickly determine the most appropriate frame set to apply and then categorize or label the input accordingly. This is how we are able to instantly recognize an object, such as a chair or a table, even if we've never seen that particular design before.

Frames are an automatic and unconscious part of our cognitive functioning; you can't choose not to apply them. In a way, that's a good thing, as frames help us create an understanding of what would otherwise be an utterly chaotic world. But there's a downside, too. Frames filter out information that's potentially useful or even necessary. As we rapidly, unconsciously select a frame, we rule out other possibilities and might ignore evidence that could lead us to different conclusions.

We all carry these frames. Organizations do, too. Take Microsoft, whose early successes were built on a clear vision: to have a Microsoft computer on every desk, in every house. You would be hard-pressed to find a better formulated, compact company vision statement; it sets direction, is aspirational, was unconventional for its time, includes a sort of noble cause, and relates authentically to what Microsoft stands for and believes in. The vision framed the company's mindset.

However, it also initially caused Microsoft to dismiss the Internet as a passing fad, because the Internet didn't fit in with its belief system, with the desktop as the central processing unit around which everything revolved. It didn't whet Microsoft's appetite to jump on the bandwagon of the emergence of the Internet in the early 1990s. This left the browser market wide open to the start-up Netscape (Microsoft recovered from its mistake while many other companies don't).

So, our frames are deeply rooted, based on a belief system developed through our upbringing, education, and experiences. Reassessing and updating our current frames can challenge those beliefs. Usually, we're not very willing to do that.

One flavor of frame blindness, peripheral blindness, is often demonstrated with a video in which two teams, one dressed in black and the other in white, throw a ball to each other. You're instructed to count the number of times the white team throws the ball. The task requires focus as the team members move around and pass the ball quickly, and you easily lose count if you don't lock your eyes on the ball. Halfway through the forty-second exercise, an actor dressed as a gorilla enters the image, stands in the middle, pounds his chest, and then walks out of the shot. Most people completely miss this very obvious distraction, exemplifying how difficult it is to see what's happening at the periphery when you're paying close attention to something else.

Even if you haven't seen the gorilla video, you are probably all too familiar with the phenomenon. While you're focused on making next quarter's numbers, it's easy to lose sight of larger long-term issues. Unsuccessfully maintaining this dual focus can lead to disastrous results, as anyone in Ireland, Iceland, or Cyprus, or the music industry, or the financial sector, the U.S. auto industry, the newspaper and magazine print business, Nokia, Kodak, or Encyclopedia Britannica can attest. And Fortis, too. But we will pick up that story later.

OVERCONFIDENCE

In addition to frame blindness, there's a second serious psychological challenge we need to deal with: our intrinsic overconfidence in what we think we know. Many psychological experiments have demonstrated the effects of overconfidence, including overestimating your knowledge and abilities, underestimating risks, and exaggerating your ability to control events. A classic example is the vast majority of automobile drivers who rate their abilities as above average (by definition, of course, a majority of anything can't be above average).

There are several aspects of overconfidence worth noting. First, we have a tendency to conceal our uncertainty. In a classroom experiment I conduct on a regular basis, inspired by the work of psychologists Marc Alpert and Howard Raiffa,[14] participants are given ten questions with a numeric outcome (e.g., what is the length of the Nile River). They're told they won't know the exact answers, which is to be expected and which is not a problem. Instead, they're instructed to give a two-number range for each answer, in which they're 90 percent confident the correct answer lies. So, their 90 percent confidence answer to the length of the Nile might be 3,000 miles on the low end and 8,000 miles on the high end. The 3,000 and 8,000 boundaries define the 90 percent confidence interval. This answer would be correct, as the real answer is 4,132 miles.

Theoretically, 90 percent confidence intervals would result in correct answers 90 percent of the time. On average, ten questions should yield nine correct answers. But this never happens. Individual scores generally don't go higher than seven correct answers, and go as low as two or three. Group averages rarely exceed five. Despite the clear prior message that they won't know the answer, people still set their intervals too narrow. What could possibly explain that?

Conceptually, the dilemma that's surfaced here is *precision* vs. *correctness*. The easy strategy to be more often correct would simply be to make the intervals wider, and hence be less precise. But wider intervals also expose your uncertainty. The experiment seems to indicate that people prefer to be perceived as precise (with the risk of being wrong) than correct (with the risk of exposing their uncertainty). Hence, they psychologically deem precision more important than correctness. Or maybe they consider the risk of being wrong less confronting than admitting to the fact that they do not know. Exposing uncertainty is apparently more concerning than giving wrong answers.

In fact, after the experiment there is often a defensive reaction. "If I'd made my margins much wider, it wouldn't have been fun," I hear people say. Or, "Since this is just a game, I tried to be accurate." With this statement, people are pretending that they would be much more willing to accept uncertainty "if this were for real." They resist acknowledging that an "irrational" human trait is brought out. After all, we operate under social pressure that we should know, or roughly know, and rather fool ourselves with overconfidence when facing the uncertainty of the unknown.

Another noteworthy aspect of overconfidence is what Ellen Langer, the Harvard University psychologist, dubbed *illusion of control* in 1975.[15] Notwithstanding our intelligence, we tend to believe we have much more control over events than we actually do, even when it's outright impossible. One of the many experiments Langer ran to demonstrate her point involved lottery tickets. Participants were either handed a ticket or allowed to pick one from a stack. All other conditions being equal (same potential price, same chances of winning), the people in the experiment were then offered a fixed small amount of money in exchange for their lottery ticket before the lottery was run. This would give them a certain small gain over an uncertain but much larger gain. It turned out that the people who had *chosen* their tickets were significantly less willing to part with them than those who had been *handed* their tickets were. In other words, despite the fact that they had no greater chance of winning, the control they had over their choice gave them the irrational illusion that the odds had shifted in their favor.

To explain overconfidence, Yale University professor of economics Robert Shiller points out that "people tend to make judgments in uncertain situations by looking for familiar patterns and assuming that future patterns will resemble past ones, often without sufficient consideration of the reasons for the pattern or the probability of the pattern repeating itself."[16] Or, to quote Edward Russo and Paul Schoemaker, "A major reason for overconfidence in predictions is that people have difficulty in imagining all the ways that events can unfold. Psychologists call this the availability bias: what's out of sight is often out of mind."[17]

As we work to improve our ability to connect the dots, we must be very aware of these dangerous pitfalls. We are all hardwired to look for familiar patterns, usually from recent history, when trying to make sense of what's coming; furthermore, we overestimate the amount of confidence we should place on these predictions. This is especially true if we had a hand in comparable strategic decisions that yielded favorable outcomes—we tend to overestimate the control we had in realizing these outcomes, believing we can apply that strategy similarly as we go forward. The phenomenon of overconfidence keeps us from seeing all possible pathways, as we zoom in on the one view closest to our experience and attach greater certainty to that view than is warranted.

With these precautions in mind as we try to connect the dots, let's look at approaches we can use to develop a coherent vision while significantly *reducing* the risks of frame blindness and overconfidence.

THE MYSTERIOUS GURU

In the late 1960s, Royal Dutch Shell was unable to accurately predict cash flows. Times with ample funds that gave the green light to drilling projects were followed by sudden periods of shortages, forcing activities to an immediate stop (only to resume once the cash position recovered). At Shell, they spoke of "cold winds" blowing through the organization during cash-poor times.

Several consultants were brought in to deal with the issue, but none of them succeeded. That's when Pierre Wack came in. As the head of the business environment division of Shell's planning bureau, Wack had a reputation for being a little "out there," especially in such a cerebral, scientific, numbers-driven organization. He burned incense in his office, went on annual retreats to consult his Indian guru, and was heavily influenced by a Russian spiritual teacher named Georges Gurdjieff.

Shell turned to Wack[18] to find a solution. He took on the assignment in his usual unconventional manner. What followed made him one of the leading management gurus of the twentieth century,[19] but, according to Hardin Tibbs, a strategy consultant with close ties to Wack, sadly also one of the least known.[20]

Instead of trying to limit, minimize, and drive out uncertainty from his view of the future, Wack embraced it, giving uncertainty a central place in his method. Think about that. It goes against most, if not all, other ways of dealing with complexity. We're used to developing models and frameworks to help us increase our control over an area of strategic interest (e.g., our competitive landscape, macroeconomic developments, production planning), aiming to make it less complex and uncertain than it appears. Wack did the exact opposite. Acknowledging that uncertainties would not go away no matter how sophisticated the model was, he placed uncertainty at the heart of his approach.

By embracing uncertainty, we acknowledge the fact of our ignorance, which in turn implies that we need to engage with more than one view in order to enrich our perspective. In other words, this approach effectively deals with the pitfalls of both frame blindness and overconfidence. Contemplating the future with uncertainties as an integral part of the package means we have to entertain multiple outcomes and work more responsibly on our ability to discover the coherences and the logic of how the future may play out. Wack called these potential outcomes *scenarios,* igniting a new discipline in strategic thinking: scenario planning.

Scenarios are imaginary yet logically consistent stories of plausible futures. The goal in scenario planning is to develop a rich set of noteworthy and equally plausible futures, including ones that don't conform to conventional wisdom and our current belief system. Essentially, it means seeking the same value Wiener and Kahn (see Chapter 4) were after: clarification and reduction of thoughtlessness, not prophecy.

CREATING MEMORIES OF THE FUTURE

Scenario planning isn't rocket science. It follows a series of logical steps that deductively bring you to the most pivotal scenarios you should take into account when envisioning the future.

Instead of covering the approach in detail (which has already been done extensively in several formidable books[21]), I'll discuss it at a high level and point out some noteworthy elements of the process and how they relate to our desire to improve our ability to connect the dots responsibly.

Since scenario planning embraces uncertainty, it can be applied to any challenge that is ambiguous: You can develop scenarios for the future of health care to the future of China, the future of civilization to the future of futurists, the future of cycling to your own personal future. Each of these areas of interest has its own set of uncertainties and therefore allow you to follow the steps of scenario planning to arrive at multiple, relevant perspectives to contemplate.

Naturally, before a scenario-planning exercise starts, the subject boundaries and time scope should be established. I usually promote three to seven years as a horizon, simply because this is far enough to see the future differently while near enough to be relevant today. With that set, let's run through the four phases of creating scenarios.

Phase 1: Understanding Key Uncertainties and Certainties

The first step in scenario planning consists of making an inventory of the most prominent uncertainties, as well as the most prominent certainties.

The first category consists of those developments for which it is difficult to predict if and how they will play out. These uncertainties become important drivers in the exercise. The second category, the certainties (Pierre Wack referred to them as the predetermined elements), are those developments that can be predicted with a high degree of certainty.

Of course, this is when you should be wary of your overconfidence and avoid labeling factors as known or knowable, when in fact they are fundamentally unknown (your confidence might stem from personal or interpersonal biases that might pressure you to avoid admitting to their uncertainty). But having said that, there are things we know for sure, or with high degrees of certainty. For instance, we are well aware that Western society is aging. We also know that obesity rates (and costs) will increase, just as we know that reserves of traditional fossil fuels are being depleted (with the exception of new findings of shale gas). On the other hand, changes such as the rise of terrorism, further integration of technology into our daily lives, and consolidation of financial markets are judgment calls and should not be confused with certainties.

With this list in place, we aim to find the two key uncertainties—or, for the more advanced reader, the two uncertainty drivers—within our scope. A productive way to find them is to position the uncertainties in a two-by-two matrix (as shown in Figure 5-2) that ranks each uncertainty first according to the level of impact it would have, and next on its level of uncertainty. This filters the set of uncertainties we identified. The group with high uncertainty and high impact (the top right corner) qualifies as the key uncertainties we're after.

In practice, it often requires deeper debate, regrouping, and sometimes rephrasing to eventually arrive at the two key uncertainties. But once you have arrived at a conclusion, you are ready to enter the second phase.

Phase 2: Developing the Scenario Skeleton

Let's put the certainties on hold for now and create a system of axes with our two key uncertainties. Each axis represents one key uncertainty. To further define the uncertainty, you will need to define the two extremes. After all, the very fact that they are highly uncertain means things can go in one direction, but also in another. So, typically uncertainties range from

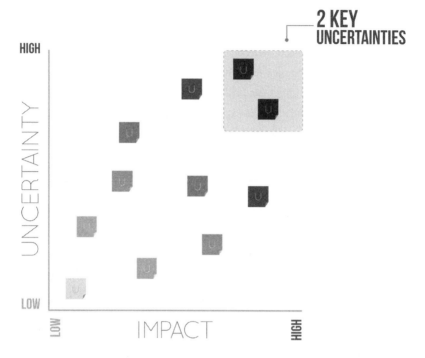

Figure 5-2. Uncertainty-impact matrix.

stable to dynamic, from evolution to revolution, from low to high, from integrated to fragmented, from growth to decline, and so forth.

With the two axes defined, and the extreme ends of each uncertainty axis labeled, we define four quadrants that, while fundamentally different, are *equally plausible*. Since we worked with the most impactful uncertainties, they are also of significant interest.

The logic once more: The two uncertainties we're working with were the most impactful (hence, of significant interest) and the most uncertain (hence, each quadrant could be "reached" in case the uncertainty were to play out in its most extreme form), so collectively, the four quadrants make up four fundamentally different and maximally interesting different future views. And, to the best of our knowledge today, each one is plausible. So, rather than placing our bet on just one of these future outlooks, we'd better understand the logic of all of them.

Let's use an example to demonstrate. In 2009, I worked with Paul Schoemaker on a scenario-planning exercise aimed at better understanding how the Western world might transform as a result of the financial crisis. The two key uncertainties we identified in our research were 1) the nature of the crisis (from deep, ugly, but essentially cyclic, on the one extreme, to systemic and transformative on the other extreme) and 2) the changing role of government influence (from temporary intervention to pull society through the hardship to a more *dirigiste,* directive role).

These defined four quadrants (shown in Figure 5-3) each represent a very different outlook. Once you've got the quadrants, what's next? Essentially, you create a story for each outlook (quadrant), starting by giving it a catchy and memorable title. Then you start painting the picture of what the world would look like: What is fundamentally different in terms of economic developments, technology, regulation, social context, and so on?

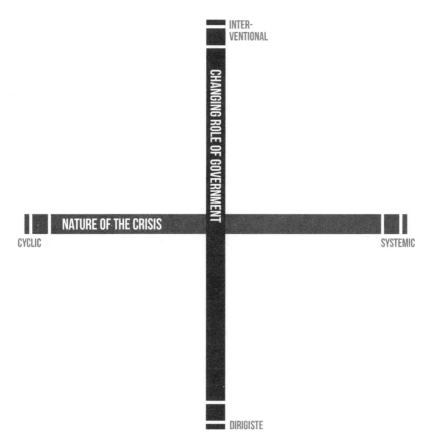

Figure 5-3. Scenario skeleton.

Good questions include: Who are the leading players? What new developments have materialized? What is it that people value? What technologies have emerged? What regulatory changes have taken place? What power balances have shifted?

Contemplating such questions will create an image of that future. Do the same for all four outlooks.

For our exercise to envision various postcrisis transformations of the Western economies (see Figure 5-4), we came up with the titles Capitalism 2.0 (for a return to free market orientation, yet with an update for the obscenities and extravagant risks), Wild Oscillation (for a future without much direction, with up and down periods rapidly alternating with each other), Visible Hand (a wordplay on the term "invisible hand" introduced by Adam Smith, alluding to a future with significant government influ-

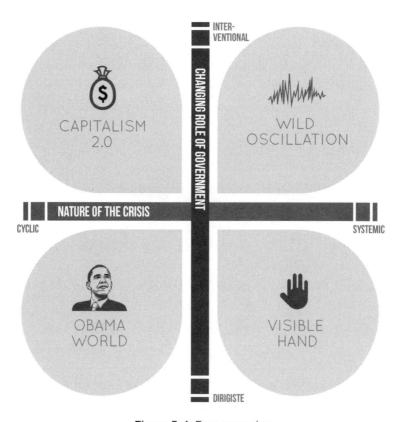

Figure 5-4. Four scenarios.

ence), and Obama World (a new generation of leadership, regained trust in government's role and policies, and more ethically and socially conscious perspectives). We further enriched each outlook with detailed highlights of that future in terms of social aspects, technological advances, and regulatory developments. So, we ended up with four future outlooks that—to the best of our knowledge at that time—were all equally plausible to anticipate.

Phase 3: Straightening the Logic

With these outlooks in place, we now seek to make each story logically consistent. This requires us to understand the path that would bring us from where we are today to that outlook. This in turn requires the identification of the dominant forces and developments that will drive the future in the direction we are trying to understand; that is, which events would be formative on that path?

Again, this is an effort to be undertaken four times: once for each quadrant. Apply the technique of *backtracking,* a kind of connecting the dots backward from a specific sketch of the future to see if you can find a path that would get you from there to here. If your outlook is set in 2020, you start wondering what would need to happen around 2019 to logically bring you to 2020. Next, you wonder what would need to happen in 2018 to bring you to 2019. Note how this technique fundamentally differs from trend analysis, which aims to say something about the future by starting with what we know about the recent past and extrapolating that forward. Backtracking does the exact opposite: It starts in the future and aims to understand what would logically get us there.

Once completed, what remains is a series of developments that, when read from now toward the future, provides the backbone to a logically coherent story. To complete the picture, you'll review and possibly integrate into your story the uncertainties you didn't identify as key, as well as the predetermined elements (i.e., trends).

This story structure, based on a logically consistent path, embellished with your informed imagination, and leading to a future outlook, is what we call a *scenario*. By doing so, you are creating several very powerful, future-oriented stories that serve as "mind hooks" to help understand, discuss, and explore the future as it emerges.

Phase 4: Deriving Implications

In the final step, with the four logically consistent, powerful scenarios in place, you now reach the essence of the exercise: You contemplate the implications of each scenario for your organization. Notice that this is the first time your own interests come into the picture. Before this step, we tried to envision what the environment—which lies largely, if not fully, beyond our direct sphere of influence—might look like, and what disruptions the unfolding future might throw your way. Now the goal becomes envisioning what you would do in each scenario in order to be successful. This outside-in perspective of scenario planning sets it apart from the inside-out approach many other techniques suffer from.

Practice 5-1.
Future scenarios.

Ask questions such as: How does this scenario impact our business and our strategy? How prepared are we for this scenario today, and what can we do to ensure that we will be successful if it were to pan out? What strategic options do we have in each story? What strategic contingencies should we anticipate? How will we respond if this scenario were to emerge? How can we best prepare and anticipate this scenario?

The former head of Shell's strategic planning group, Arie de Geus, a scenario-planning veteran and scholar, calls the exercise "creating a memory of the future," a wonderful phrase that alludes to the essence of the exercise: creating mental preparedness by anticipating multiple relevant futures. He asserts that an organization's ability to learn faster than the competition may be the only sustainable competitive advantage, and scenario planning is a pivotal method in developing this future-readiness. Moreover, it battles in a most deliberate way the ever-present pitfalls of overconfidence, frame blindness, peripheral blindness, and cognitive dissonance—the forces we were up against in our attempt to connect the dots responsibly.

SHELL'S AWAKENING

To round off our exploration of scenario planning as a method for developing our ability to connect the dots, I must wrap up the story of the "mysterious guru" Pierre Wack. Dealing with the complex issue of improved cash flow projection, Wack developed the scenario-planning method to understand where the future of Shell might be heading. His first effort involved oil price scenarios in 1970.

On the demand side for oil, everything seemed stable and predictable: Growth in oil demand had been consistent in the late sixties, and there were no indications that the situation would change radically in the next few years. Demand for oil was a predetermined element.

On the supply side, however, there were a few unsettling developments. Despite the planning department's initial assessment that it was stable (resources were plentiful and drilling capacity was productively utilized), Wack took a deeper look. Contemplating the key uncertainties they were facing, he noticed two developments that he considered to be potentially disruptive, but he couldn't predict with a sufficient level of certainty how they would play out. He noticed how the United States was gradually moving from an oil-*exporting* country to an oil-*importing* one—which, considering the growth of oil consumption vs. production capacity, was a fairly predictable trend. Wack flagged this development as a potential indicator of a geopolitical power shift, decreasing the West's dominance as it grew more dependent on other, less-developed parts of the world. He aimed to get under the hood of how these new realities might impact leadership behaviors, especially of those who controlled oil supply.

In *Scenarios: The Art of Strategic Conversation,* Kees van der Heijden points out: "It was one of Pierre's great contributions to the scenario process that he insisted in looking at *people* behind decisions, not just the technical or macro phenomena."[22] It seems Pierre Wack was an early behavioral strategist.

In the same vein, Wack wondered if it would make sense for these oil-producing nations, from their own perspective, to continue to increase supply. He doubted it: Sooner or later those governments would start to question their long-term income from the assets in their ground. However, the argument could still be brushed aside; if any individual country were to step out of the delivery process, others would happily step in. More would be needed to upset the future of oil supply.

That's where the second development came on his radar screen. Wack noticed that several oil-producing countries—including Venezuela, Iran, and Saudi Arabia—were regularly meeting and exchanging views. As this seemed a somewhat odd group of nations, nobody was paying much attention to their meetings; the group was viewed as a tiger without teeth as far as policy was concerned. But Wack contemplated a different run of events. He realized it would take very little for the group to turn into a governing body for oil-producing nations. We now know that this was the beginning of what would become OPEC, which fully reshaped the oil industry by controlling supply and, by extension, price. At the time, though, it was all in Wack's imagination.

Altogether, these uncertainties about a possible power shift due to the loss of independence and the option of more controlled production formed the basis of a set of scenarios. Among them was the "crisis scenario," in which oil-producing countries teamed up and would no longer increase capacity beyond what made sense for their own development. The story turned out to be a very accurate prediction of the oil crisis just a few years later.

The fact that Wack accurately predicted this scenario makes it an intriguing anecdote, but that's not the point of the story. What he *did* with his early insights was what *really* made the difference. Wack didn't just create scenarios, he used them to engage senior leaders in simulation exercises to gain insights and aid decision making. When the oil crisis actually happened in 1973, Shell executives had already given considerable thought to a future that had been unimaginable within their traditional frame. They were mentally ready to act once the new reality hit. In a way, they had already rehearsed the future.

Van der Heijden tells the story:

They interpreted the October 1973 events in the Middle East as the unfolding of this scenario, and were to quickly shift their investments. While most of the refining industry needed years to decide that something really fundamental had happened in the industry, Shell moved immediately, switching investments from expansion of primary capacity to upgrading the output of refineries, well ahead of the "pack." As a consequence of industry inertia, refining capacity in the industry ran into considerable oversupply, with disastrous consequences for profitability, but due to Shell's early adaptation of alternative policies they suffered much less from overcapacity and outperformed the industry by a long margin. This later was shown to have had a fundamental impact on the way the company as a whole came through the turbulent 1970s and early 1980s.[23]

After this initial success, Wack's team foresaw the more severe price shock of 1979, the collapse of the oil market in 1986, the fall of the Soviet Union, the rise of Muslim radicalism, and the increasing pressure on companies to address environmental and social problems. Even today, Shell still periodically produces and publishes future scenarios. It has institutionalized the practice as part of its strategic rhythm: When new scenarios have been created, Shell executives worldwide must gather with their management teams and deliberately spend time debating and analyzing the possible implications of each of these scenarios for their part of the business. This is how Shell continuously ignites internal strategic dialogue and reflection, and assures that its senior leaders—who are, at the end of the day, only human—do not fall victim to tunnel vision.

Shell's managing director in 1980, André Bénard, commented, "Experience has taught us that the scenario technique is much more conducive to forcing people to think about the future than the forecasting techniques we formerly used."[24]

THE FALL OF FORTIS

Let's pick up the Belgian tale where we left off and examine whether the collapse of Fortis could be blamed on its leaders or if they just fell victim to extreme and unforeseeable circumstances. Recall some key facts: The economy was booming, confidence was very high, and there was a widespread, unquestioned belief that the European banking industry was going to consolidate to a handful of main players.

Soon after Fortis announced its participation in the Consortium in early 2007, doubt started seeping into the organization. The initial euphoric mood shifted to one of concern as management and staff realized that the deal would mean an integration process unlike any they'd ever done. They did have extensive experience—in fact, in its two-decade history, the company had been built through a series of mergers and acquisitions—but the new deal was different. It was bigger and more complex in terms of the size of the acquired company, the three-company Consortium that was making the deal, and the entrenched ABN AMRO culture.

ABN AMRO's reluctance to cooperate was clear from the start; its CEO labeled it aggressive, challenged Fortis's ability to afford the takeover, and was unambiguous in his preference to consolidate with Barclays. Moreover, in the months following the announcement, it became obvious that the Consortium's price was astronomic. ABN AMRO's value had never seriously exceeded 40 billion euros on the stock exchange, and the Consortium had offered nearly twice that much. Let's also not forget Fortis's lack of capital to pay for the acquisition and its (over)confidence that it would be able to raise the money.

But the executive committee, headed by Jean-Paul Votron, wouldn't hear of any criticism or doubt. There was no room for negativity. They grasped at every occasion to rally the troops and explain the upcoming success; they preached and expected an optimistic "we can do this" attitude.

The real moment of truth arrived when ABN AMRO, in an attempt to fight off the Consortium, sold off one of its crown jewels: its U.S. LaSalle Bank brand. The operation, which represented a stronghold in Chicago and the Illinois and Indiana region, had been one of the selling points in the deal. ABN AMRO announced the sale to Bank of America weeks after the Consortium had declared its intention. The Consortium responded with a court case, challenging the legality of the sale of strategic parts of the organization without approval from its shareholders.

Initially they won, but on Friday, July 13, the Consortium lost a final appeal. The ruling came as a serious blow. On top of the hostility from ABN AMRO, growing internal doubts, falling stock prices, a simmering internal concern about its portfolio of subprime mortgages, and the realization that the bid had been astronomic, loss of the court case looked like a face-saving end of the battle for the Consortium. Most people who were closely following the case figured that an announcement that the deal was called off was imminent.

But on Monday, July 16, the Consortium announced it was sustaining its bid. Behind the scenes, Fortis is said to have in fact threatened one of the other members of the Consortium, Royal Bank of Scotland (RBS) (which was to obtain LaSalle Bank) if it decided to withdraw now that the ruling was final. ABN AMRO's tactic to brush them off had failed.

In the light of the developments, the position Fortis took was hard to comprehend. In order to get some understanding of the phenomena that were quite likely at work here, we must turn to the field of psychology once more.

GROUPTHINK

The "what if" game is particularly harsh on the Consortium that Fortis was part of. What if the company had walked away at that moment of truth? The Fortis brand and independent operation would probably still be around, instead of having vanished into—mostly—BNP Paribas and ABN AMRO; RBS would probably not be government-owned, as it is today; tens of thousands of (mostly Belgian) families would still have their pensions and life savings; and the RBS CEO at that time, Fred Goodwin, would still be Sir Fred.[25]

But that's not what happened. Against mighty adversarial forces and surrounded by some of the smartest, best-paid financial advisers, the Consortium chose to push the deal. Was it just bad luck that caused the story to unfold the way it did in the year following the decision? Or did the players mentally dig themselves into a tunnel from which it was impossible to escape?

In 1952, William H. Whyte Jr. coined the term *groupthink*. It was picked up in the seventies by Irving Janis, a Yale professor, who provided an academic foundation for the concept, focusing on the causes of groupthink and how to recognize and prevent it. He originally described groupthink as "the mode of thinking that persons engage in when concurrence-seeking becomes so dominant in a cohesive ingroup that it tends to override realistic appraisal of alternative courses of action. The more amiability and esprit de corps there is among the members of policy-making ingroups the greater the danger that independent critical thinking will be replaced by groupthink, which is likely to result in irrational and dehumanizing actions directed against outgroups."[26]

The Fortis senior leadership team, with its strong Belgian majority, qualifies as an ingroup. (There was a small Dutch subset in the executive committee (ExCo), but they were no counterforce to the Belgians.) However, there was a more important, cohesive subgroup in the ExCo: those who had been crossed by ABN AMRO in recent years. Jean-Paul Votron himself used to work at ABN AMRO, where he sought to become a board member in the late 1990s. He left after two years when it became clear to him that he didn't stand a chance. Votron shared his story with Lex Kloosterman, who had recently joined Fortis as a strategist (after he, too, was denied a top spot at ABN AMRO) and was closely involved in realizing the deal. They were joined by Chairman Lippens, who had gone head-to-head with ABN AMRO and its chairman approximately ten years earlier in a nasty battle over De Generale Bank (an early acquisition win that put Fortis on the map and left the two chairmen with bitter memories). So the Fortis chairman, the CEO, and the ExCo member responsible for strategy—not an unimportant subset, mind you—all held a grudge against ABN AMRO.

Let's get back to Janis. He identified eight symptoms that indicate groupthink, organized in three categories:

Type 1: Overestimation of the group
Type 2: Closed-mindedness
Type 3: Pressures toward uniformity

You can probably spot the interesting connections with the challenges of connecting the dots: Type 1 overlaps with overestimation/overconfidence, and type 2 with closed-mindedness/frame blindness. Type 3 adds the group dynamics element. In Janis's theory, the more symptoms at play, the higher the risk of groupthink.

How could these symptoms apply to the story of Fortis? The illusion of invulnerability—one of the two type 1 symptoms—was clearly present at the top of the organization, as it continued to stress Fortis's legacy of successful acquisitions and integrations. This integration was just bigger than any the company had done before, but nothing to be alarmed about. Or at least that's what they convinced themselves.

Executive committee members discouraged criticism, even though there was ample reason to question the morality of individual members and the revenge factor in getting back at ABN AMRO (the second type 1 symptom of unquestioned belief in group morality). The warnings that started trickling in after the announcement of the Consortium were rationalized away (a type 2 symptom of rationalizing warnings); doubts about the height of the bid were dismissed as it would have taken too much time to back-pedal and put in a new, more realistic bid. A critical stance was considered negative and ill-intended and simply not acceptable (the second type 2 symptom of stereotyping opposition).

Above all, though, it seems irresponsible that Fortis entered the deal without funding. It had raised less than half the capital required. The case of Northern Rock, which caused an immediate lockup of interbank lending, should have set off alarms at Fortis. How could they be certain that they would be able to raise the necessary capital in the current and possibly emerging environment? And so Fortis stepped into the monumental deal without heeding this early-warning signal.

The type 3 symptoms, which consist of four forms of pressures toward uniformity (self-censorship, illusion of unanimity, direct pressure to conform, and self-appointed mind guards) are easy to spot when studying the case.[27]

Collectively, the situation provided the perfect setup for groupthink to kick in.

SO WHAT?

What does Janis teach us about the potential consequences of groupthink? In essence, it boils down to bad judgment in decision making. Groupthink creates a strong, positive bias toward the information that favors the pre-ferred choice, keeping you from effectively considering alternatives and objectives and from effectively weighing the risks. When the conditions change, options are not reevaluated, which prevents the group from ac-knowledging the need for—much less working out the details of—contin-gency plans.

Let's consider that last point in more detail. What can we learn from the Fortis case? What if they had managed to avoid groupthink? Would they have decided not to join the Consortium? At that time, they were under the very reasonable impression that the neighbor's house is only for sale once. The opportunity to acquire ABN AMRO was unique. It's probably unfair to blame the executives for their thirst (even though this completely contra-dicted their freshly announced strategy to expand *outside* the Benelux).

But, to get back to Janis's findings, one of Fortis's major mistakes was that the company never seriously considered contingencies and exit strategies. It never returned to the drawing board, not even when the conditions changed significantly and the initial assumptions were proven false. Imagine if Pierre Wack had been in the room with the Fortis executives, helping them develop several scenarios of possible futures, gain strategic clarity on when to reassess their options, and define under which (changed) conditions they would remove themselves from the bidding process.

Had Wack been there, the only time they might have listened to him would have been at the *beginning* of the process, when Fortis was still considering its participation in the Consortium. After that, groupthink sank in its claws. The pressure and incentive to realize the "deal of a lifetime" made it virtually impossible to back out—even if the conditions changed, which they did for Fortis. They got a perfect opportunity to step away from the bidding process when the court ruled against them, but psychologically it was too late. They had already paralyzed themselves by reinforcing, over and over again, the singularity of their vision.

BRILLIANT OR FOOLISH?

If the Fortis senior leaders had developed a set of scenarios at the early phase of their adventure, and diligently identified under what conditions they would need to reconsider or change course, chances are that they would have allowed much more mental agility into their vision.

So that seemed to have been the wiser way of working. But a question we struggle with is whether developing multiple future outlooks fits with the expectations we have of a leader and a leadership team. Don't we admire those leaders who emanate confidence in the path they have set out for the organization, rather than those who don't disguise their doubt and anticipate various different future outlooks? Aren't those that explore exit strategies before they even get started in realizing their vision just too insecure to stand the heat of resolute decision making? Wouldn't it therefore be detrimental to their leadership persona if they exposed their uncertainty by anticipating multiple futures?

Simon Sinek, the author of *Start with Why,* fittingly observed that "one of the best paradoxes of leadership is a leader's need to be both stubborn and open-minded. A leader must insist on sticking to the vision and stay on course to the destination. But he must be open-minded during the process."

In June 2013, the Indian School of Business released a thought-provoking case study on Glenmark, an India-based pharmaceutical company that followed a high-risk innovation strategy in drug discovery.[28] Named one of "Asia's 200 Best under a Billion" by *Forbes* in 2008, this company triggers an insightful discussion on entrepreneurship, leadership, innovation, and success factors in emerging markets. But above all, it is a case study on vision—or perhaps tunnel vision.

In 2001, under the leadership of the founder's son, Glenn Saldanha, the company reoriented itself from the generic drug producer it had been since its founding in 1977 to an innovator, focusing on drug discovery and research. The strategy yielded great success during the 2004–2007 period, when it generated substantial income in up-front and milestone payments in four different drug innovations from out-licensing deals with powerhouse clients such as Merck and Eli Lilly.

But then the odds changed in 2008. Amid the turmoil of the global financial crisis, one licensee changed strategy and discontinued its commitment; another drug stalled after hitting unfavorable research outcomes. The market and belief changed radically overnight. "From 2000 to 2008, whatever we touched turned to gold. In 2008, when all these transactions started falling apart, it brought a hard reality to our business models," CEO Saldanha recalled. "There was disappointment within the management team and people were worried about whether we would or could continue the research effort. Many analysts felt we should shut down research because it was not productive or spin it off." To make things worse, the third deal fell apart in 2009, changing the promising outlook of four serious opportunities to a gloomy image of one remaining innovation candidate in a matter of twelve months.

That's where the case ends, and the conversation in the classroom starts. What would you do? Stick to the plan and continue the high-risk strategy? It's tempting to take the position that one could have known all along that intense risks are part of an innovation strategy. Undoubtedly someone will call out that if you can't stand the heat, you should stay out of the kitchen. Macho determination always works well when reviewing cases. But really? If it were your own money, your own job, would you still think the same?

Alternatively, you could change course. But what route should you follow? Should you make a radical shift away from innovation and abandon all you have learned over the years? Reduce or minimize your innovation agenda for a while, so the company has time to settle and come to terms with the new reality? But what would that do to the talent you attracted and the culture you developed? Maybe you should spin off or sell off the innovation operation—although, at its lowest value in years, would that be a smart thing to do?

It's a great case for discussing matters such as risk appetite, surfacing leadership dilemmas, generating options, and other valuable strategic conversation themes.

Fortunately, the Indian School of Business also released a successor case on the company, which tells us what Glenmark actually did.[29] This case study focuses on the leader, Glenn Saldanha. In short, he persevered with the innovation agenda. He did plug a few holes that had come to the surface, reducing costs and altering some of his bets, but he held on to his fundamental belief in and commitment to innovation. When reviewing the course Glenmark took after the challenging 2008–2009 period, and listing critical success factors for innovation-based organizations, Saldanha said, "The first and most important thing is that a long-term focus is very critical to create value. The second is to create an organizational culture right from the leadership down the line. People have to stay for the long term, because continuity is very critical for innovation. Our commitment and passion for research has never died. Failure is part of it."

What should we think of this leadership position? Dedicated or stubborn? Driven by passion or blinded by passion? Heroic confidence or irrational overconfidence? A leader who stands for what he truly cares about, or a leader unwilling to challenge his own assumptions? It's Sinek's leadership paradox in action. We tend to admire leaders who dare to make bold decisions and take courageous positions. In Saldanha's defense, the company dug itself out of the hole and reported licensing successes again in 2010, 2011, and 2012. On the other hand, he "bet the house" by continuing the high-risk innovation strategy and seriously jeopardized the futures of many. One more failure in the last remaining innovation trajectory and the company might have ceased to exist. Based on the outcome, we might be tempted to conclude that he did the right thing. But that's only with the benefit of hindsight. We are careful about the benefit of hindsight when things turn out wrong, and we should be equally careful about it when things turn out favorable.

So, brilliant or foolish? Contemplate that question for a while—what do *you* think?

Here's what I think. The case doesn't mention whether Saldanha truly, with an open mind, considered alternatives, eventually leading to this strategy of continued dedication to innovation as the best-option outcome, or whether his mind was more or less fixed and determined all along. I'm inclined to believe the latter, judging by the full version of the case, although I can't be sure since it's not documented. That, to me, would be the point of the case. Being dedicated, persistent, and decisive is admirable and undoubtedly a leadership quality, but it becomes foolish when it arises from stubbornness and a fundamental, dogmatic unwillingness to change course—even if in hindsight that strategic choice turned out to be successful. If Saldanha carefully and without preconception reviewed his options and alternatives, including exit conditions and strategies (possibly using scenario planning as a technique), and eventually, with an open mind, arrived at the conclusion that continuing his path was the best alternative at that point in time, it would lean toward brilliance. Unfortunately, the case does not reveal this part of the story. But as the remarkable British thinker Gregory Bateson once said, "There is no wisdom in only one point of reference." I think that is what Saldanha opted for: overconfidence in the point of reference to which he attached his beliefs, persona, and self-esteem. If I am right, it would have been foolishness—and in some way mere luck that things turned out well. We should not confuse luck with brilliance as we try to distill lessons from a case like this one.

RESPONSIBLE VISIONARY LEADERSHIP

We reviewed a case where the story took a wrong turn (Fortis) and a case where the story took a favorable turn (Glenmark). Considering multiple plausible scenarios—including some that are different from your preferred view—and working your way through their implications is a smart thing to do when you are entering into a process of decision making under great uncertainty. It need not be a formalistic scenario-planning process. When

Chanda Kochhar, who leads India's ICICI Bank, reflected on the company's success in the highly volatile markets of emerging India, she commented:

> We have a team of people who do scenario planning and stress testing. That's important for any bank. But one can't just leave everything to the process, because things are changing every day. One day, I might see something that happens to another bank and think, "That could happen to us." So I call the team. We brainstorm, we discuss. So there's an institutionalized process but also a constant on-the-fly process that's much less structured.[30]

An established process might help, if only to safeguard you from the overwhelming pressure to just focus on the now. But more important is a mindset and attitude that's willing to explore various perspectives on how things might proceed. This multiple-futures attitude helps you combat these very human tendencies that lead to overconfidence and frame blindness.

When you enter a strategic decision-making phase, facing a decision that will have significant impact on the future, and when your visionary capacity is most called for, the right moment to envision such multiple futures is when you are not yet tunneled in. At that point, you're still "sane" and open-minded enough to fully comprehend the alternatives and their implications. It's also the moment where you are still psychologically willing to review exit strategies from your expected decision, and identify the points where you should change course. Once you have made your decision, and voiced it to others, the phenomenon of consistency and commitment will kick in, pressuring you to remain consistent with what you have stated, even if that becomes ill-considered consistency at a later stage.

Now, you might be wondering if you can afford to create future scenarios in these pressure-cooker times, such as during mergers and acquisitions, or when suddenly the odds of success seem to shift dramatically. It seemingly distracts you from focusing on what's most urgent, and it's pretty impossible to find scenario-building reflection time when everyone is preparing for the successful realization of the merger or acquisition, or fighting the fires of terminated strategic client relationships. Right?

The answer depends on how you define the role of senior leaders. I believe that the top people in a company have one major task in such periods of change: namely, to be the guardians of a strategically responsible process. To accomplish that task, you have to understand the phenomena that might delude you (and your people) and do whatever it takes to prevent that from happening. People in less senior positions can get away with the fact that their vision was blinded by circumstances, but at the top you can't escape the responsibility. You are in charge. You are expected to be diligent and responsible in your role—not to gamble with the jobs and lives of large numbers of people.

I fully agree that there is real strategic and motivational value in having a powerful story on how to go forward, and radiating confidence and determination—all that is indeed part of the leader's role. The point is that leaders should not get fooled by their own confidence. Keeping an open mind and changing course accordingly is a more impressive form of strategic leadership than dogmatically holding on to one worldview when the odds have shifted.

You might also ask, won't wise people with wise advisers automatically come to new conclusions if conditions change and dictate a new perspective? They don't need early-stage scenarios and exit strategies to deal with alternative circumstances if they adjust their views in time, right? Well, psychologically, that's nearly impossible. Fortis's leaders grew accustomed to their mental models that developed over a period of months as they explained the "logic" of the acquisition over and over again. And they weren't corrected by their intelligent, high-profile advisers, either—the same advisers who had considerable personal financial incentives to close the deal. The title "adviser," which implies both knowledge and impartiality, is clearly ironic, given that a tremendous amount in fees was at stake if the deal was completed successfully. And the incentive trap didn't stop there. The leadership team, most notably the CEO, had a significant personal financial interest in going forward with the deal.

Fortis's fatal errors could possibly have been avoided. The story is a classic example of the dangers of groupthink. It works like quicksand once you get involved in a large deal or some other project. Your blind spots, your inherent irrationality, and your overconfidence prevent you from making sound decisions. It's only at the start of such a process that you can clearly and rationally take a step back and develop a series of future outlooks, connecting the dots to other futures than the one you are hoping for, so that you can see what else might happen. This is also the time to heed early-warning signals and develop contingency plans for them, growing your own mental agility to change course if necessary. Possibly you assign the role of maverick to one or two of your trustees and allow them to play the role of the devil's advocate. Or you install any of many other ideas that demonstrate your awareness of these dangers, and that highlight your responsible attitude (Figure 5-5) toward safeguarding the process from our inherent human imperfections.

That's what *responsible* visionary leaders do: They keep in mind their responsibilities as well as their human flaws, and take steps to prevent those flaws from misleading them in such strategically critical circumstances.

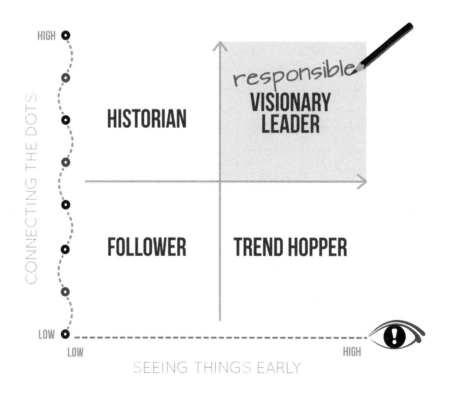

Figure 5-5. Improved visionary framework.

Connecting the dots once we've become adept at seeing things early isn't easy. Due to the complexity and uncertainty of the future, we can only have a limited perspective on what might lie ahead. Psychological factors like frame blindness and overconfidence add to the confusion, producing a distorted view of the uncertainties, events, and forces that might shape a very different future than the one we envision.

Ideally, we should be able to adjust our views easily to incorporate these changing realities if and as they unfold. But our human tendency to cling to our existing belief system stands in the way. We often end up with a very limited vision, sometimes even tunnel vision; even highly capable individuals and groups get locked in outdated belief systems that, despite clear signals that indicate that circumstances have changed, are unable to update their vision to incorporate these new realities.

To protect yourself against these risk factors, you must connect the dots in multiple ways and work intelligently with uncertainty. Don't brush uncertainty aside, or expect that you have covered for it because you have added some error margin into your model or calculations. Grow this dimension of your visionary capacity by entertaining multiple, significantly different outlooks on the future. Engage with scenario planning, a proven methodology that requires existential open-mindedness, agility, and creativity. These qualities are extremely helpful in improving your visionary abilities. In a way, you are productively using doubt as a growth factor in your strategic reasoning.

The philosopher Bertrand Russell once said, "The whole problem with the world is that fools and fanatics are always so certain of themselves, but wiser people so full of doubts." Some people say that doubt is a true sign of intelligence; that's simply because you cannot connect the dots with unwarranted certainty looking forward, you can only connect them with absolute certainty looking back. Just as the legendary Steve Jobs explained so wisely on that sun-drenched June day in Palo Alto.

PART 3

6

Your Visionary Self

Developing character and vision is the way leaders invent themselves.

—WARREN BENNIS

ON BECOMING A VISIONARY LEADER

When it comes to the important personal dimensions of leadership, and the pivotal role you play yourself in enacting what you stand for, I'm a big fan of the work of Warren Bennis, one of the most eminent thinkers in this field. His landmark book *On Becoming a Leader*—the title of which inspired the heading of this section—is one I often recommend. In it, Bennis promotes an integrated perspective on leadership, consisting of four essential competencies: vision, adaptive capacity, voice, and integrity.[1] Vision and adaptive capacity already feature prominently throughout this book; in this chapter, we'll explore the relationship between your visionary capacity and Bennis's concepts of voice and integrity—the identity-oriented aspects.

Recall that followers look to your vision as a guiding light for the decisions they make, the initiatives they start, the priorities they set, and so on. These uses correspond to the Logos side of your vision (see Aristotle's classic three elements of persuasion explained in Chapter 1). In addition, followers need to *feel* something in order to become ignited to follow you. That's the Pathos dimension.

But there is a third critical element that has been missing from our exploration so far: the integrity, credibility, and authenticity of the leader. This is what Aristotle meant by Ethos in his memorable triad: "Persuasion is achieved by the speaker's personal character when the speech is so spoken as to make us think him credible."

This is where your personal character enters the equation. Bennis asserts that "timeless leadership is always about character, and it is always about authenticity."[2] And Harvard professor John Kotter adds that acceptance goes deeper than message alone: "Whether delivered with many words or a few carefully chosen symbols, such messages are not necessarily accepted just because they are understood. Another big challenge in leadership efforts is credibility—getting people to believe the message."[3] So in order for your vision to evoke energy and provide the many invaluable benefits we have examined, it must be aligned with your authenticity, credibility, and behavioral integrity.

YOU!

Your followers will be watching to see if you really mean what you say. Are you really willing to pursue that—possibly unconventional—path? They'll want to see if you are prepared to make the required sacrifices, to change your behavior, live by your vision, and stand by your vision when you're under pressure. It's the classic walk-the-talk, practice-what-you-preach thing.

This means that the importance of *you* in your vision cannot be underestimated. You play a critical role in making your vision powerful through the way you show up, the way you behave, and the way you accept the consequences of your words. A CEO whose New Year's speech professes the incredible importance of sustainability and the realignment necessary to build a green business for future generations can get the logic right (it's backed up by enough evidence) and present a noble cause (leaving a habitable planet for our children is noble enough). But if that same CEO is unwilling to draw personal implications, change some behaviors, or make sacrifices or, worse, acts as though the vision does not apply to himself, the CEO will fail to persuade, and thus energize and inspire, others.

I'm still astounded to see companies whose leaders preach "putting the customer first in everything we do," yet keep the five best spots in their parking lot reserved for senior leadership. Companies with deep-rooted beliefs don't need posters on the wall to remind them of their values. IKEA's founder Ingvar Kamprad lives and breathes these values in everything he does (or used to do; he stopped his active involvement in the company in 2013, at the age of 89). Cost-consciousness is at the core of the IKEA model. Without this, it would be impossible to deliver on IKEA's enduring intent to make well-designed furniture easily accessible. One of the richest men in the world, Kamprad is known to fly economy class and to take the bus instead of a taxi from the airport to the hotel. His actions, in other words, are in alignment with the values he preaches. Which means IKEA has no need for coffee mugs or artistically designed gadgets to spread its core messages and beliefs.

The values you live by and emanate are part of your story already. They must also become part of your identity as a leader. In this chapter, we'll dig deeper into this *self-dimension* of your visionary capacity.

First, we'll take a look at two very different visionaries: not all-too-familiar, overused, larger-than-life examples, but leaders in their own right who come from nonmainstream worlds. Let's see what we can learn from them in terms of authenticity, values, and behavior.

UTZON'S MASTERPIECE

Imagine you are an architect living in the 1950s. You are about a decade into your career, and so far you haven't established a big name for yourself. The world you live in differs greatly from the way it is today. Letters still get written by hand or typewriter; color television is a novelty; phone booths dot street corners; news travels slowly; the world has not globalized in any significant way; many words—the Internet, frappuccino, iPhone, Dubai, and even Walkman, video game, laser printer, credit card, and McDonald's—have yet to enter our vocabulary. In your world of architecture, the focus is predominantly on postwar housing projects in a society trying to recover from the Second World War. Even the ugly concrete jungles of the 1960s and the 1970s have yet to be designed.

As you are trying to build your business, you notice a little announcement in your favorite architect's monthly. There's an international competition for a new project, on the other side of the world. You decide to enter, spend time creating a number of sketches, and submit them as requested. But your expectations are modestly low. After all, your portfolio is still limited, your name is unknown internationally, you submitted only a few drafts, and you live far away, two full days by air travel (remember, it's the 1950s), from where the building is to be erected.

But to your surprise, six months later you are declared the winner, beating 233 competing designs from around the world. Apparently, you submitted something that stood out.

Fast-forward more than half a century. Today your building stands as one of the most beautiful ever created. American architect Louis Kahn has been quoted as saying that "the sun did not know how beautiful its light was, until it was reflected off this building."[4] Your name is Jørn Utzon, the competition is for a national opera house at Bennelong Point, and the building is the magnificent Sydney Opera House.

The conception of the Sydney Opera House is a fascinating tale of visionary thinking with, at its center, the Danish architect Jørn Utzon. What kind of person, what kind of brilliant mind, and what kind of creative process did it take to design something so beautiful and complex, a structure that half a century later is still considered futuristic, and still stands out as one of the most acclaimed and recognizable buildings in the world?

When the Sydney Opera House was declared a World Heritage Site in 2007, Utzon became only the second person ever to receive such recognition during his lifetime. And when he was granted architecture's highest honor, the Pritzker Prize, in 2003, one of the judges declared that "Utzon made a building well ahead of its time, far ahead of available technology, and he persevered through extraordinarily malicious publicity and negative criticism to build a building that changed the image of an entire country."[5] And he sure did, because Sydney, and in fact Australia, will never be the same without it.

The tragic backstory is that Utzon never saw his masterpiece with his own eyes. After spending a few years creating the detailed plans in Denmark, he and his family emigrated to Australia in 1962 to be present during construction. But a redesign dispute with the newly elected Liberal Government in 1965 threw his life upside down. With his payments withheld, Utzon was forced to close his office, lay off his staff, and retreat from the project in March 1966. He returned to Denmark with his family and vowed to never set foot in Australia again. And he never did. For many years, his pivotal contribution was even omitted from the official Opera House history; in fact, during the grand opening by Queen Elizabeth II in 1973, his name was never mentioned. The wrongdoing was only corrected in 1999, when he was approached by the New South Wales government and the Sydney Opera House Trust to help with some necessary redesign work. But at that point he wasn't able to travel to Australia anymore due to his age.

Utzon passed away in 2008 at the age of 90, having only seen his amazing creation in pictures.

But the fascinating question that arises out of Utzon's story is: What allowed him to invent such an elegant and unique structure, without any real reference points and without the technological means available today? We marvel at his creativity, imagination, and visionary capacity, and speedily file it away as purely a stroke of genius (which it was). But now, let's instead try to figure out how Utzon's process of unconventional thinking might have happened.

First of all, the architect had a deep appreciation for nature. His designs mimicked nature's patterns of growth, an approach he called Additive Architecture. He famously said, "If it grows naturally, the architecture will look after itself." In Katarina Stübe's impressive photographic testimony to the beauty of the Sydney Opera House and a true tribute to Jørn Utzon's life (created in cooperation with his son Jan), Utzon says that "nature knows nothing about compromise, it accepts all difficulties, not as difficulties as such, but rather as new factors that configure a totality."[6]

Thus, his inspiration came from a source very different from those commonly used for other designs. Before the Sydney Opera House competition, Utzon traveled the world, from China to Africa, with a mind open to vastly different construction principles. He purposefully rid himself of traditional constraints, finding ideas and drawing parallels from nature to feed his imagination. Utzon's open-mindedness, curiosity, and willingness to recategorize his thinking are important aspects of visionary behavior that we will review in more detail in Chapter 7.

Utzon possessed another crucial quality, however—one that is held by most (if not all) visionaries. When you hear how he was ousted from his masterpiece project after having relocated his family to Australia, and how he was relentlessly pestered by government officials who seemingly robbed him of his dream, you might assume that Utzon became a bitter and cynical man. It seems all too reasonable, in light of the hardships he endured.

But he didn't. Instead, he always communicated positively about the project and about the people he worked with, even those who stood in his way. His son Jan Utzon recalls, "He was the most positive person I've ever met. He never talked about things or people he did not like. Always only positively about what interested him."[7]

Jan also recounts an anecdote that speaks to his father's character. As they walked together around Palma, Mallorca, Jan and Jørn paused to admire the wonderful building of the great Palma Cathedral. His father stopped one of the custodians and asked him when construction of the cathedral had begun. Somewhere in the twelfth century, the man replied. Jørn then asked when it had been completed. The custodian smiled and answered that it hadn't been completed yet—"It's an ongoing process." Jørn turned to his son and said, "This is why I think the Sydney Opera House has been a wonderful event in my life. To have been allowed to conceive the idea of it. To have been permitted to work there for so many years. To know that it is continuing and that people are fond of the building."[8] Jørn Utzon believed that the building was more important than the architect, and he was proud of his contribution. Some might say that he was too modest, and perhaps he was. But his character and values—his *ethos*—prevented him from projecting his ego and self-esteem onto the building, and therefore from becoming cynical and negative.

The outlook of a visionary is positive, optimistic, and hopeful (we're going to call it "mindful" in Chapter 7). In fact, as we discussed in Chapter 3, cynicism is among the biggest drains on one's leadership, and definitely on one's visionary capacity. Remember the Historian archetype? The one whose strength lies in connecting the dots but whose weakness is seeing things early—and who's prone to cynicism? Those who exhibit this destructive quality can't succeed as visionaries. Even if they suffer life events that give them good reasons to become cynical and negative, visionaries resist these tendencies, as Utzon did.

JUMPING OFF THE EIFFEL TOWER

Let's take a look at another unorthodox visionary: an extreme sports practitioner who goes by the name of Taïg Khris. His vision? Jumping off the Eiffel Tower on in-line skates. Or, more specifically, jumping off the first platform of the famous landmark, some 40 meters above the ground, and landing on a ramp that would break his speed and allow him to conquer the jump. To make that more visible to you, the reader: That height equals that of a twelve-story building. If successful, the stunt would break the world record of the highest unsecured jump on Rollerblades. Without the full story of Taïg Khris, this seems like an absurdly dangerous idea, easily dismissed as the errand of a fool with a death wish.

But that could not be further from the truth. Taïg's life had been one of overcoming obstacles. For him, this was simply the next one he wished to conquer.

Born in Algeria, he had no formal education as his Greek mother and Algerian father decided not to send him to school. They believed it would be better for their son to use his own intellect, imagination, and self-confidence to make it in the world.

During his youth, Taïg developed an interest in the half-pipe, the U-shaped construction used by in-line skaters, snowboarders, and skateboarders. He proved to have a real talent for it, becoming the first person to successfully perform a double backflip in competition in 2001 and winning gold medals in the X Games. But he yearned for more. Realizing that in order to make a name for himself (roller skating doesn't lead to instant fame, even with his track record), he needed to do something even more remarkable. So he envisioned jumping across the river Seine in front of the famous Notre-Dame Cathedral in Paris. He designed a ramp that would launch him off one bank at the right speed and send him flying across the Parisian river to land on the other side. He set his dream in motion, pulled a team together, found a sponsor, and put in eighteen-hour workdays to overcome the many obstacles in his path toward achieving his goal.

However, one obstacle turned out to be insurmountable: In the end, the police department of Paris refused to authorize the event. The constructions on both sides of the river would block traffic for too long. His team evaporated, the sponsor withdrew, and the idea seemed a lost cause. The lack of cooperation he got from the officials and their unwillingness to support his highly unconventional plan could have rendered Taïg negative and cynical. But that's not the kind of person he is.

He redirected his dream (or maybe, better put, his vision), still aiming for an outrageous stunt but jumping off the Eiffel Tower instead. He approached the council of Paris, who gave him a list of conditions that rendered the feat virtually impossible. But when you meet Taïg, you know one thing for sure: The word *impossible* is not part of his vocabulary. He doesn't overcome barriers by being blunt, brutal, or forceful. Instead, he's extremely respectful and empathetic to the opposing view, and that attitude has helped him get what he wants. Taïg understood why the mayor of Paris was reluctant to agree to a radical stunt, which, if it went wrong, would taint the image of the famous Parisian monument. He was able to put himself in the shoes of his opponents; rather than seeing them as adversaries, he embraced their arguments, and positively looked for ways to satisfy their needs.

And there is something else.

One of Taïg's distinctive weapons to overcome his barriers is an all-encompassing passion. The passion he radiates makes you *want* him to be successful. It's exactly that passion that allowed him to retrieve his sponsors, convince the mayor of Paris, meet with and gain support from the then-president Nicolas Sarkozy at the Elysée, and eventually realize his envisioned "dream."

Now, is Taïg just a crazy guy with no fear? Absolutely not. He is unconventional for sure, but he is also pragmatic. He comes up with an idea, pours his full passion into it, and taps into all the expertise he can find to make it work. He doesn't quit easily, but neither does he dogmatically hold on to something that has proved to be impossible. And when he runs into obstacles, he doesn't become cynical and negative, but is instead considerate toward his opponent and looks for ways to reconcile and meet their needs. This is how he turns his wild dreams into challenging visions into reality.

And that is exactly what happened on May 29, 2010. In front of a crowd of 100,000, Taïg successfully made his jump off the Eiffel Tower. And he lived to tell the tale, as you can see when you look him up on YouTube.

Wait for Taïg to come to a monument near you: His new dreams include jumping off other buildings around the world, including New York's Rockefeller Center. And he is the kind of person who perseveres.

What does Taïg's story teach us? Surely, his dreams are very different from ours, at least most of us. And most of us do not face the death-defying challenges he faced. Nor do we desire to. But his story is equally a story of a man with a clear image of what he wants to achieve, who overcomes seemingly impossible barriers, who inspires and mobilizes people to support him, and who taps energy from a source that seems to withstand even the biggest setbacks. So, what is that source that allows him to persevere?

PASSION AND AUTHENTICITY

Although their daily lives, occupations, and talents could not be more distinct, Jørn Utzon and Taïg Khris, as visionaries, have several characteristics in common. Above all, they are passionate about what they do. They uphold a set of deeply felt values and beliefs that provides them with a virtually endless source of energy and direction. This helps them do what they want to do, deal with setbacks, overcome barriers, know when to draw the line, and maintain a hopeful outlook. The same applies to Peter Kapitein, whom we met in Chapter 1. The connection between what he does and his core beliefs fuels a passion that helped him conquer the famous Alpe d'Huez by bike to raise money for cancer research. When you care deeply about what you do, your passion propels you toward achievement.

But how can you unleash your passion and let it ignite and inspire your followers? Gaining clarity about your beliefs and values is a critical step in providing the power Simon Sinek talks about in his best-seller and popular video *Start with Why*. Authenticity arises when people can see, smell, and feel that what you say is entwined with something you truly care about—that is, your "why."

The former CEO of Ford, Alan Mulally, echoed the importance of authenticity when he reflected on how he

Practice 6-1.
It starts with why.

managed to turn the ailing company around, saving it from the brink of bankruptcy in 2006 and bringing it back to profitability three years later. "A big part of leadership is being authentic to who you are, thinking about what you really believe in and behaving accordingly," he said in an interview.[9] Mulally's fundamentally believes that it is an honor to serve. In spite of the many tough decisions he had to make to rescue Ford, this value inspired him to develop an inclusive culture in which everyone's contribution is respected. "When people feel accountable and included, it is more fun. It is just more rewarding to do things in a supportive environment," he reflected in that same interview. This is his deeply felt, authentic belief, translated into a personal core value of being of service to others.

DISCOVERY MODE

No one can be authentic by imitating someone else. Authenticity is about knowing who you are, what you stand for, and what you care about. Those who have developed this sense of self-awareness know what they want to achieve, what they want to focus on in their professional and private lives, and what they want to be remembered for. "People with strong self-awareness are neither overly critical nor unrealistically hopeful. Rather, they are honest—with themselves and with others," wrote Daniel Goleman,[10] author of the landmark book *Emotional Intelligence*.

But achieving clarity on your purpose and values isn't easy. In their acclaimed *Harvard Business Review* (HBR) article "Discovering Your Authentic Leadership,"[11] Bill George et al. report a study of 125 leaders, selected for their reputation for authenticity and effectiveness. Yet even these successful leaders did not always have crystal-clear answers to questions about their drives and core values—despite frequently reflecting on them. "Analyzing 3,000 pages of transcripts, our team was startled to see that these people did not identify any universal characteristics, traits, skills, or styles that led to their success. Rather, their leadership emerged from their life stories. Consciously and subconsciously, they were constantly testing themselves through real-world experiences and reframing their life stories to understand who they were at their core."[12]

In other words, discovering your core values is a journey of learning and self-reflection—you probably won't gain instant clarity. Without dedicating time and attention to it, the picture of what your core values really are is likely to be a bit blurry. I'll share some practices to help you get the process started, but beware that it's not a simple 1-2-3 exercise. Even leaders renowned for their authenticity are in ongoing discovery mode, as the HBR study suggests.

Moreover, the journey to discovery can be painful, confusing, and possibly upsetting. But those who are willing to embark on it and to discover more about their core selves find it very fulfilling and even liberating. Not only does awareness of your core values deepen your understanding of yourself; it also translates to more radiant, clear, and energetic leadership. And, therefore, into a more radiant, clear, and energetic vision.

I know from experience that many people find this step of developing their visionary side challenging. To bring meaning to your vision, you must determine what you fundamentally stand for, what you care deeply about, and what most ignites passion in you. What values do you embrace? How do you substantiate them so that your followers perceive them as truly and authentically yours?

Some people find such questions too mellow, and reject the journey of discovery altogether. Some ridicule it as soft and esoteric (and I must admit that I have seen coach types who go over the top with it). But an unwillingness to give depth to this discovery process, whether out of ignorance or self-defense, will very likely lead to a shallow and unauthentic version of the Vision Thing. You need a sound self-awareness of your core values in order to create personal focus, direction, and resilience.

COVEY, STORIES, AND PEARLS

How do you discover your deep-rooted values? If you answer quickly, you'll probably come up with qualities such as honesty, professionalism, dedication, creativity, and so on. Great values, but not very distinctive, and possibly even the product of wishful thinking. Such a generic list won't give you much insight into your true self, so it will be of little use to proceed this way. How do you dig deeper, then?

I'll share three practices with you that can help you in your process of discovery. They are really worth a try, and I encourage you to take some time to explore them.

Practice 1: Obituary Exercise

The first practice is often called the obituary exercise or the funeral exercise (although you could alternatively picture less morbid circumstances, such as a farewell to a group of people you worked with for a long time and whom you truly care about). It's frequently attributed to the late Stephen Covey, who popularized it in his landmark work *7 Habits of Highly Effective People*, but notwithstanding Covey's great work, it had been around long before.

Paradoxically, thinking about your death is actually a good way of identifying the core purpose and values of your life. The exercise goes like this: Imagine your time has come, sadly, and you need to write your own obituary. What will it say? To help you reflect deeply on what is really important to you, contemplate and answer the following questions:

- What have been your main accomplishments in life? Once you've listed them, examine what connects them.
- What has been your greatest achievement of all? Why did you pick this one?
- Who are you leaving behind, and who will miss you the most? What will they miss you for?
- List the people you've helped in your life. How did you help them?
- What has been the main question that life has asked you? How did you respond?

In the process of answering these deep questions, values will surface. What should people really remember you for? That you excelled at project management, processing invoices, or creating marketing strategies? Probably not, right? It's not that your day job is not important, but your life has more depth than that. But in what way? What will your loved ones miss you for?

Make a list of the values that come up in this exercise. When you're finished, check it for authenticity. The list shouldn't contain what you think you *should* say, given your role and your responsibilities (both private and professionally). The value needs to feel like your favorite sweater: It

Practice 6-2.
Obituary exercise.

has to fit just perfectly. Eliminate any values that don't really fit, although they might look wonderful on paper.

Now, run your edited list through a final reduction. Evaluate each value, asking yourself: In the one life you've been given on this planet (or so we think), is this value important enough to be remembered for? Your aim should be to limit yourself to a maximum of three to five values. The end result should be a set of values that you feel warmhearted about, that inspire you, that define what you truly care about and resonate with your character. The true core values of your life.

You were warned: Going through this process, digging into your core values, is not easy. And using your death as a starting point feels unpleasant. But if you make the effort, and work through the exercise seriously, the results will give you very valuable insight into the real authentic leader within you.

Practice 2: Stories

A second way of exploring your values is through storytelling, since your stories say a lot about you. We've all experienced monumental moments in our life that taught us something profound. Warren Bennis calls these stories crucibles:[13] intense and unplanned experiences that transform us and become sources of distinctive leadership.

Several years ago, I worked with twenty-five senior leaders of a global company. Halfway through the retreat a Q&A session was planned with the CFO. The questioning started as a conventional exercise: We covered financial results, outlooks, economic trends, and more of the same. As the session drew to a close, and the business stuff had been dealt with, one of the senior leaders asked the CFO what he thought the *true* purpose of the organization was. As he thought for a minute, we prepared ourselves for a response about customer value, market share, and sustaining margins (he was the CFO, after all). But instead he answered that for him, the true purpose of the company was creating happiness for its employees.

Somewhat startled, we listened to him acknowledge that clients and numbers were very important. But he went on to recall the story of an early career experience: One of his first tasks in a new job had been to lay off a third of the existing team. At this early stage, he came to realize how tremendously important the workplace is in people's lives, and how taking it away from them utterly devastated their self-worth, dreams, and happiness. The experience helped him discover the value of caring for people. Even though reality is sometimes harsh and unavoidable, as he knew all too well as the CFO, he decided that on his watch, layoffs would be the absolute last resort. He finished by saying he hoped that in fifteen to twenty years, everyone in the room would look back on their time spent at the company with happiness. In the end, that was what mattered most to him. You can imagine how silent the room grew in admiration of the honest, value-driven, and unexpected answer from the CFO. And how the perception of his leadership blossomed with the group.

You too have stories—stories that say a lot about who you are and what you care about. They often emerge from situations in which you were tested, but they can also center on happier occasions. Think of the "crucible" definition from Bennis, and look for intense and unplanned experiences that transformed you.

Here is a way to get to your core purpose and values through stories. Ask a friend to interview you. Your role is to respond honestly to the questions; your friend's role is to identify the values in your responses. The questions are straightforward:

- Describe three different situations in which you:
    1. Were truly at your best. Think of moments or occasions when you were in a state of flow (as athletes call it), when things seemed to go effortlessly and your actions were spot on; that is, exactly what was needed.
    2. Learned something profound that has stayed with you ever since.
    3. Were caught in a conflicting dilemma between something that was expected from you and something you really believe(d) in.
- Ask your friend to help you delve deeper into these stories by asking more probing questions, such as: Why did you feel that way? What made this situation so important to you? What were you experiencing?

When you describe these situations, you will convey a lot about yourself, what motivates you, and what is important to you. With your friend helping you to uncover the hidden layers of your stories, your personal values will be revealed. Appendix B contains a list of values— make a copy for your friend to have available while identifying your values. If your resulting list is too long

Practice 6-3.
Your stories.

(again, the aim is to get to three to five values), go through the validation process, as described in the obituary exercise, to reduce your list to its core.

Practice 3: So That What?

The last method was created by my good friend, the very gifted artist-turned-business-consultant David Pearl. As a former opera singer, his inspiration predominantly comes from the world of performing arts. Primed with Joseph Campbell's story architecture *The Hero's Journey*, and with his keen eye for spotting hidden dimensions, Pearl noticed something very interesting about Hollywood's great movies. Movie "heroes" only really come to life if we, as an audience, develop an understanding of what drives them. What is it that the hero really cares about? Why is the hero willing to undergo the ordeal set out for him or her? Great movies communicate this why of the hero in very subtle ways. Heroes who have "strong" and "invincible" written all over them can make entertaining movies (think of *Mission Impossible* and *Die Hard*), but there is shallowness to it. As an audience we lack an understanding of why they are truly fighting their fights. However, heroes who are driven by powerful, identifiable values are very attractive to us, since we are able to associate with their character.

Take *Gladiator,* a well-known blockbuster action movie awash with violence that, at first instinct, might fall into the *Mission Impossible* category. But if the hero, General Maximus Decimus Meridius (played by Russell Crowe, who won an Academy Award for the role), had merely been portrayed as strong and incredibly brave, our connection with him would have been weak. Yet, what makes this such a powerful movie is that we can easily associate with the hero, even though his day job is very different from ours. The famous opening scene very subtly shows us the Gladiator's true values as he walks through a farm field in the early, prebattle morning, his hands touching the tops of the crop. We see a wedding ring on his finger; in the background, almost imperceptibly, we can hear the sound of children playing, and we see the Gladiator deep in thought. His eyes lock in on a beautiful bird that's sitting on a branch and flies off, and as he watches the bird fly, we can distill from the expression on his face that he would love to have the freedom the bird has. And then we are off to battle.

In less than thirty seconds, we are shown what the Gladiator truly cares about, what drives him to join the battle, and what is hidden from his day job of fighting disloyal Romans: his wife, his children, his life on the farm, and the freedom to go where he wants to go. In this sense, *Gladiator* is essentially a love story about a man who wants nothing more than to return to the life he had on his farm with his loved ones and to once again be free.

Now, let's try Pearl's exercise. His approach to bringing out a person's core values, that hidden layer that goes deeper than the day job, is to engage in a conversation that starts by completing this sentence: "The deep intent of my working life is . . ." Once you have formulated your sentence, a partner asks just one question: "So that what?" And you respond by reformulating the "deep intent" sentence you came up with before. Then you repeat the sequence multiple times.

For example, let's say your first response is as follows: "The deep intent

Practice 6-4.
So that what?

of my working life is to provide innovative services to our clients and to ensure the continuity of our company" (hey, not everybody is a gladiator . . .). Not bad, but your partner should not let you get away with it. She asks: "So that what?" You respond, "So that I can drive our business forward into new directions." *So that what?* "So that I can grow and explore new opportunities." *So that what?* "So that I can satisfy my curiosity." *So that what?* And so on.

You need to repeat the "So that what?" sequence five or more times until you arrive at a point where you can't go any further. This is typically the moment when you have arrived at your core. If done right, your resulting "deep intent" sentence is followed by a compact statement of ten words at most. And just to clarify, it need not be a noble or politically correct statement. It's something that you truly care about, and if that is about satisfying your curiosity, or being acknowledged, or creating freedom for yourself, or another more self-oriented cause, that's perfectly fine.

MEDIATING REALITY

The three practices described help you go beyond the obvious responses that come to mind without deeper reflection. One last warning, though. Some people mistakenly believe that these self-awareness exercises uncover the one and only truth about them, and that the core value(s) they identify will point to what they should exclusively do in life. I think this is naïve, because life is more complex than that. Operating with your values at heart implies that you have more clarity on what anchors you, but you will always need to interpret these values in context.

The art of working with your values is to integrate them into your life, finding the right balance between what you must do and what you truly care about. Of course there will occasionally be conflict, as short-term interests bump up against long-term desires. Or the demands put on you, such as a stringent reduction of your department's budget, bump up against your deep-rooted value of caring for your team members. Or loyalty toward one of your closest friends conflicts with your value of honesty when you learn that he has been involved in a fraud scheme.

As a leader, it is your task to resolve these dilemmas in the way you see fit. Your first strategy might be one of reconciliation. You'd start by acknowledging the conflict, since you can only deal with it productively once you understand what the opposing forces you're experiencing are really about. Then, you would aim to reconcile the conflicting sides, seeking alternative solutions that placate both interests in what might be a novel, unexplored direction. It doesn't always work, but it's worth a try.

What do you do when you can't reconcile? What happens when your role and responsibilities demand things of you that compete with the personal values you like to maintain and live by (and that you've perhaps integrated so well into your vision)?

Yale economist Albert O. Hirschman captured the options in *Exit, Voice, and Loyalty,* a 126-page masterpiece of lucid thinking that reaches far beyond what I will allude to here. If you *really* cannot reconcile in a creative way, you have three options left: Draw the line for yourself and exit; voice your position and live with the consequences; or accept and settle. These options aren't easy, and there is no right or wrong choice.

The exit option safeguards your honor, but its consequences might not be attractive. This is the reality whistleblowers face. We also saw it in the Jørn Utzon story, when the architect chose the exit option rather than accepting the changes the government of New South Wales proposed to his design for the Sydney Opera House, which he considered thoughtless. Clarity on his values helped him understand where to draw the line for himself. But the consequence was that he never saw his unique creation with his own eyes.

The second option, voicing your opinion, could result in a change of course, but it could just as well lead to endless complaining, which is generally neither productive nor appreciated. You might be admired for your principles, but sidelined for your unwillingness to capitulate. And the third option, accepting and settling, will probably mean you get to keep your job, role, and responsibilities, but at the cost of your self-worth and often at the cost of the perception of your leadership by others, as you did not "walk the talk." In other words, there is no simple answer to dealing with situations in which you experience friction between your personal values and what you are asked or expected to do. You will need to mediate reality and come to a conclusion that seems fitting, understanding the pros and cons of each of these three options in your given situation.

So how can clarity on my personal values be helpful then, you might ask. Despite these potentially damaging consequences, getting clarity on your values can serve you well. Understanding your purpose and core values helps you navigate in such challenging times; it reminds you of your boundaries, protecting you from behavior you really do not want to be known for. Moreover, it serves as a prevention device: When you identify conflicts that might arise early, it gives you time to find reconciling solutions and take preventive action. And when you integrate your values into your vision, it becomes a manifestation and reminder of the things you stand for and believe in. Your vision can become a long-term aspiration and guiding light for yourself as well as your followers, even if it must occasionally be mediated in face of the short-term pressures and conflicting interests reality throws at you.

And mediating these pressures is not impossible, as the story of Franck Riboud shows us.

DANONE'S ECOSYSTEM

Franck Riboud heads the Danone Group, the French firm headquartered in Paris and marketed in the United States as the Dannon Company. The multinational organization is best known for its yogurts and other fresh dairy products, but is also big in water, baby food, and medical nutrition. It boasts a proud history that dates back to 1919, when it was founded in Barcelona as a small yogurt factory. But its current success really started in the 1970s, when Riboud's father, Antoine Riboud, took the helm after merging his industrial glass company, Boussois-Souchon-Neuvesel, with Gervais Danone, following up with a string of mergers and acquisitions.

In 1996 Riboud succeeded his father as the CEO, divested a lot of the company's activities, and brought it to where it is today: a food- and nutrition-focused company. So much for yet another corporate history.

Where does this story get interesting? Let's take a look at Danone's mission statement: "Bring health through food to as many people as possible." You're probably thinking, nice words, slick corporate slogan, great marketing department at work, but really? Isn't it just like any other company, only interested in annual (or worse, quarterly) results?

Yes—and no. The company is publicly held, so quarterly results are important. But what does Riboud stand for in terms of the mission statement? Can he maintain credibility as a figurehead of a public company while speaking passionately about Danone's role in society and his motivations to advance Danone's mission?

"Corporate responsibility does not end at the factory gate or at the office doors," Riboud said. "The jobs it provides shape whole lives. It consumes energy and raw materials, and in doing so alters the face of our planet. The public will remind us of our responsibilities in this industrial society." Sounds like any CEO in the past decade, jumping on the "corporate responsibility" bandwagon, right?

But wait. Riboud said this in 1972, nearly forty years before it became fashionable to make such statements. It wasn't *Franck* Riboud I quoted, but his father, Antoine Riboud, in a speech to the French employers' federation that was both controversial and visionary at the time. And these perspectives have become rooted in Danone's company persona, most notably by the selection of "humanity" as one of its core company values—a rather exceptional choice among the usual suspects we find at most companies (think professionalism, customer focus, integrity, flexibility, entrepreneurship, passion, and commitment).

These company values are not merely posters on the wall at Danone; they are deeply held by Franck Riboud. In 2009, he echoed his father's words when he asked the question, "How can a company hope to develop in an economic and social desert? It is in a company's best interest to take good care of its economic and social environment, in one word its *ecosystem*." But wait—he said this in 2009? Remember 2009? Didn't we have something else on our minds as the world found itself in the worst economic storm since 1929? It speaks for authenticity and true core values when under such dire circumstances you hold on to your beliefs, even if they are not fashionable at such times. Core values are enduring commitments that *can* weather a storm.

What does Danone do to live up to its self-declared role as a frontrunner in social responsibility? In fact, it's a long list. And when you look into Franck Riboud's personal life, you'll find that it goes much deeper than a tick-the-box kind of corporate social responsibility. It's embedded in the leader's DNA, and therefore also in the company's DNA.

Among many things, Danone runs an initiative called Danone Communities, which operates as an investment fund for social businesses. It runs Livelihoods, a carbon investment fund aimed at creating social value in rural areas. And in 2009, amid the most devastating economic storm the world ever witnessed, it donated 100 million euros into the Danone Ecosystem Fund, an endowment that fosters projects and initiatives aimed at societal improvements.

The endowment's mission is "to fund and co-create local socioeconomic capabilities through inclusive partnerships that reinforce the Danone ecosystem and contribute to common interest." Its funding prerequisites dictate that a project must generate jobs and income (for members of society), develop competencies, and/or create capabilities. Among the nearly fifty projects it supported in 2013 were children's metabolic disorder prevention in Turkey, milk collection communities in Egypt, waste pickers in Mexico, caregivers in Brazil, and farmers in Indonesia. Senior leaders launch internal projects to make use of this resource and are accountable for them. To successfully apply for funds from the Danone Ecosystem, it is a prerequisite that your project does *not* make a profit.

Riboud's story is an inspiring one of balancing real-life executive requirements for business continuity, shareholder value, and profits with social responsibility and an authentic desire to contribute to society. And Riboud is doing this in the phase of his life in which he can make a tremendous impact. I've heard too many CEOs say that when they retire, they really want to give back to society. But why wait? If you are truly passionate about society, why not make the effort while you are at your influential peak? Sure, after your career it's great to use your network and start worrying about your grandchildren's future. But with clarity on your values and the things you truly care about, you can have more impact by integrating it into your leadership—and your vision—when you are most influential. Fortunately, people like Franck Riboud do.

———

Uncovering your most fundamental "whys" and "hows," your core values and beliefs, is key to understanding your authentic self. When your projects, initiatives, and actions are linked to you authentically, passion follows. People notice; your eyes start to shine, your tone of voice changes, your energy is virtually limitless, and your passion comes to life. Authenticity radiates.

After Taïg Khris jumped off the Eiffel Tower, he declared that his "jump was to give youth the desire to reach beyond their limits, to follow their passion, their dreams." You could be cynical about this statement, but given Taïg's life story (a young guy with no formal education, with a lifetime pursuit of overcoming barriers and a deeply felt desire to be acknowledged), you can see the authenticity. Jørn Utzon's objective was not to become an acclaimed architect, but to be a part of a creation that would be enjoyed by many generations. While their projects are vastly different, both Taïg and Utzon were in touch with their values (as is Franck Riboud). That's how they tapped into their energy and passion, how they coped with setbacks, and how they succeeded.

Having clarity on your core beliefs and values will be a tremendous help in furthering your leadership agenda and developing your visionary self.

Connecting your vision to these roots is the key to making your story authentic, passionate, and inspirational. And these three qualities matter big time in making your vision fly.

Note that this doesn't mean you can only work on things that are connected to your purpose and values. By no means. We are all called on to devote time to things we don't care deeply about. But when it comes to your leadership, and in particular your vision, being able to connect to your truest self creates the essential credibility, energy, and inspiration for the Vision Thing.

7

Mindful Behavior

If your actions inspire others to dream more, learn more, do more, and become more, you are a leader.

—JOHN QUINCY ADAMS

In Chapter 6, we began the discovery process into your visionary self. We saw that having clarity on what you truly care about and what forms your values relates to passion and authenticity, which are essential for rallying the troops and persuading them to follow.

But leading with authenticity also means you must practice what you preach. The best evidence of your true feelings and beliefs comes less from your words than from your deeds. When your words are believably connected to what you do, when you *behave* in line with your vision, only then do you display integrity and build trust with your followers. This is especially the case when it comes to so-called moments of truth, when you are confronted with a difficult choice or dilemma. In these defining situations, confidence and trust in your leadership either increases or evaporates, depending on how you act.

Moreover, and far less obvious, researchers have found that your own behavior not only informs *others* about what you really stand for, but it also informs *yourself*. The evidence of your own behavior, what you truly do in practice, is a primary source of information about your own beliefs, values, and attitudes[1]—and the more reason to take notice of Kurt Vonnegut's warning that "we are what we pretend to be, so we must be careful about what we pretend to be."

In this chapter, we take a closer look at what *visionary behavior* really means. What behaviors are essential for growing your visionary leadership? What should you be conscious of, and which practices can help you in your journey toward mastery?

But first, it's time to look at something unconventional.

SOLAR ROADWAYS

Can a road generate energy? It's a question you probably won't spend much time thinking about. What could a road—black, dirty, and virtually immovable—possibly have to do with the dynamic, motion-oriented concept of energy generation? Why waste brain power thinking about such an incongruous idea?

In 2007, Scott Brusaw and his wife, Julie, started talking about global warming. It alarmed them that despite the scientific community's dire predictions and celebrity-infused media attention, very few real solutions were surfacing. One day at their home in Idaho, Scott and Julie were discussing their concerns and started brainstorming. Scott, who is an electrical engineer, had always been fascinated with cars and innovation. As a child, he'd dreamed of building electric roads on which slot cars could drive.

Suddenly, Julie wondered if this childhood dream could be made out of solar panels. Scott immediately dismissed the idea, laughing: "There's no way you can drive on a solar panel." But then he reconsidered. Sure, there were barriers to overcome, but ultimately, why wouldn't it be possible? There are over 28,000 square miles of roads in the United States alone, continuously exposed to the sun, collecting heat. Why not capture and store that free energy?[2]

Scott's reversal of opinion is a familiar pattern of creativity and breakthrough thinking. The first reaction is dismissive—the idea sounds too far out to even entertain. There are massive constraints and plenty of reasons why it *wouldn't* work. Until someone says, "But if you did it this way . . . ," and all at once the radical idea seems plausible.

Even now, you're probably still doubting the idea of solar panels instead of asphalt. It's your assumptive framework working against you, thwarting your acceptance with a combination of conceptual assumptions ("Solar panels are for roofs, not for roads," "Why use them as roads? Put them out in the desert instead"), technical assumptions ("Glass can't withstand a fully loaded truck," "Wouldn't the surface be too slippery when it rains?"), and experiential assumptions ("There is no way to efficiently transport the energy from far out places to a home").

But if you distance yourself from those "truths" for a moment, you can start appreciating the brilliance of the idea. Roads need to be built and eventually replaced anyway, so if it could be economically feasible to make them out of something other than asphalt, why not?

Scott and Julie Brusaw didn't let the potential barriers stop them. Solar Roadways started in 2007, and since then they have successfully involved universities and young engineers. They were awarded a significant grant from the U.S. Federal Highway Administration in 2009, which allowed them to develop the one missing link: the specially textured glass strong enough to hold a fully loaded truck, rough enough to not be slippery, transparent enough to allow the sunlight to come through, and matte enough to prevent the sun from glaring in the driver's face. Their story, featured in many news outlets, from CNN to the *Moscow Times,* is now supported by GE. Solar Roadways participates in contests of world-changing ideas and is a showcase for creative and imaginative visionary thinking. Apparently the idea wasn't so bizarre after all.

Their story lends us another example of how purpose fuels vision. All the elements are there: from sense making and exploiting imagination, to challenging assumptions, to embracing unconventionality and a noble cause.

MINDFULNESSLESSNESS

What do we know about the mindset and attitudes that produce such visionary insight? And how can we adopt such a mindset ourselves? Obviously there are no easy answers, no magic pills that guarantee instant brilliance. But we can see how we might start to develop our visionary thinking by exploring the work of Harvard psychologist Ellen Langer.

Her research on what she calls "mindfulness" spans a time period of over thirty years. Langer's term doesn't refer to the Buddhist version of mindfulness that's popular today, describing a state of active attention to the present moment; rather, Langer says mindfulness encompasses a mindset and attitude that leads to discovery and noticing new things.

To illustrate Langer's mindfulness, let's first look at *mindlessness*. Imagine you are walking down the street in a busy city and you see a woman sitting on the sidewalk. Clearly, she must have tripped and hurt herself. She explains to you that she sprained her knee and needs help. You ask her what you can do and she asks you to get an Ace bandage from the drugstore just a few steps away. You head into the drugstore and ask the pharmacist for an Ace bandage, and he tells you that, unfortunately, he's out of them. What do you do?

This is the exact experiment Ellen Langer ran,[3] with a simulated victim and a pharmacist instructed to say that he was out of Ace bandages. Langer wanted to see what people would do when specific instructions could not be fulfilled. She found that none of the twenty-five people approached on the street asked the pharmacist if he could recommend something else. People left the drugstore empty-handed and returned to the victim to tell her the news. Langer concluded that highly specific instructions—go to that store and get one particular item—encourage mindlessness. In her work, Langer explains that we operate mind*lessly* when we:

1. Are trapped by categories
2. Run on automatic behavior
3. Operate from a single perspective (as in the case of the sprained knee)[4]

The first might need some clarification. A *category* is the psychological term for the necessary labeling of things that allows us to create a picture of the world around us. Something is a coffee cup, a door, a boss, French, dangerous, and so on. This is a necessary process, because otherwise the world around us would be incredibly chaotic. But once pictures are created and categories are applied, the category starts living a life of its own. We become victims of our categorizations, blinded by the fact that they're not real but simply mental constructs. When we operate mindlessly, these categories dominate how we perceive things, and often become more rigid than is justified.

You've probably noticed that *categories* are similar to the mental *frames* we explored in Chapter 2. I'll keep the terms so as not to upset the purists among us. Categories are similar to frames in that they stand in the way of our creativity and therefore of our ability to develop a full picture of the challenge at hand. Discovering new things and contemplating unconventional thoughts and ideas is only possible when we recategorize, rethinking the automatic labels we have applied over time. It is very similar to what we mean with the term *reframing,* which was introduced in the What Would Google Do exercise (Chapter 2): Seeing or presenting reality through a different frame set can help uncover new insights and new ideas.

In addition to categorization and single perspective, the other trap identified by Langer is automatic behavior. This is the mindless conduct of someone operating without much deliberate thinking, which psychologists call *stereotyped responses*. "It is odd that despite their current widespread use and looming future importance, most of us know very little about our automatic behavior patterns,"[5] says Robert Cialdini, emeritus professor of psychology and thought leader in the art of influence. If you drive long distances, you've probably caught yourself suddenly realizing you've progressed much farther than you were aware of. You were driving mindlessly. This is a rather harmless form of mindlessness, as your inattentiveness usually doesn't cause major problems.

But, as Langer points out, "the consequences of mindlessness range from the trivial to the catastrophic."[6] You are behaving equally mindlessly—although in a much more concerning way—when you respond to a need or request seemingly without thinking, simply because you didn't assess it critically. Let's look at a classic and dreadful example.

In 1961, Yale University psychologist Stanley Milgram demonstrated a dramatic case of mindlessness in a controversial study. The Milgram experiment, which was designed to study and understand obedience, revealed that up to 65 percent of its subjects became mindlessly alienated from their own conscience by the presence of an authority figure and the repetitiveness of a routine. In the experiment, ordinary people were instructed to apply an electric shock every time a "learner," who was out of their line of sight, gave a wrong answer to the questions they had to ask them. As wrong answers increased, subjects were told to "apply" increasingly stronger shocks. The out-of-sight learner (who wasn't actually enduring the shocks and was part of Milgram's team) responded with fake cries of pain. His shrieks intensified as the shock levels increased, to horrifying levels, but the authority figure instructing the people continued to reassure them that everything was fine—even up to the point where the majority of subjects eventually "applied" shocks that would have killed the learner. The presence of the authority figure was enough to keep subjects from questioning the procedure.

Milgram's experiment also highlights the power of routine. Once we fall into a routine, we often don't question our behavior as we progress, especially when supervised or sanctioned by an authority figure. It's only later, when we've broken out of the routine and can purposely reflect on our actions, that we realize how far we've come. That's how companies like Enron develop a culture of fraud. The culture didn't emerge because the company recruited people eager to start a scam. It crept in via small unethical behaviors at first, and as bosses applauded the "entrepreneurial" spirit, it progressed to a level at which it became very difficult to stop. Mindlessness doesn't take over only when we're not concentrating—it can also surface when we're fully focused and aware of what we're doing.

FOOLISH CONSISTENCY

The Consistency Principle, introduced in Chapter 5 when we discussed tunnel vision, explains where some of these mindless, automatic behaviors come from. Once we have committed ourselves, we have a strong tendency to act in accordance with that commitment. Especially when this commitment is made verbal and public, and is realized through some effort. The verbalized commitment alters our self-image and informs others as well as ourselves on where we stand. Since we do not want to do the hard labor again of thinking over the issue, the commitment provides a shortcut for thinking about our actions and behaviors.[7]

Often this is for good: We're faced with a challenge, think it over, arrive at a conclusion, commit ourselves to it, and start working in accordance. But beware that mindlessness can quickly creep in. When more complete information becomes available after we've made up our mind, chances are significant that we do not want to reconsider our position. We mindlessly keep heading in the direction our behavioral shortcut tells us to, since we want to sustain our image of consistency.

Being inconsistent actually feels wrong and foolish. We sometimes go to great lengths to avoid this unpleasant feeling. And it therefore might be mindlessly guiding our behavior more than we would consider desirable.

This tactic—often exercised by salespeople—has a name: foot-in-the-door technique. I once had an experience that undoubtedly most of us have had at some point. A salesman from a telemarketing firm called me in the evening. Immediately recognizing that it was an undesired call, I waited for a chance to interrupt his opening flow to tell him I wasn't interested. (I could have disconnected or rudely interrupted, but deeply ingrained patterns of decency, probably going back to my childhood upbringing, stopped me from being that rude.) But then he did something very clever. Rather than selling me his product or whatever it was he was trying to promote, he got me to agree that nobody could disagree with something that was totally free, with no strings attached. Knowing I was getting lured into something, my mind was racing ahead, thinking of where this call was heading. But *in the moment,* I could indeed not think of any reason why anyone would be against a totally free, no-strings-attached proposition. So I said he was right, but now that I had the word, I immediately added that I wasn't interested in whatever he had for me, trying to bring the conversation to a close. He bounced back and said with convincing bewilderment that he could not understand how I could not be interested given that I had just said that nobody could be against something totally free, with no strings attached. He had me there: I was inconsistent. And it felt wrong; I felt bad about myself. Not so much because he lured me into something (that realization came later), but more so for being inconsistent. It doesn't feel right to be inconsistent, and there is a strong desire to correct it when it appears. Which is exactly what this salesman wanted, since becoming consistent would mean I needed to listen and undoubtedly accept his offering. I rambled something incoherent, stepped over my childhood-ingrained decency, and hung up. Feeling stupid. But I realized how easy it was to fall for this nifty application of the Consistency Principle.

The last mindlessness trap derived from foolish consistency is that we might commit to something without even being aware of its profound implications to our future behavior. A striking example was given by social scientists Jonathan Freedman and Scott Fraser in 1966.[8] They had a re-searcher, who pretended to be a volunteer working for safety, go door-to-door in a Californian residential neighborhood. The request he made was rather outrageous: He asked the residents if they would agree to post a very large sign in their front garden that read DRIVE CAREFULLY. He showed them a picture of what it would look like, with a house virtually hidden behind the sign. Naturally, hardly anyone agreed (83 percent de-clined). But one particular subgroup was not unwilling. Of that group, 76 percent agreed to the sign. What was special about this group?

Two weeks before, people in this subgroup had been approached by a different "volunteer," who was also part of the research team. He had come by and asked them if they were okay with having a very small three-inch-square sign affixed to their mailbox that read: BE A SAFE DRIVER. It was one of these things you could hardly be against, being a good citizen and caring for the children in the neighborhood, so indeed nearly everyone approached agreed to that small sign. But little did they know that agreeing to this trivial request two weeks earlier played such a big role in evaluating the preposterous request later. The first request had informed them of their values and what they stood for (safe driving is important in the neighbor-hood), which had in a way informed their self-image. When it came to thinking through the second request, the consistency shortcut freed them from thinking it through and led them to accept something fairly ridicu-lous. They had previously informed themselves that they stood for safe driving in the neighborhood and now felt compelled to act consistently.

Foolish consistency stunts the growth of our visionary capacity by lim-iting what we take into account, hampering our willingness to challenge conventional perspectives and our tendency to stick to the knitting of our consistency. Langer points out that this leads to a mindless stance: "When faced with something that hasn't been done before, people frequently ex-press the belief that it can't be done. All progress, of course, depends on questioning that belief. Everything is the same until it is not."[9]

This concerns us, mortal souls, and it equally applies to organizations at large. And we've already known it for a long time. In *The Second American Revolution,* published in the seventies, John D. Rockefeller observed that "an organization is a system, with logic of its own, and all the weight of tradition and inertia. The deck is stacked in favor of the tried and proven way of doing things and against the taking of risks and striking out in new directions."[10]

Overcoming mindlessness and pursuing behavioral mindfulness is therefore a vital step in working on our visionary selves, and mindfulness is one of the true traits of great leadership.

MINDFULNESS, TAKE TWO

So what is leadership mindfulness exactly, then? Let me introduce it with an anecdote. One of our family friends has been a flight attendant for over twenty-five years and is now a purser on a Boeing 747. It's a serious responsibility; she's the one in command when things go wrong, and she has to make decisions and take action (together with her team on duty, of course) under intense pressure to uphold the safety of her passengers. And although this dramatic situation is extremely unlikely to happen, if it were to happen, she would want to be at her very best. So, it is not a responsibility to be taken lightly.

You would imagine that countless takeoffs and landings, as well as the safety training sessions she attends regularly, have provided her with the experience she can readily and instantly tap into in an emergency situation. Right?

Well, she knows experience alone is not enough. Mindlessly relying on it to help her act in times of stress would be too risky, regardless of how well trained she is. Instead, she has adopted some purposeful practices she applies on every flight. Because takeoff and landing are the riskiest moments of a flight, she takes thirty seconds once she is seated to mentally rehearse the emergency procedures. On every flight. *Every* time they take off and *every* time they land. That's a form of mindful leadership put into practice.

It's important to understand that mindlessness is part of the natural human condition; it would be difficult to find anyone who doesn't fall victim to it at times. The best way to avoid falling into ever-present mindlessness traps is to first become aware of them; you can grow this awareness through periodic assessment and honest reflection on your recent actions and behaviors. Next, you can develop some practices that will help you reduce the risks of mindlessness in your own role and responsibility, just like our family friend has done, since she knows that her automatic behaviors might not cut it when she needs her mindfulness most.

But what exactly is this mindful state we should aspire to? Growing your mindful state boils down to three behaviors, according to Langer:

1. Creating new categories
2. Welcoming new information
3. Adopting more than one view

The first has to do with relabeling, reframing, and recategorizing—an existential awareness and willingness to challenge the mental constructs that drive your thinking. It's what children do automatically as they engage with their creative and imaginative side, but adults often lose this capability over time. The experience we gained throughout our lives has been categorized and fixed in our minds, creating a belief system that we depend on and feel motivated to keep as is. Mindful recategorization will bring us new insights and more options to consider. But it requires a willingness to challenge our belief systems.

This is what Jørn Utzon (Chapter 6) practiced when he turned to nature for inspiration and envisioned the Sydney Opera House. It's also what the inventor of containerization, Malcolm McLean (Chapter 3), practiced when he played around with the idea that his truck's backend—until then categorized as a trailer—could become a stackable structure, which eventually became the container. And this is what Scott and Julie Brusaw practiced when they recategorized a solar panel from rooftop to road.

Second, a mindful state implies openness to new information. This might sound simpler than it actually is. Most of us consider ourselves to be open-minded, but we all get used to a set of "truths" we discover in our lives that become helpful, reassuring, and practical to hold on to. We dislike when this "truths set" is challenged or dismantled. It's unsettling and results in an unpleasant state of confusion. That's why we have a natural tendency to shield ourselves from information that doesn't conform to what we like to believe. We maintain a status quo of beliefs amid a deluge of new information.

Let's look at the physical analogy of this phenomenon, since this protective behavior is not unlike what happens to you when you are thrown off balance. Literally. In an experiment to study motion sickness, people were blindfolded and strapped in chairs that rotated swiftly around a vertical axis. As the chair started circling, subjects reported their sense of the rotations. But after some time, usually a minute or two, their internal biological balancing mechanism adjusted itself and started sending signals to the brain that made them think the chairs were no longer rotating.

When participants were next asked to tilt their head forward, they suddenly experienced the rotation again. The movement threw their internal balancing mechanism off and led to instant sickness and nausea. The primal reflex is to withdraw from that state and return to the steady one, to avoid the discomfort of exposure to dynamics.

This metaphorically represents our openness to new information. We like to live in a steady state, where we operate in balance even if things are spinning around us. When we stick our heads out of the window and get exposed to new information, it can be so off-putting that we quickly retreat to our steady state. We prefer to avoid the unpleasantness of engaging with the dynamic state of new information. Sometimes we ridicule it, and sometimes we simply dismiss it. It takes high levels of mindfulness, courage, and self-confidence to productively deal with the issue, consider different ways of looking at it, and question what we believe.

Remember Scott Brusaw's initial reluctance about the idea of driving on a solar panel? You can't drive on a solar panel, he laughed, as his mind quickly contemplated all the potential problems this new information presented. But he soon recovered from that reaction and began to consider how it *might* work. We can't be sure, but chances are if Scott hadn't challenged his initial dismissive reaction, and hadn't asked himself how solar panels could be used as road building blocks, the ideas that led to the Solar Roadways system might never have reappeared in his mind, since he had filed it away as too ludicrous.

The point is that even if we believe we are fully open to new information, we could very well be in an illusionary state of balance, avoiding exposure to new information that would throw us off balance. It's something to think about.

The third aspect of mindfulness as defined by Langer is the adoption of more than one view, and being mindfully aware of and open to other views. Once we realize and embrace that there are as many different views as there are observers, we allow ourselves to see a more complete picture. Pierre Wack's quest, which led to the art of scenario planning as discussed in Chapter 5, is fully in line with this aspect: Exploring scenarios and preparing for different futures is mentally liberating, providing you with a richer palette of options to consider.

The in-line skating champion Taïg Khris, whom we met in Chapter 6, did not welcome the news that he would not be permitted to fulfill his envisioned "dream" of jumping over the Seine, nor was he overjoyed with the near-impossible constraints placed on his redirected plans to jump from the Eiffel Tower. But he was empathetic to the views of others and did not perceive the Parisian officials as adversaries or make them his enemies; he adopted their frame sets, looked at it from their perspective, embraced their arguments, reached out to them, met and conversed with them, and looked for new ways to make his dream a reality. It was this combination of mindfulness and passion, rooted in existential open-mindedness and clarity on purpose, that got him to overcome the barriers he faced. Which is a lesson we can take from him and his story, even if our challenges concern less dangerous ventures.

CURIOSITY

Let's turn to curiosity, the quality that motivates you to explore, entertain alternatives, and seek new ways of understanding. Curiosity is imperative for finding and developing unconventional ideas to fuel your vision. When I was in college, students from the university's school of law organized a series of theme evenings based on legal topics. Each night started with a Hollywood movie that matched that night's theme. Being mildly interested in law (but more in good movies at that point in my life) I attended the series. One night, they screened *Presumed Innocent*, a legal suspense thriller directed by Alan Pakula and starring Harrison Ford. Just before the movie started, I overheard someone in the row behind me saying to her friend, "You know that _____ did it, right?" She was giving away the plot before the movie had even started. I remember instantly losing interest in the movie—my curiosity and excitement vanished when I learned the outcome beforehand.

Which brings us to an interesting question: What is it that makes us curious? We go to the movies to watch stories that satiate our curiosity. We like to spend ninety minutes in the painful clutches of suspense, not knowing how the story will end. In fact, we *pay* good money for our desire to be cast into the unknown. Apparently, the experience of having our curiosity satisfied is a pleasant one, since we tend to repeat it often.

American economist George Loewenstein formulated a theory of curiosity, which is remarkably simple: Curiosity occurs when we experience a gap in our knowledge.[11] It's that nagging feeling that there is something out there you haven't grasped yet, but *could* grasp with some effort. This is the art of soap opera writers who leave you hanging day after day, giving you just enough information to keep watching. So, when our current knowledge is artfully questioned, our curiosity gets triggered and we become motivated to take action to resolve our—now apparent—knowledge gap.

William James commented in *The Sentiment of Rationality* that "the transition from a state of puzzle and perplexity to rational comprehension is full of lively relief and pleasure."[12] We enjoy being perplexed and get energized by the journey toward closure. But, as it turns out, this is only true when a few conditions are met. Above all, the closure or "knowledge completion" must be within reach, both in terms of filling our knowledge gap as well as in terms of the effort it will take us to reach it. Most of us lose interest in quests that we know will be unsolvable. The same thing happens if we know the solution will take longer than we are willing to wait. But with both conditions in place, we have an intrinsic motivation to discover.

POWERFUL QUESTIONS

If curiosity kicks in when the right question exposes our knowledge gap, that means the quality of our thinking and imagination depends on the quality of the questions we ask ourselves. Good questions trigger us to explore and seek out new territory, innovative solutions, and unconventional ideas.

As noted in the story of Solar Roadways, the right questions can have a significant impact on what we allow ourselves to contemplate and "see."

Replace the question *Can a road generate energy?* with *How can a road generate energy?* and your mind would probably have entertained and explored it. It's a simple rewording, but it can make the huge difference between dismissing the question and piquing your curiosity.

In fact, this book began with a question I asked myself years ago:

> *Why is it that we theoretically consider vision to be key in leadership,*
> *but find very few leaders actively, consciously, and structurally*
> *developing visionary capacity in practice?*

It's questions like these that captivate your thinking, stimulate your curiosity, and stay with you for a long time. Sometimes even to the point where you feel the odd desire to write a book about it.

Artfully crafted questions generate curiosity, are thought-provoking, and invite creativity, as conversation specialists Eric Vogt, Juanita Brown, and David Isaacs have explored.[13] Moreover, such questions give energy, as the right question makes us aware of the fact that there is something to explore that we hadn't fully grasped before. Powerful questions also "travel well," which means that they easily include and appeal to others. They can draw in a larger group of people who feel intrigued by the question and energized to explore it with you.

So, it would be very valuable if we could improve our "questioning ability" by designing better questions. Vogt, Brown, and Isaacs promote a three-dimensional architecture (shown in Figure 7-1) that helps you evaluate, and possibly redesign, questions to make them more powerful.

Dimension 1: Construction

To construct a question that opens up, you need the right interrogatives. (Remember the earlier example: "How can a road generate energy?") How, what, and why are particularly useful and much better than the less exploratory who, when, where, and which. But even these are better than the closed yes/no questions we tend to formulate.

For example, think about the following question: *Can our team become more innovative?* Asking your team this closed question will probably get

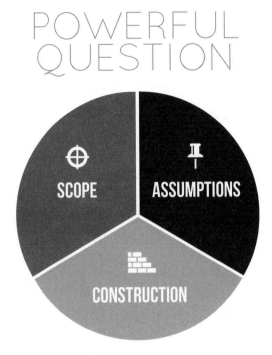

Figure 7-1. Question validation dimensions.

you a "yes," and you might feel satisfied with the agreement you have reached. "So let's work on that, then!" could be your concluding words of encouragement as you wrap up your meeting, assuming that your team has now adopted some miracle mindset shift toward innovation. Chances are high that three months down the road you will have experienced no change, to your frustration. You might inappropriately draw the wrong conclusions and start believing your team is not willing to work on this goal or is not capable of thinking-out-of-the-box. You might even conclude that the team is noncommittal to your leadership.

If you had instead asked *How could our team become more innovative?* you would have gotten a richer picture, and your understanding of the areas of improvement would have been far better. But even that's not as powerful as asking *Why is it that our team is not as innovative as we would like it to be?* Or, *What do we need change to ensure our team can become more innovative?* These are vastly different questions that target the root cause of the apparent problem, and they are much more engaging and explorative. But if you don't ask them, probably nobody will. Unnecessary frustration, affecting your leadership, grows.

Dimension 2: Scope

Once you've chosen effective interrogatives, you are ready for the second dimension: stretching the scope and boundaries of your questions. Questions we ask ourselves are often unintentionally limited by boundaries. The question as framed in the previous example is limited to our team. These kinds of unintentional boundaries are quick to creep in. It was seemingly appropriate to limit the question to "our team"—you probably didn't even notice it as we worked from can to how to why. Expanding the scope expands creativity and imagination. "What do we need to change to ensure that we can become more innovative for our customers/in our domain/in our company/in our industry?" This question vastly widens the mental boundaries and yields much more space to explore.

Dimension 3: Assumptions

The third, and often most difficult, dimension to catch is to examine the assumptions made in the question itself. For example: What could we do to deliver our products faster to our customers? A question like this one is built on the assumption that customers want faster delivery. Maybe instead they'd prefer cheaper or less erroneous deliveries. Or perhaps they do not even want delivery at all—maybe our customers would be most satisfied if we delivered to some nearby convenient location, where they could collect our products at their convenience.

Even the previous question—How can our team become more innovative?— contains an implicit assumption: becoming more innovative is important. Questions can inadvertently confine our exploration to something that isn't one of our biggest challenges. Perhaps the real challenge is that we do not get along as team members, and hence, things like innovation and customer satisfaction suffer. By limiting our focus to innovation, we might be overlooking the essence of what is truly holding us back.

CONVERSATION SURPRISE

One of the leaders I used to work with applied a leadership style probably best described as leading by questioning: He has built up a repertoire of powerful questions for various occasions. For example, when something has gone wrong, as inevitably happens in the real world, he invites the person involved for a conversation. He puts two powerful questions on the table: 1) What have you learned from what happened? and 2) What options do you see now that you did not see before? This way, he aims to build a learning culture and to encourage entrepreneurship, which he considers vital for his organization. He's well known for never penalizing anyone for making a mistake; in fact, you might even get rewarded if the failure involved entrepreneurial risks. But he does expect people to reflect and learn, and to be able to demonstrate increased insight. It really ticks him off when someone doesn't learn mindfully from a mistake.

Some companies have institutionalized the art of powerful questions, knowing that asking the right question is a critical element in process improvement. Carrefour, the French retail giant, has a "conversation surprise" (which is just the reverse in English, but try it with a French accent) with all new hires within their first six weeks. The conversation focuses on only one question: "What has surprised you since you started working with us?" Knowing that most people adapt to company culture rather quickly, Carrefour wisely exploits the fact that in their first few weeks, newcomers still dare to challenge the assumptions older employees live by, so they are, in that short time frame, a great source of ideas for improvement.

At Hertz, the largest publicly traded rental-car operator in the United States, the main senior leadership team does formal "skip level" reviews at least twice a quarter. They interview frontline staff members, without their managers or HR representatives present, using only a handful of powerful questions such as, "If you were the CEO for a day, what would you do?" and "If you had a magic wand, what would you change about Hertz?" This institutionalized process of inquiry ensures that the executives at Hertz do not alienate themselves from reality, and allows them to initiate—and possibly sponsor—high-impact changes.

The field of productive questioning has become academic terrain since Frank Stowell and Daune West developed the Appreciative Inquiry

Method in 1991. Their approach broke with tradition, since most business improvement disciplines focused on those things that are *not* functioning optimally. However, an excessive focus on dysfunction can easily lead to paralysis, frustration, and negativism, which creates a less productive atmosphere. Appreciative inquiry (AI) is instead concerned with what is going very well. Based on research revealing that a focus on strengths and positive attributes motivates people to understand and value the best features of their culture, AI encourages improvement by creating a very clear understanding of what works well and focusing energy on those things people seem to do effortlessly.

Developing a set of appreciative inquiry questions could alter your leadership behavior in a very favorable way. By appreciating and acknowledging others' strengths, by focusing on the positive, you can better inspire and engage them. And, by the way, this applies equally to your nonbusiness role as a partner or parent. Try it tonight. Rather than asking your loved ones how their day was, or how they are doing, ask this appreciative inquiry question: "What was the very best thing that happened to you today?" Pay attention to the conversation that unfolds and explore if and how it differs from the usual one.[14]

Philosopher Ralph Waldo Emerson was known to greet friends and visitors with the question: "What has become clear to you since we last met?" It might be a bit intimidating while you're hanging up your coat, but it's a great question that sparks interest and curiosity straight away.

WORKING YOUR SWING

At this point you're probably wondering: How do I integrate all this information into my leadership practice? We have seen that mindfulness is imperative to growing your visionary capacity, and Ellen Langer provides a solid theoretical framework for the various dimensions, but the practical question remains. How do we get to that state?

My good friend and actor Bruce van Barthold once explained how actors can learn "to live inside the character." His acting instructors taught him that you cannot think yourself into a new way of acting, but you *can* act yourself into a new way of thinking. He had to repeat it to me twice, but once I got it, it made a lot of sense. Developing a mindful mindset is similar: There are behaviors and practices that can help you. You can't simply tell yourself to start "recategorizing" from now on, or to be open to new information, or to stop taking a single perspective. That wouldn't work, and Langer's three elements of mindfulness would remain purely theoretical. But you *can* use a repertoire of behaviors and practices that, through repetition and perseverance, will help you develop that mindset.

Here are eight original, easy-to-integrate behavioral change practices (summarized in Figure 7-2) that you can incorporate in your daily leadership to *act yourself into a new way of thinking*.

RECATEGORIZING PRACTICES

1. *"Yes, and . . ."* This powerful practice can help you liberate yourself from your current belief system. In the next few days, try catching yourself when you say "Yes, but . . ." (it's only human, and it *will*

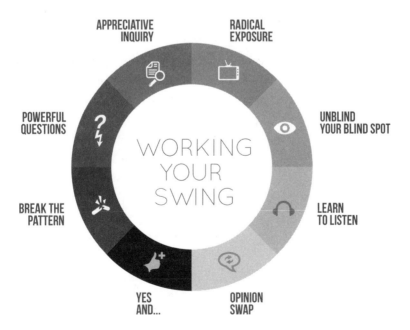

Figure 7-2. Practices.

Practice 7-1.
Yes, and . . .

happen). Nine out of ten times you will be stopping a thought or an idea that isn't in line with your current thinking and is blocking a creative idea or alternative perspective in the process.

To combat this tendency, immediately rephrase your reaction to "Yes, and . . .," allowing you to make your point by remaining open rather than closed. Keep up this practice until "Yes, and . . ." becomes your default reaction. It should not take you more than two weeks of practice to make this saying a habit. Remember, just one word can make a huge difference.

2. *Break the pattern.* A deceptively simple practice to increase your chances of seeing things differently is to deliberately break your normal pattern of working, communicating, thinking, reacting, and responding. For example, if you are normally the first to volunteer, hold back. Or if you are always the one who holds back, now volunteer. If you're very punctual, arrive late (as confronting as it might sound). If you like things to be done exactly your way, allow it to be done differently this week. If you always take the same route to work, choose a different one. Sit in a different part of the canteen. Change where you sit. Raise or lower the height of your chair. Part your hair differently.

Practice 7-2.
Break the pattern.

In fact, you can start right now. Do you wear a watch? If it's on your left wrist, move it to your right, or vice versa. You'll quickly find yourself looking at the wrong wrist, which will be a constant reminder that you easily, unconsciously, fall victim to mindless routines. You'll prompt your internal alert system to wake up and start seeing things differently.

NEW INFORMATION PRACTICES

3. *Powerful questions.* As we discussed earlier in this chapter, artfully designed questions generate curiosity, are thought-provoking, challenge underlying assumptions, and invite creativity. Moreover, they

give us energy, making us aware of the fact that
there is something to explore that we hadn't fully
grasped before. So train yourself to catch poorly designed questions, asked by you as well as others, and
reformulate them. Keep the three dimensions in
mind: 1) *why*, *what*, *how* constructions, 2) scope, and
3) underlying assumptions.

Practice 7-3.
Look OUT!

4. *Appreciative inquiry.* Develop a set of appreciative
questions aimed at discovering what is going well,
and why. Use them when analyzing problems, with-
holding the temptation to first ask what went wrong.

Practice 7-4.
Appreciative
inquiry.

5. *Radical exposure.* Author and self-made millionaire
Jim Rohn once said, "You are the average of the five
people you spend the most time with." Although this statement
doesn't have academic validity, it is true that we are strongly influenced by the small group of people we have direct contact with—
for better or worse. And since we tend to hang out with people who
are fairly similar to ourselves, chances are we are limiting our perspectives and excluding information. The radical
exposure practice promotes a deliberate effort to engage, with some frequency (e.g., once a month),
with a subgroup that is profoundly different from
the usual suspects you hang out with. Visit a conference of a very different profession, hang out with
skaters, join an arts club, buy a magazine randomly
off the shelf, things like that.

Practice 7-5.
Radical exposure.

6. *Unblind your blind spot.* Group dynamics often make what's on the
table appear as though it's the only possibility. But it rarely is. It's
just what the group is most comfortable with; once an option is chosen, the group is unlikely to consider anything else. Whenever you
engage in a conversation aimed at clarifying or making a decision,
ask, at the appropriate moments:

Practice 7-6.
Unblinding your
blind spot.

- What other options exist?
- What are we not seeing or saying?

When you ask about other options, you go beyond what is currently being considered. Asking about what's not being seen or said prompts consideration of whether judgments are based on the best available information. Are we well informed enough to make the decision? Or are we running a high risk of tunnel vision? In their *Harvard Business Review* article "Before You Make That Big Decision...,"[15] Nobel laureate Daniel Kahneman and coauthors Dan Lovallo and Olivier Sibony offer a checklist of great questions that check for various biases that might keep you from seeing the full picture. For example, "If you had to make this decision again in a year's time, what information would you want?" aims to avoid availability bias. Developing a repertoire of such questions and using them actively reduces the risk of falling victim to blindspots.

MULTIPLE VIEW PRACTICES

7. *Learn to listen.* We've all been taught the importance of listening, but in reality many of us struggle to do so. When listening mindlessly, we are mostly—consciously or unconsciously—looking for a way to take back the conversation, and we jump at the first opportunity to share our story, our opinion, or our experience. That's not listening—and it can prevent you from understanding a different perspective.

You can train yourself to listen consciously and mindfully by choosing to engage in three *pure listening conversations* a week. They don't need to be longer than fifteen to twenty minutes; they can be at the coffee machine; they can be formal or informal; and your conversation partner does not need to know you are practicing. But you do.

Here's how it works: Consciously and deliberately go into *listening mode*. This means not taking over the conversation with your

ideas or observations, no matter how much you
want to. Just keep asking questions, and don't dismiss anything your conversation partner mentions,
no matter how odd it sounds or how disconnected
the person's views are from yours. Learn to listen for
other people's insights, hunches, and observations.
Ask simple, open questions such as:

Practice 7-7.
Learn to listen.

- What has changed in our world/industry since the last time
  we spoke?
- What surprises you about the way things are progressing
  with our clients, competitors, and suppliers?
- What signs do you see today that might be early signals of
  change?
- How have your life and ideas changed in the last five years?

Once your conversation has ended, take a few minutes to reflect
on what you've learned. Don't dismiss any ideas or views that don't
align with yours. Consider what truths they might hold, and research them a little further. Dare to challenge your own assumptions and reframe your beliefs if that is what is called for.

8. *Opinion swap.* Choose someone at work who is least like you—not
   someone you dislike, just someone very different. You two might
   differ in character, taste, thoughts, or actions. Think of a subject
   you normally disagree on. It might be something simple, like a
   product, marketing message, or television program that you avoid
   or find trivial and the other person really likes. Imagine yourself
   adopting this person's opinion, like you'd try on an
   outfit. See things from this person's point of view
   and come up with some reasons why he or she loves
   what you hate, or vice versa. Once you are comfortable, do the same exercise—live. Have a real conversation with the person, and gradually let go of your
   opinion and take the other side. Just experiment—

Practice 7-8.
Option swap.

what do you have to lose? You don't even need to explain what you're doing. When you try this practice with people, they might think they've won you over, and you may learn something valuable about your own opinions.

You could also revisit the practices we discussed in Chapters 4 and 5, FuturePriming and scenario planning, which strengthen these behaviors as well. FuturePriming gets you to explore new information, possibly recategorizing your current perspectives, and scenario planning explicitly helps you adopt more than one view.

Understandably, some of these practices will be out of your comfort zone. You might not be ready to try all of them right now. I'm not suggesting you implement them all at once. Grow into a more mindful, visionary leader one step at a time. Work on these practices over the next few weeks and months. Collectively, they play an important role in developing your visionary self. Acting out these practices for real will help you find out where your personal growth opportunities lie.

PART 4

1 VISIONARY CONTENT

2 VISIONARY PRACTICES

3 VISIONARY SELF

4 VISIONARY COMMUNICATION

8

Igniting Your Followers

Thought is born through words.
—L. S. VYGOTSKY

So far, we've covered a lot of terrain on growing your visionary capacity: content prerequisites and ways to unlock your imagination, development dimensions and practices, character and behavior. But we haven't addressed one final, critical dimension essential to developing your visionary swing. You can do all of the above par excellence—you can have great ideas, make the powerful practices second nature, have clarity on your core purpose and values, and exercise the right behaviors for growth—but if you are unable to communicate your vision in a way that engages and energizes others, the Vision Thing still won't work for you.

There are several specific visionary communication qualities that, when done right, will transform your story from something future-oriented but technical and uninspiring to something that invigorates your followers. Let's start by reviewing some minimum requirements, the so-called hygiene factors, before we explore more elaborate aspects in powerful visionary communication.

HYGIENE FACTORS

Hygiene factors is a term introduced by Frederick Herzberg in 1959 that's often used in management literature to label those aspects whose presence alone does not provide positive satisfaction, but their absence results in dissatisfaction. For example, a hygiene factor in a restaurant is clean tableware. Restaurant guests simply expect clean tableware, but they won't return to the restaurant just because of it; however, if the tableware is dirty they will avoid the restaurant the next time. Similarly, hygiene factors in visionary communication are important necessities: Getting them wrong will decrease the impact of your story, whereas getting them right merely provides a foundation to work from.

Three of the most important hygiene factors in your visionary communication are:

1. *Short and crisp.* You must be able to communicate the core message of your vision in just a few minutes. (PowerPoint-free!) This doesn't mean it should merely be a sales (or elevator) pitch, a series of superficial slogans, or a content-free rallying cry. In two or three minutes you can have a tremendous impact. But you need to carefully choose your words and what you want to communicate for this "minimum words, maximum impact" version, demonstrating real focus and crystal clear clarity on what's at the heart of your vision. It also means you should prepare and rehearse your story—it's too important to the perception of you as a leader to wing it or leave it to luck.

   Of course you can have more extensive versions available for when you have time to elaborate and want to describe the implications in more detail. I'd still encourage you to go PowerPoint-free, since sharing your vision is a leadership moment, and your authentic self gets more chance to shine when *you* speak than when your projector does most of the communication.

   Having said that, some well-designed slides might prove helpful when you've got the opportunity to go into depth. But those extended versions are familiar territory for most leaders. The real struggle is to resist the temptation to present all of the logic and key points in your story, to instead boil your message down to its essence while maintaining gravitas and radiating authenticity.

There's actually a neuroscientific explanation for this necessity to reduce your message to its core. Remember the default and control network introduced in Chapter 2 (in the section titled Neural Networks)? The control network, which overrides our habits and impulses and aligns our behavior with our goals, suffers from mental fatigue. "When overwhelmed, the control network loses the proverbial reins, and our behavior is driven by immediate, situational cues instead of shaped with our priorities in mind," Waytz and Mason assert.[1] Since your vision should decrease complexity in the decisions your followers face going forward, a clear image of what you're aiming for is pivotal in helping their (as well as your own) control system maintain its focus.

2. *Positive and hopeful (better: mindful).* As Ford's former CEO Alan Mulally, who headed one of the most impressive corporate turnarounds in history, points out: "Positive leadership, conveying the idea that there is always a way forward, is so important, because that is what you are here for, to figure out how to move the organization forward."[2] A powerful vision leaves no room for negativism or cynicism; recall the draining effect of cynicism with the Historian archetype that I introduced in Chapter 3.

There is, however, a limit as far as optimism is concerned. An unrealistic amount of it can be equally harmful to your cause. Leaders who are all smiles, who habitually joke legitimate problems aside and maintain an overly optimistic, quixotic attitude are not effective. We're therefore better off using the word *mindful,* a concept we explored in Chapter 7, rather than *positive.* Jim Collins called this the Stockdale Paradox in his leadership bestseller *Good to Great.* Jim Stockdale was the highest-ranking U.S. military officer in the "Hanoi Hilton," the prisoner-of-war camp during the Vietnam War. He was held there for eight years, was tortured over a dozen times, and had little reason to believe he would ever get out. But he always kept faith. "I never doubted not only that I would get out, but also that I would prevail in the end and turn the experience into the defining event of my life, which, in retrospect, I would not trade,"[3] he told Collins.

It was a heroic mindset, given his situation, yet the real value of this terrible anecdote lies in Stockdale's second reflection: The most optimistic prisoners always failed to get out alive. "The optimists were the ones who said, 'We're going to be out by Christmas.' And Christmas would come, and Christmas would go. Then they'd say, 'We're going to be out by Easter.' And Easter would come, and Easter would go. And then Thanksgiving, and then it would be Christmas again. And they died of a broken heart."[4]

The famous Austrian psychiatrist Viktor Frankl similarly reported the importance of believing you have a choice in every situation, even under the most dreadful circumstances. Frankl was held in four different camps, including Auschwitz, between 1942 and 1945. He survived and described his Nazi death camp experiences and the spiritual lessons it provided him in *Man's Search for Meaning,* a book that continues to inspire and provide direction in understanding what is truly important in life.[5]

Both Frankl and Stockdale stressed the importance of facing reality. Frankl writes that suffering is inevitable and that avoiding suffering is futile. But knowing you can still choose how to behave, choose how to engage with and be helpful to others, choose how to communicate, provides mental strength in dealing with the situation. This "mindful" point of view—following Ellen Langer's approach to mindfulness as introduced in Chapter 7—allowed Frankl to psychologically sustain himself, despite the ordeals he endured. Under these extraordinarily horrendous circumstances, wishful thinkers failed to endure the continuous setbacks to their unrealistic outlooks.

The problem with delusional, over-the-top optimism is that it fails to acknowledge reality. Stockdale accepted his situation, and chose to do what was in his power to boost morale and provide hope to others and himself. "You must never confuse faith that you will prevail in the end with the discipline to confront the brutal facts of your current reality, whatever they might be,"[6] Stockdale pointed out.

Rather than positivism, what matters for your vision is an acknowledgment of the reality of your situation and the full range of choices available, as well as a believable sense of hope, ambition, and confidence. As Mulally stresses, the leader's role is to find the hope-giving hook that propels people forward, moving beyond today's occasionally daunting reality. It's what worked for him at Ford, and for Frankl and Stockdale during their nightmarish experiences in imprisonment.

3. *Future-oriented*. This might sound like stating the obvious—and, really, it is— but I'm emphasizing it because I've seen too many leaders fail to take this point into account. When given the opportunity to communicate their visionary ideas, they take their audience into the past, missing the opportunity to inspire and demonstrate their leadership.

Practice 8-1.
Moments of truth.

The tendency to drift toward the past is understandable from a risk-aversion point of view. The past provides facts and experiences that can help you develop a valid, indisputable, logically consistent story. It's safe ground to build on. But explaining "where we came from," even when you continue the story into the future, sets an unimaginative, unexciting tone.

Instead, start with the future. Describe where you're headed. This is much riskier territory—you'll have to tap into your imagination and creatively paint a picture of what tomorrow could look like without the logic and certainty that facts can provide. But it's vital for a vision intended to recast people's thinking and point their minds forward.

GETTYSBURG ADDRESS

Abraham Lincoln's Gettysburg Address superbly demonstrates the three hygiene factors (and several others, as we will soon discover). Overlooking the battlefield where a fierce and historic battle between the Northern Union forces and the Southern Confederacy took place four months earlier, costing 51,000 soldiers their lives, Lincoln delivered his speech on the afternoon of Thursday, November 19, 1863.

In just a few minutes, using only 272 words, Lincoln expressed his views on America's purpose in a way that still guides thinking about democracy. It made Garry Wills, the author of the Pulitzer Prize–winning book *Lincoln at Gettysburg: The Words That Remade America,* conclude that "the power of words has rarely been given a more compelling demonstration."[7] Edward Everett, the president of Harvard and principal speaker at the Gettysburg cemetery dedication who preceded Lincoln with a two-hour speech, was clearly impressed and wrote to Lincoln the next day: "I should be glad if I could flatter myself that I came as near to the central idea of the occasion, in two hours, as you did in two minutes."[8]

What makes the Gettysburg Address so powerful is Lincoln's successful reframing of the tremendous agony of the battle fought on those Pennsylvanian fields into a hopeful, forward-oriented perspective on America's future:

> It is for us the living, rather, to be dedicated here to the unfinished work which they who fought here have thus far so nobly advanced. It is rather for us to be here dedicated to the great task remaining before us—that from these honored dead we take increased devotion to that cause for which they gave the last full measure of devotion—that we here highly resolve that these dead shall not have died in vain—that this nation, under God, shall have a new birth of freedom. . . .

The Gettysburg Address, engraved on the wall of the colossal Lincoln Memorial in Washington D.C., set the path for generations to follow. A century later, Martin Luther King Jr., standing on the steps of the same monument, referenced Lincoln in his own historic speech, recalling the "great American in whose symbolic shadow we stand today." Even today, the rhythmic conclusion of Lincoln's speech, "that government of the people, by the people, for the people, shall not perish from the earth," continues to inspire and move.

Practice 8-2.
Elevator pitch.

There is much more to be said about this speech, and we will explore it further, but the point here is that short, positive, and future-oriented can fit together perfectly and have tremendous impact. Even for us mortal souls who don't have the rhetorical skills Lincoln possessed, this is a valuable lesson. In visionary communication, less is always more.

THE POWER OF LANGUAGE

Therefore, language really matters. Especially if you intend to bring people on board and persuade them to follow you and your ideas. Read the line below, and see if it does anything for you, emotionally:[9]

> *"Around ninety years ago our ancestors initiated an innovative new political process in our country, produced in an unconstrained mindset and based on the concept of equality."*

Inspired? Energized? Probably not, right? But why not? Why does this sentence lack emotional engagement? It can't be the message, since that exact message has inspired millions of people throughout the years.

But it inspired using different words. Here's the same message in its original form:

> *"Four score and seven years ago, our fathers brought forth on this continent a new nation, conceived in liberty, and dedicated to the proposition that all men are created equal."*

How does this feel? It's more of Lincoln's Gettysburg Address—his first words, actually. Content-wise, the two messages are pretty much the same. But one is rather boring and uninspiring while the other is uplifting and almost poetic. That's the power of language: It can touch us and re-frame our thinking.

Language also shapes our memory. This was first observed in 1974, when Elizabeth Loftus and John Palmer, researchers at the University of Washington, conducted an experiment to better understand the effects of language on memory.[10] They wanted to see if leading questions could dis-tort eyewitness accounts and reconstruct memories. To test their hypothesis, Loftus and Palmer asked forty-five students to watch a short video of a car accident. They then asked each of the participants to estimate the speed of the cars, using five slightly different questions. One-fifth of the group was asked the question, "About how fast were the cars going when they *smashed* into each other?"

Another group of nine students was asked a slightly different question: "About how fast were the cars going when they *collided* into each other?" The remaining variations used the verbs *bumped, hit,* and *contacted.* Interestingly, the average speed estimates correlated with the severity of the verbs. Those asked the "smashed" question estimated 40.5 miles per hour, while those who heard the "contacted" version estimated 31.8 miles per hour. That's more than a 25 percent difference. (See Figure 8-1.)

It's a remarkable finding, but the study didn't end there. A week later, the participants were invited back and given a new question. This time, the researchers asked, "Do you remember whether you saw broken glass in last week's film?" It turned out that the students who had been asked the "smashed" version of the speed estimate question a week before answered yes in significantly greater numbers than those who had been asked the other variations of the question. (If you're curious, there was no broken glass in the video.)

Just think about that for a moment: Forty-five people all saw the same short video. The only difference was the slightly altered questions they were asked following the video. Not only did that small language difference affect their speed estimation immediately after watching, but the verb used in the question also affected their memory. Those who had been given a question that alluded to more damage ("smashed") remembered the film differently than those who had answered a less dramatic version of the same question. Loftus and Palmer showed that language affects how we *perceive* as well as how we *remember*.

A YouTube hit features a blind beggar, sitting on a sidewalk with a cardboard sign saying: "I'm blind. Please help." It looks like a typical day in the life of a beggar; he receives some small change every now and then. Until a woman walks up, looks at his sign, picks it up, and changes the wording. After she leaves, he suddenly starts receiving more donations. When he recognizes the sound of her shoes returning, he asks her what she did to his sign. She replies, "I wrote the same, but in different words." As

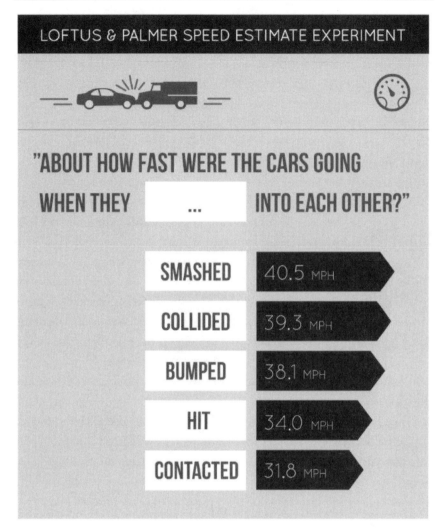

Figure 8-1. Loftus and Palmer speed experiment.

she walks away, the camera shows the new message: "It's a beautiful day, and I can't see it."[11]

Even though the video was orchestrated, it holds an important truth. Some words move us, and others don't. It's not just the message that needs to resonate; the way it's translated into words also shapes its impact and the actions it inspires. That's the hidden power of language: The words we choose affect our emotional state and memory, and can result in noticeably different outcomes. If you want your vision to reframe people's mindsets and move them to act, you need to use productive, active language.

WORKHORSE VERBS

One of the first lessons you're taught in writing class when your text lacks pizzazz is to scrutinize your verbs. Verbs carry sentences, and the ones that do the heavy lifting, bringing energy to your message, are called "workhorse verbs" or "powerhouse verbs."

Practice 8-3.
Verb-alize.

By consciously incorporating a number of these verbs into your message, you will create a profoundly different effect on your listeners. Your language will become more colorful; your listeners will become more perceptive. Compare these sentences: "He quickly sat down on his chair" with "He launched into his seat." Entirely different, right? The latter probably created a different image in your head, one of energy and motion. The message is the same, but the energy, image, and imagination are quite different.

Let's get more businessy. Compare these two statements: "We discussed the opportunity to develop a new product" with "We explored boosting our offering." Quite different again, right? How about these: "He addressed the future opportunities" vs. "He galvanized with a compelling vision." Or, "She discussed the differences and came to an agreement" vs. "She conquered the discussion and harmonized their views."

Workhorse verbs move your story forward, create powerful imagery, and convey a confident tone. The novelist Rudyard Kipling once remarked, "Words are the most powerful drug used by mankind." Sometimes workhorse verbs are criticized for being too smooth, too salesman-like. This kind of language often doesn't come natural to numbers-and-facts-prone individuals like engineers, accountants, and scientists (sorry for the generalization)—and most business folks today, who typically evolve in an environment that fosters the humdrum of charts, bullet points, and logic. They often lean toward facts and statistics as their primary weapons of persuasion.

Workhorse verbs should therefore indeed be used with caution. The counterproductive "overselling perception" becomes particularly apparent when you *overdo* it, and your language runs the risk of being perceived as unauthentic. I would therefore recommend to use powerhouse verbs sparingly and precisely to preserve their impact. But don't forget, sharing your vision is about selling your idea of the future, and creating excitement through language is part of your role as leader. Your intention is to unlock people's imagination and get them to associate, maybe even "dream" of the compelling tomorrow you paint for them.

Here's how to grow your ability to make your speech more colorful: Create a list of verbs that attract you but are not yet part of your everyday vocabulary. Pick one a day, and set a target of using it at least three times that day. You'll find that over a short time many of these words will become part of your regular repertoire.

Figure 8-2 gives some examples of energizing verbs (and their more mundane counterparts).

Figure 8-2. Workhorse verbs.

NOTIONS OF LOSS

There is a final aspect of language and wording worth noting for our purpose of influencing and persuading with our vision, one that brings together two psychological concepts: the Contrast Principle and notions of loss. Paradoxically, there is real value in including a negative picture in your vision. But, in line with what I have been advocating, it's not a negative (or cynical) picture of what is or what might be if we change in your intended direction, but a negative picture of what might be if we do not change. Let's see how that works.

The Contrast Principle refers back to the automatic behaviors discussed in Chapter 7, only this time not as a negative factor in our own behavior, but as an activation factor in the automatic behavior of others. After all, irrationality might be unfavorable for ourselves, but we can use it productively to influence others if we are aware of its hidden powers. Cialdini aptly calls these ingrained automatic behaviors "weapons of automatic influence" that "possess tremendous ability to direct human action."[12]

So here's the idea. Our evaluation of things is not based on their objective value, but on how they stand out *between* other things. If you'd like to experience this firsthand, take three large bowls of water: one really cold, one hot (so hot you can *just* bear it), and one at room temperature. Put one of your hands into the cold water, the other in the hot water and leave them for a minute. Then take them out and put both in the bowl of lukewarm water. You'll notice that the hand from the cold water now feels hot and the other now feels cold, whereas in reality they are feeling the same temperature. Apparently it is not the objective temperature you experience, but how it feels compared to the previous experience.

Smart salespeople use this as a tactic. A clever real estate agent who wants to promote a particular house will first show you two clearly overpriced houses. This setup will make you much more likely to agree to the third one you're shown, which will now feel like a bargain. You'll walk out satisfied, happy with your "bargain deal" (which, in reality, might be at or even above market value), and tell others how lucky you were to find this unique house. Similarly, when suggesting project names to your team, you should suggest one or two obviously unsuitable names first, and then the one you prefer. Undoubtedly, they'll like the third option more than they "objectively" should. That's the Contrast Principle in action.

How does this principle relate to our intention to persuade with our vision? Contrasting your desired future direction with the one that is undesirable to you—most likely the status quo, no change option—will unknowingly add more appeal to your story. It'll get people to agree with your version of the future much easier. Remember how Steve Jobs was successful in winning over John Sculley (see Chapter 2) by asking him, "John, do you want to sell sugar water for the rest of your life, or do you want to come with me and change the world?" That's another example of the Contrast Principle in action.

Negative contrast has a second advantage as well, which brings us back to the original work of Daniel Kahneman and Amos Tversky on framing (see Chapter 2) and what has become known as the "Asian disease problem."[13] Participants in their experiment were asked to "imagine that the U.S. is preparing for the outbreak of an unusual Asian disease, which is expected to kill 600 people. Two alternative programs to combat the disease have been proposed. Assume the exact scientific estimate of the consequences of the programs are as follows."

For their two alternatives, one group had to make a choice between:

- Program A, which will save 200 people
- Program B, which has a one-third probability that 600 people will be saved, and a two-thirds probability that no people will be saved

What would *you* choose? Read it once more, and determine what your preference would be if you were responsible for this decision and these were the only two options you had. Kahneman and Tversky found that 72 percent of participants preferred program A, which provided a sure bet to save 200 people.

Another group was given the same challenge, and also had to make a choice between two programs. However, their choices were formulated as follows:

- Program C, in which 400 people will die
- Program D, in which there is a one-third probability that nobody will die, and a two-thirds probability that 600 people will die

In other words, the groups effectively had the same choice. In the first group the choice was framed positively, using the verb "save." For the second group, the choice was framed with a negative decision frame, using the verb "die." But effectively, the choices were identical.

Remarkably, the second group preferred option D over C (78 percent opted for D). As it turns out, when the choice is framed positively, people become risk-averse (as the first group demonstrated), but when framed negatively, people become far less risk-averse and maybe even risk seekers (as the second group demonstrated). Psychologically, we perceive the notion of loss differently than the notion of gain.

Robert Cialdini, already introduced as a thought leader in how these psychological concepts play out in influencing and persuading people, explains the usefulness of this knowledge in getting people to change. He says that "moving people under conditions of uncertainty is difficult—the first thing they do is freeze. They're scared of what they might lose. Therefore, it's good to tell people what they will lose if they *fail* to move."[14]

Alluding to this notion of loss is psychologically very powerful and helps battle the status quo bias that people fall victim to when evaluating their options. Setting up a negative frame by painting what failure to change would look like is more likely to lure them into action and free them from their risk-averse reflex to keep things as is. At the same time, you are exploiting the Contrast Principle, which will make the future you paint seem even more compelling and persuasive.

A PICTURE IS WORTH A THOUSAND WORDS

Now that we've seen that language, wording, and framing matter and how far well-chosen verbs can take you, let's look at one final characteristic of energizing and inspiring communication. It's the part that focuses on that mysterious, emotional spark that triggers your followers to commit not only with their heads but also with their hearts.

For this, let's turn to what might be the most famous speech of all time: Martin Luther King's "I Have a Dream." Spoken on the steps of the Lincoln Memorial, it deeply moved millions of people, uniting them in a vision of a more just and decent world. Decades years later, King's words and his delivery of them still move people. But what accounts for this effect?

Other than the allure of the message—that of a more equitable world—he uses specific language to "sell" this message. King rarely used a sentence that didn't include *pictorial language*. He speaks of "the bank of justice," "insufficient funds," "great vaults of opportunity," "cash a check," "tranquilizing drug of gradualism," "the dark and desolate valley of segregation," "the sunlit path of racial justice," "the quick sands of racial injustice," and the "solid rock of brotherhood"—just a few of the many, many images and metaphors he evokes for his audience. In fact, even the title of his speech is metaphorical, referring not to a real dream but to a vision of a more honest and equitable tomorrow.

Notwithstanding King's pure rhetorical brilliance, stemming from years of training as a Baptist minister, his excessive use of metaphorical language serves a real purpose in uplifting the audience. Why is that?

A clue may be found in Chapter 2, where we discussed Fred Polak's early work *The Image of the Future* on the importance of future orientation. He coined the term "image" to describe future-oriented perspectives (visions). And it should be no surprise that the word *imagination* is etymologically related to the word *image*.

When describing the future, you can't use facts and figures. You don't have statistics to prove your points. You must largely rely on your imagination. And to convincingly bring your audience into the future, you must unlock *their* imagination, helping them *envision* a different world. Every nationality I've worked with has a proverb along the lines of "a picture is worth a thousand words." So it shouldn't be a surprise that images, and visual language such as metaphors

Practice 8-4.
A picture is worth a thousand words.

and analogies, are of vital importance in bridging the gap between the cerebral and the imaginative. They help people "see" it. To quote George Lakoff and Mark Johnson: "If a picture is worth a thousand words, then a metaphor is worth a thousand pictures."[15]

MEMORABLE METAPHORS

Metaphors do more than just informing and making the message stick. They also add a layer of emotion to the content. By accessing your associative brain, a metaphor immediately hitches emotions to the message.

King's "bank of justice" is a fabulous example. Most of us will instinctively and immediately imagine a bank building, grand and enduring, guarded, protecting things of real value. Once he's established that image in our heads, he takes it further, saying he refuses to believe this bank has insufficient funds. We're thinking, "Indeed, a bank with insufficient funds . . . that cannot be true." Maybe there is an unwillingness to open the locks, but there must be funds in the "vaults of opportunity." The United States is, after all, the land of opportunity. King leads his listeners to feel the injustice and to long for rectification. It only seems right and just that "we've come to cash this check." We become intellectually, but even more so emotionally, convinced that his cause is right. "Feelings inform thought, not the other way around," Waytz and Mason indicate.[16]

The dream metaphor of the title—which King reinforces throughout the speech—also carries important emotional associations. Automatically and subconsciously, we associate dreams with emotions such as hope, renewal, optimism, and wonder. Imagine how different it would have been if he had titled his famous speech "I Have an Action Plan!"

At this point, you're probably wondering where to find metaphors or which ones would work for your story. There's no magic answer. You'll need to search, experiment, and practice actively. To expedite your search, try using the Zaltman metaphor elicitation technique,[17] named for its inventor Gerald Zaltman. In a simple version of the technique, you gather several very different magazines and cut out pictures that represent the key message of your vision. Since almost anything could be a potential metaphor for your story, exposing yourself to random images will increase your chances of finding something. That something will be visual, and often also unconventional and rich. What matters is that it carries the right associations with your message and has no obvious associations that counter what you have to say.

No time to get magazines? Then just look around you right now and consider the objects you see as metaphors. Create a sentence for each: "Our future is like . . . a telephone," "Our future is like . . . a watercooler," "Our future is like . . . a vase of flowers," and so on.

Clearly, not all potential metaphors will work well. The ones that immediately trigger negative associations are especially unhelpful. You could probably make all sorts of positive associations with a fax machine (reliable, instant communication, multifunctional), but the fact that it's yesterday's news renders it useless as a metaphor for a vision. Using it would plant the wrong image in people's minds, and they would instantly dismiss your story.

Finding the right metaphor is a delicate, creative process. Edward de Bono (see Chapter 2 on lateral thinking) taught us not to make it too easy by dismissing words that appear unsuitable at first. Kickstart your creative side, explore, and let your mind freely associate. Don't deductively analyze which one would work best. It's a messy, slightly frustrating process of trial-and-error at times, but great fun once you find a metaphor that resonates with your story and provides the hook that will help people remember it.

You don't need to limit yourself to objects, either. Consider categories such as nature (rainbow, whirlwind, dawn, oak tree, flower, etc.), animals (lion, dolphin, falcon, butterfly, etc.), travel (journey, adventure, sailing, Eiffel Tower, Egyptian nights, Venice), sports (chess, Olympics, swimming, archery, kite surfing), food (pasta, Château Margaux, cheesecake, fortune cookie), or other interesting parallels (orchestra, solar system, community, pendulum).

ACTIONABLE ANALOGIES

Getting people to see things differently, or to align their view of the future with yours, is often the key challenge in visionary communication. The very phrase "seeing things differently" brings us back to our earlier discussion on frames. To see things in a different light, your audience must reframe their minds. This requires insight plus an acceptance of the fact that there is a different way to look at our future, and even at ourselves.

Metaphors are analogies that help us "see" such things that are not immediately obvious. Jack Malcolm, a communication specialist, explains, "Analogies are useful mental shortcuts that we take when we encounter new and unfamiliar situations that require judgment."[18] (By the way, notice how closely Malcolm's comment resembles the shortcuts in automatic behaviors stemming from the Consistency Principle of Chapter 7. So, as powerful as they can be, use them with care and watch out for "foolish consistency" with your analogies and metaphors!) If used well, analogies can be very instrumental in achieving the desired mind shift.

For example, if you are responsible for a hospital, a hospital division, or a medical team, and you state that you want to be considered the Singapore Airlines of the health care industry, people will get it. They will immediately understand that quality of service matters to you. The analogy, and the image it conjures up, tells the story, decreasing the need for rational and factual points that explain why quality of service is important.

Intel long maintained a strategy of producing high-end products only, and frowned upon cheap microprocessors for inexpensive PCs. It was not part of the company's mental model; the corporate assumption held that "cheap" was not for them. Until Intel's top management attended a seminar in 1997, run by Clayton Christensen, Harvard Business School professor and author of the influential *The Innovator's Dilemma*. Christensen explained how, in the 1970s, the traditional steel industry frowned upon small steel mills that were producing cheap concrete-reinforcing bars (rebars). It was an attitude the industry leaders soon regretted when the minimills moved into high-end products and ate their cake. The analogy clicked with Andy Grove, Intel's CEO, who declared in the meeting: "If we lose the low end today, we could lose the high end tomorrow." Soon after, Intel broke free from its constraining mindset, which had served the company well for a long time, and pursued a low-end strategy with cheaper Celeron processors.[19]

This story demonstrates the reframing power of an analogy, and how it can be used to bridge two realities. Don't expect ingrained belief systems to be easily upended; we've seen too many companies hold on to outdated belief systems despite reality clearly catching up with them. They often need a startling wake-up call. It's in these pivotal moments that deep-seated neural pathways get rewired, creating a new understanding that leads to revised strategies and actions. Unfortunately, a crisis is often required to get to a willingness to rethink that mindset, not only for the leader, but also for the followers. As long as things appear to continue more or less as before (even if business is suffering from a slow but certain decline), the sense of urgency is missing and getting followers to change is very difficult. As the leader, trained to anticipate and see things early, you need ways to help your followers to "see" the changing reality. Analogies and metaphors have this power to rewire, as the Intel story shows, and should become an integral part of your visionary communication repertoire.

So, strengthen your visionary story and make it actionable with analogies. Look for analogies in car or airline brands, sports teams, animals, pop bands, cities, or industries. What car brand provides the best analogy for the future we aspire to? A Lamborghini? A Tesla? A Toyota? A Bentley? As you start associating, more suitable peripheral candidates might surface, such as a bicycle, an autonomous car, a hybrid, or a Dakar Rally race truck. Once you've found the right one, you're holding the key to getting your followers to recast their image of the future.

LET ME TELL YOU A STORY . . .

Logos is focused on setting direction and ensuring the validity of our vision's content. Pathos activates our audience's creative, pictorial, and emotional attention. That leaves Ethos, which is about the speaker's character, credibility, and authenticity. How do we communicate authenticity? How do we convey our character and credibility to our audience? This is where stories come into play.

The art of storytelling is witnessing increased popularity in the business world. And for good reasons, since stories have a lot of valuable features that can be helpful in conveying our message and persuading people into the direction we aims for. We all *love* stories. They have intrigued and entertained us from our earliest days. We used to love bedtime stories in our childhood, and today we pay good money to go to the movies or the theater. Stories inspire; they're catchy and heighten our natural curiosity. According to bestselling author Margaret Parkin, they bring out our youthful emotional state of curiosity, and "once in this childlike state, we tend to be more receptive and interested in the information we are given."[20] So stories have the capacity to switch on that exploratory, mindful state we were after in Chapter 7.

Moreover, stories communicate values and make them accessible, understandable, and believable. The best stories often come with multiple meanings that go beyond the literal surface. In fact, cultures communicate their values through stories. Joseph Campbell documented universal story architectures, used in myths around the world, in *The Hero with a Thou-*

sand Faces. These myths often serve to preserve cultural legacy and to share values across generations.

Stories are also memorable. Psychologist Jerome Bruner estimates that facts are twenty times more likely to be remembered when they are part of a story.[21] Speaking from personal experience, I can vouch for this. Several years ago, I was involved in an initiative to increase customer focus and intimacy at an organization. They weren't doing all that bad: Their net promoter scores (a customer feedback metric often used to determine the level of expected customer loyalty) were okay—above industry average, in fact—but not spectacular. We presented some research findings from Jones and Strasser[22] showing that customers who are merely satisfied are prone to leave, while those who are at times surprised by surpassed expectations become truly loyal. This was the message we wanted them to take in, so they would discover their own options for performance improvement. How could they exceed their customers' expectations from time to time?

But we ran into a problem. The data didn't excite them. Everyone agreed that outperforming expectations was important, but the organization's leaders weren't very inspired to figure out how *they* could do it. The exercises we ran felt obligatory rather than exciting and exploratory, as we had anticipated. Then we ran a new session, and I shared an anecdote of something that had happened the week before. One of my boys, four years old at the time, was a Lego fanatic. And, as everyone who has ever stepped on a piece of Lego knows, those bricks never break. That is, until the day my wife dropped one of our son's Lego trains when cleaning his room and a small but critical component broke off, rendering the train useless. As good parents, we wanted to make it right, but buying a completely new expensive train set to replace that one little piece felt a little over the top. In a state of light despair, my wife called the Lego customer service department and explained what happened. They gave us the typical response: "We'll see what we can do." We were convinced we wouldn't hear back from them—we were just one customer out of millions, and wasn't it our own fault that we dropped the train?

Three weeks later, an envelope came in the mail, addressed to my son (four-year-olds love getting mail!). The beautifully drafted letter greeted him by his first name and mentioned how sad he must have been when his mother had dropped his train (an unexpectedly personal touch in these computerized times). Lego was happy to provide him with a spare part, and threw in an extra one, just in case it happened again. The letter also mentioned that, given how much he loved Lego, they were giving him a one-year subscription to Lego magazine. And although we would have been happy to pay for the spare part, plus shipping and handling, all of it was free. The experience completely surpassed our expectations, and even though we don't expect Lego to outperform on every occasion, it significantly increased our customer loyalty. (And I feel compelled to tell this story to audiences around the world—talk about free PR!)

After I finished the story, the executives became instantly excited about what outperforming expectations would mean for their business. They recognized what I was talking about, often threw in one or two similar stories that had happened to themselves, and eagerly started to explore ways in which they could create similar experiences for their clients. The story carried the same idea as the research did, but it made a huge difference between mere acknowledgment and real action.

DATA WITH A SOUL

So how do you use the art of storytelling to make your personal character, authenticity, and values come to life? Brené Brown, a research professor at the University of Houston, says, "Stories are data with a soul. Data wrapped in stories have the ability to move people, to inspire people to take action."[23] For your visionary communication to become authentic, you need to integrate a special type of story—the personal anecdote. We all have anecdotes about moments in our lives that gave us wisdom and personal lessons that we still remember and apply today. These experiences often provide anecdotal evidence of why we think and behave in certain ways—they reveal the values, beliefs, and ideas that we care deeply about.

Your personal anecdotes are much more than just insightful recollections; they communicate something about your character. In other words, they provide your story with a soul. Sharing a meaningful personal anecdote shifts your rhetoric from the head to the heart. After all, the story has stayed with you for a good reason: You experienced it and attached significance to it. And when you share it, you'll relive the emotions and show what you truly care about. This kind of honesty automatically makes you and your story truly authentic.

One of the CEOs I worked with had a hard message to sell: Business was going down and it wasn't expected to improve. The traditional business model was being challenged by changes to the industry caused by the Internet. In addition to cutting costs, the company needed to reorient itself, completely overhauling its business model. This transformation would cause a lot of uncertainty, and there was no guarantee that the new direction would yield success right away. The next few years would require a lot of energy, persistence, and support from everyone, especially the company leaders.

The CEO asked me to sit in on a critical, much-anticipated meeting in which he would share his views with his leadership team. He started by taking them through the numbers. Judging by all the nodding, everyone agreed something would have to change. Intellectually, they understood.

But you could sense the message hadn't sunk in completely. There was still an element of self-interest in the room. One executive claimed he represented the last, lone growth engine. Another complained he'd already suffered significant cuts in a previous round. Yet another one argued that reducing head count in his group would be like throwing out the baby with the bathwater, as finding the highly experienced specialists he was leading would be impossible once growth resumed.

They all saw the need to cut costs, but "not in my budget." It sounded like a mix between cognitive dissonance and self-defense. They understood the situation intellectually, but they weren't behaving like a team. The CEO realized that this lack of team spirit would seriously harm the much-needed transformation. Somehow, he would have to get them on board for real.

And that's when he did something brilliant. From his hard disk he retrieved a picture of himself, taken a few weeks earlier, and projected it on the big screen behind him. We saw a man with a frozen face, caught with a bewildered look and a bad-looking scratch on his cheek. It instantly shocked us. Despite the large-size projection, it was hard to recognize him. The picture had been taken a several weeks before, during a 200-kilometer ice-skating marathon on the lakes of Finland. The CEO, a skating fanatic, had entered the race with a group of friends. It'd turned into a true ordeal. They lost their way in the darkness, fell constantly because of the poor ice conditions, underestimated the tremendous cold, and miscalculated their food supply. He admitted that there were moments he'd feared they wouldn't return safely. The only reason they had survived was the fact that they formed a team. They stuck together, kept each other out of the wind, waited for and supported each other when someone tripped, and occasionally sacrificed their own needs to make sure everyone would make it through. He closed by saying he was proud they had finished, but he was even more proud to have been a member of such a determined, collaborative team in which everyone kept his ego in check. He was convinced that that was what had pulled them through.

His eyes became watery when he retold the story, and at times you could sense he was actually reexperiencing the emotions. When he finished, you could have heard a pin drop.

Practice 8-5.
Let me tell you
a story.

The story illustrated the invaluable importance of teamwork in such critical times. The members of his leadership team would need to stand up for each other, support those who would come under pressure, and refrain from serving their own interests. The personal anecdote communicated it all, in a way no factual argument ever could. And the CEO left an important leadership mark about the values he stood for and aspired to.

I encourage you to dig into your personal database of life lessons. Seek out these memorable, meaningful moments and experiences; they taught you something important that still resonates with you today. Maybe it was a comment from a parent at a point in your life when you were stuck between a rock and a hard place. Or maybe it was something you did that failed miserably. Or a worry that turned out to be unfounded and taught you not to let your fears hold you back. Or maybe even something one of your kids said to you recently.

Try to discover why you remember the story—what is the real meaning of this experience to you? Be honest and authentic. And don't ignore your database of mistakes: What were your expectations, what went wrong and why, and what did you take away from it?

When you integrate a meaningful, personal anecdote into your message, the vision you have for the group will carry your Ethos, your character and credibility, and will authentically transform your story from the conceptual to the inspired and actionable.

JOBS & PAUSCH

Steve Jobs's memorable 2005 Stanford commencement speech is a marvelous example of radiating ethos through anecdotes. "Today I want to tell you three stories from my life. That's it. No big deal. Just three stories," he began. Jobs recounted the story of dropping out of Reed College and how it taught him to have faith in destiny. Then he described getting fired from Apple and how it devastated him, but also how it shaped his belief that you've got to find what you love to do. "If you haven't found it yet, keep looking. Don't settle. As with all matters of the heart, you'll know when you find it." His last anecdote was about death, the diagnosis of pancreatic cancer he'd received a year before, and how it made him reflect on the importance of making your own choices in life. "Your time is limited, so don't waste it living someone else's life," he points out with unchallenged authenticity.

It was three brief anecdotes, told in less than fifteen minutes. Of all the wisdom Jobs could have shared, listed in bullet points or framed into a model, backed up with convincing statistics, he simply chose to tell three stories. And everybody got it. Moreover, everybody was moved, and the speech continues to inspire people around the world today. The messages he shared are inspirational, but the form of very personal anecdotes made them utterly credible and convincing. And it elevated the speech from well-intended advice to motivational genius.

Professor Randy Pausch had been teaching computer science, human-computer interaction, and design at Carnegie Mellon University for two decades when he was asked to speak in a series of inspirational lectures at the university. The series' theme was what you would share if you were asked to give a final lecture. In August 2007, just before Pausch was to give his "Your Last Lecture" speech, he was diagnosed with terminal pancreatic cancer.

On September 18, 2007, in front of an audience of hundreds of students and colleagues, Pausch delivered his lecture, "Really Achieving Your Childhood Dreams." It's another example of the power of anecdotes. Despite the tragic circumstances, his moving, inspirational speech—delivered in an incredibly upbeat style—stands as a tribute to life. In little over an hour, he shared several life stories, from his love for stuffed animals to his early dreams of working in Disneyland and becoming an "Imagineer." He shared valuable insights and lessons learned from his experiences, his achievements, and his setbacks. The authenticity of his words and insights are unquestionable.

Pausch concluded, "If you lead your life the right way, the karma will take care of itself, the dreams will come to you." A video of the speech became an Internet phenomenon, captivating millions (I encourage you to watch it—you won't be able to turn it off), as did his bestselling book of the same title and his television appearances. Pausch passed away in July 2008, but his anecdote-drenched speech will continue to inspire.

VISIONARY CHECKLIST

I've spoken of various hygiene factors, workhorse verbs, language, the Contrast Principle, metaphors, analogies, and anecdotes; they all have the potential to transform your story into something that inspires, unlocking the imaginative side of your audience and becoming truly authentic and convincing. Growing this capacity to communicate requires practice and rehearsal, reflection and feedback. Developing a vision is not a onetime thing, but rather a continuous process of reformulating your story; integrating new insights; letting go of ones that are no longer valid; imagining manifestations of changing realities; thinking through alternative scenarios; and revitalizing your story with new language, metaphors, and anecdotes.

Then, you'll need to share your story. This might be during a formal planned event, such as an annual or quarterly meeting. Or it could be unexpected, on an occasion when you're asked without warning to share your vision. Both are important leadership moments. With a touch of drama, we call them Moments of Truth. They are markers you can either hit or miss. Hitting them will consistently build your leadership persona; missing them will consistently deplete it.

The chances of hitting these Moments of Truth increase when you prepare and rehearse your story with some frequency. As Louis Pasteur famously said, "Chance favors the prepared mind." So as we wrap up our exploration of the art of visionary communication, let's bring it all together into something usable and tangible, something that will help you prepare for your own Moments of Truth.

Starting Point: Content

Your vision starts with your ideas. What is at the heart of your future-oriented message? What do you believe in and stand for as you go forward? What could be (as opposed to what is)? To generate these unconventional ideas, think back to the FuturePriming exercises I encouraged you to engage in. Making that practice part of your daily leadership routine, and logging the unconventional thoughts that surface with some frequency will help you build a good platform of ideas to work from.

In a few weeks, FuturePriming should help you uncover at least five, but hopefully more (around ten to twenty) unconventional thoughts. Consider them in terms of what they might mean for your part of the organization going forward. You don't need to work with all of them; start with the ones that will have the greatest impact, and that you feel powerful about in terms of the changes they stand for, and that you want to highlight to engage your followers into action.

You'll need to feel confident of using these changing realities as ingredients for your story—just beware that you should not become overconfident! Radiate excitement, but don't become dogmatic. Force yourself to engage in a scenario planning exercise with some frequency, and enter it fully open-minded—regardless of your story until then. It's only healthy to be confronted with different perspectives every so often, and the more serious you consider them, the richer your future-oriented perspective will become.

Once you have the ideas for your vision, it's time to turn them into an inspiring story. For that purpose, I developed a checklist (shown in Figure 8-3) to help you deliver on Aristotle's classic triad, using the ideas we discussed in this chapter.

Logos

Logos is about sense making. Can you make the case sufficiently believable? People will need to understand it intellectually, so your content needs to make sense. Ask yourself questions such as:

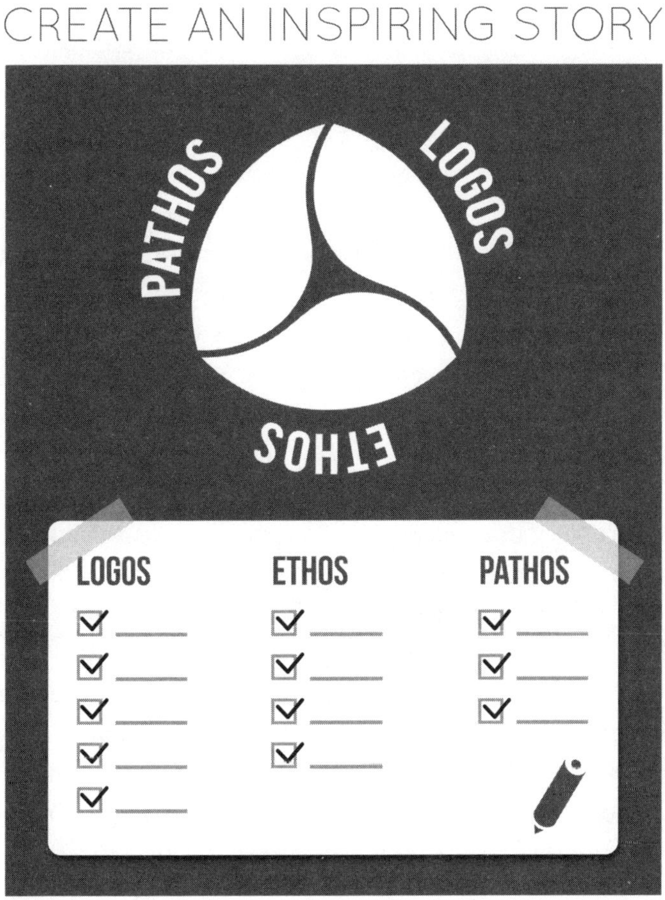

Figure 8-3. Visionary checklist.

- What is the essence of my vision? What is the key idea or key change that I'm envisioning?
- What is a hopeful formulation of this idea? Remember, positivism and optimism in themselves are not enough (and will be considered insincere if they fail to correspond to the brutal reality), but mindfully paint a picture of what *could* be.
- What developments or trends are—or will be—happening around us that support this direction?
- What are the clear choices made in this vision? What is not included?
- What are the consequences of *not* going in this direction? Remember the Contrast Principle.

Pathos

Your vision is a break from today. This means you are taking people into uncertainty, and their reflexive reaction might be defensive. So you'll need to work to get them excited about it. Your passion will help, but you'll also want to intrigue, excite (through your story's unconventionality), and/or inspire feelings of belonging and bonding (through your story's noble cause).

- What is exciting about my vision? How does it generate energy? How can I make it more exciting, hope giving, and/or energizing? (Don't be vague here: Change is frightening for some people, so be as clear as possible about why your perspective on the future is appealing for them personally.)
- What will happen once we are successful in realizing this vision? How will it concretely affect my followers' lives?
- What image, metaphor, or analogy best suits my vision, and how can I integrate it into my story? What positive associations does it conjure up? How can these associations help people to envision the story?
- How does my vision fit with our legacy, core values, and purpose? How does it relate to the "why do we exist" question?

Ethos

Finally, Ethos is where "you" enter the equation. Inserting yourself into your visionary communication requires honesty and vulnerability. Beware that people quickly see through artificial authenticity; rather than uplifting your story, it will deflate it. So, reflect honestly on why you really care, and make that tangible through anecdotes and stories in which you are the main actor. Picture the situation, describe the outset, name the people involved, mention your senses and feelings; in other words, make the story come to life.

- Why do I personally care about the success of this vision?
- What deeply felt personal value(s) does it relate to?
- What anecdote—from my personal past (private or business)—explains my caring? When and how did I discover this personal value, and how has it served me so far? (In short, tell stories!)
- What will I personally change or be willing to sacrifice (or have already sacrificed) to better align my behavior with my vision? Do I have a tangible example?
- What behavior(s), attitude, or habit(s) do *not* fit with the vision, and what will I do (differently) to ensure that I will not exhibit them?

We have reached the end of our journey, in which we have explored the various dimensions of developing your visionary self. It has been my intention to provide you with a sense of direction about how to do that, since it is one of the most critical aspects of leadership—and one of the least understood. As a final comment, growing your visionary capacity requires effort, practice, and reflection. It will not happen overnight, and you should not aim for unrealistic results. The larger-than-life leaders are not good examples to focus on; they may be interesting to observe and take some cues from, but as we have seen, the "usual suspects" have a dark side you should wish to avoid. Their narcissism and tendency toward grandiosity is something to steer clear of. It has been *responsible* visionary leadership we have aimed for, which in many ways is more difficult and challenging than pitching a one-dimensional sound bite version of a vision.

A truly powerful vision provides direction and is emotionally engaging and authentic. It's an invaluable tool for (aspiring) leaders that allows you to do what leadership is all about: to ignite others. Deep down, we all desire to live purposeful lives. If you are a leader and intend to make the lives of your followers, as well as your own life, more meaningful and inspired, I hope this book has been useful to you.

Strategic Questionnaire

GENERIC

- Do you have a particular vision for the development of your part of the business (or the area you are interested in) in the next three to five years?
- What are the key differences from today?
- What breakthroughs are needed to achieve that vision?
- Can you describe intermediate states on the road to your vision?
- What current boundaries are likely to have disappeared in the next few years?
- What paradigms are up for renewal?

CUSTOMERS AND MARKETS

- What will be the growth areas in your industry in the next three to five years?
- What changes in customer needs and preferences do you see emerging?
- What are the drivers of these changes?
- Do you see new types of customers emerge? Do you see old types disappear? How do new types differ from existing ones?

- What kinds of new developments will most benefit customers? Can the developments be assigned to specific segments of the market?
- What will successful companies be doing right in three to five years? What will the unsuccessful ones be doing wrong?

INTERNATIONAL

- What geographically related changes do you anticipate?
- How do you expect the U.S., European, and Asian marketplace to evolve?
- What will be the driving economies, and which ones will lag behind?
- What global regulations/policies/practices do you expect to see changing?
- What role do you foresee for emerging economies?

INDUSTRY STRUCTURE AND COMPETITION

- How will competitive factors affect the pace of change or level of innovation?
- What entirely new kinds of competitors do you envision?
- Which types of companies will lead the markets in three to five years' time?
- What (and who) is likely to be your biggest competitive threat in five years?

INNOVATION

- What innovative new products, services, and business concepts do you expect to see in the coming years? Will they replace or complement existing concepts?
- Who will be the early market adopters for these concepts?
- How will the new products, services, and business concepts be brought to the market?
- Will any new business models be required or take hold?
- What role will technology play in your business area?

- What are the relevant, fundamental, new technologies that are likely to reach commercial viability in the next three to five years?

CONCLUSION

- In your wildest dreams, what would be the most fundamental change that would redefine your business or market (it need not be realistic!).
- What are the greatest opportunities if this change would take place?
- What do you think is *not* an issue that is getting too much attention today?
- What do you think about that no one else sees?

Values List

- ❑ Accountability
- ❑ Accuracy
- ❑ Achievement
- ❑ Adventurousness
- ❑ Altruism
- ❑ Ambition
- ❑ Assertiveness
- ❑ Balance
- ❑ Being the Best
- ❑ Belonging
- ❑ Boldness
- ❑ Calmness
- ❑ Carefulness
- ❑ Challenge
- ❑ Cheerfulness
- ❑ Clear-Mindedness
- ❑ Commitment
- ❑ Community
- ❑ Compassion
- ❑ Competitiveness
- ❑ Consistency
- ❑ Contentment
- ❑ Continuous Improvement
- ❑ Contribution
- ❑ Control
- ❑ Cooperation
- ❑ Correctness
- ❑ Courtesy
- ❑ Creativity
- ❑ Curiosity
- ❑ Decisiveness
- ❑ Democratic
- ❑ Dependability
- ❑ Determination
- ❑ Devoutness
- ❑ Diligence
- ❑ Discipline
- ❑ Discretion
- ❑ Diversity
- ❑ Dynamism

- ❏ Economy
- ❏ Effectiveness
- ❏ Efficiency
- ❏ Elegance
- ❏ Empathy
- ❏ Enjoyment
- ❏ Enthusiasm
- ❏ Equality
- ❏ Excellence
- ❏ Excitement
- ❏ Expertise
- ❏ Exploration
- ❏ Expressiveness
- ❏ Fairness
- ❏ Faith
- ❏ Family Orientation
- ❏ Fidelity
- ❏ Fitness
- ❏ Fluency
- ❏ Focus
- ❏ Freedom
- ❏ Fun
- ❏ Generosity
- ❏ Goodness
- ❏ Grace
- ❏ Growth
- ❏ Happiness
- ❏ Hard Work
- ❏ Health
- ❏ Helping Society
- ❏ Holiness
- ❏ Honesty
- ❏ Honor
- ❏ Humility
- ❏ Independence
- ❏ Ingenuity
- ❏ Inner Harmony
- ❏ Inquisitiveness
- ❏ Insightfulness
- ❏ Intellectualism
- ❏ Intelligence
- ❏ Intuition
- ❏ Joy
- ❏ Justice
- ❏ Leadership
- ❏ Legacy
- ❏ Love
- ❏ Loyalty
- ❏ Making a Difference
- ❏ Mastery
- ❏ Merit
- ❏ Obedience
- ❏ Openness
- ❏ Order
- ❏ Originality
- ❏ Patriotism
- ❏ Perfection
- ❏ Piety
- ❏ Positivity
- ❏ Practicality
- ❏ Preparedness
- ❏ Professionalism
- ❏ Prudence
- ❏ Quality Orientation
- ❏ Reliability
- ❏ Resourcefulness
- ❏ Restraint
- ❏ Results Orientation
- ❏ Rigor
- ❏ Security
- ❏ Self-Actualization
- ❏ Self-Control

❑ Selflessness
❑ Self-Reliance
❑ Sensitivity
❑ Serenity
❑ Service
❑ Shrewdness
❑ Simplicity
❑ Soundness
❑ Speed
❑ Spontaneity
❑ Stability
❑ Status
❑ Strategic Outlook
❑ Strength
❑ Structure
❑ Success
❑ Support

❑ Teamwork
❑ Temperance
❑ Thankfulness
❑ Thoroughness
❑ Thoughtfulness
❑ Timeliness
❑ Tolerance
❑ Traditionalism
❑ Trustworthiness
❑ Truth Seeking
❑ Understanding
❑ Uniqueness
❑ Unity
❑ Usefulness
❑ Vision
❑ Vital

25 Visionary Development Practices

Scan the Quick Response (QR) code to access these twenty-five practices. Alternatively, go to www.visionarycapacity.com and enter the practice number displayed under the QR symbol.

Chapter 2			
2-1	Story Pace	Telling a good story requires not only content, but also speed and timing. This practice will help you develop pace in the stories you tell.	
2-2	Assumption Bowling	Discovering new insights requires knocking over some ingrained beliefs. Assumption bowling is a powerful technique that challenges some fundamental assumptions you might be holding on to, and that stop you from seeing "new" realities.	

| 2-3 | Business Upside Down | This powerful practice forces you to suspend traditional perspectives and take an opposite view. | |

| 2-4 | Lateral Thinking | Consciously stretch your imagination by applying one of Edward de Bono's lateral thinking practices. |  |

| 2-5 | WWGD | A playful practice using the power of associations. Try it with your team. |  |

Chapter 3

| 3-1 | Your Current Visionary Self | Where are you currently in the visionary landscape? Honestly assess yourself in order identify your growth dimensions. | |

Chapter 4

| 4-1 | FuturePriming | The power practice to develop your ability to see change early. | |

Chapter 5

| 5-1 | Future Scenarios | This practice describes the four most fundamental steps in scenario planning. Unlike other practices, this one will require some designated time. | |

Chapter 6

| 6-1 | It Starts with Why | An easy practice: It just requires you to sit back and contemplate the ideas expressed by Simon Sinek in a world-class video. | |

| 6-2 | Obituary Exercise | A reflective practice to discover what is truly important in your life. |  |

| 6-3 | Your Stories | Another reflective practice that helps you identify the values that drive your thinking and behavior, using the art of storytelling. | |

| 6-4 | So That What? | A quick practice to guide the discovery of your deep personal motivations and purpose. | |

Chapter 7

7-1	Yes, and . . .	A great practice to help you transform a bad habit into a productive one.	
7-2	Break the Pattern	Deliberately break your normal routines in order to discover how your routines shield you from observing the full picture of opportunities and perspectives.	
7-3	Look OUT!	Pick a couple of discovery questions every day, and keep them in mind when you are in conversation, meeting clients, surfing the Internet, watching TV, or just relaxing.	
7-4	Appreciative Inquiry	A practice around the academically grounded principles of appreciative inquiry.	
7-5	Radical Exposure	A practice to engage with subgroups you do not ordinarily hang out with—to deliberately expose yourself to those who think and act differently.	
7-6	Unblinding Your Blind Spot	A routine-building practice aimed at incorporating two fundamental questions into your leadership repertoire.	

| 7-7 | Learn to Listen | A practice aimed at developing a critically important leadership skill: listening! |  |

| 7-8 | Opinion Swap | Experience what "the truth" looks like from the point of view of others. |  |

Chapter 8

| 8-1 | Moments of Truth | A fun practice to break from the conventional and do something remarkable at all-too-common moments. It offers a great idea to develop your future orientation. |  |

| 8-2 | Elevator Pitch | Deliver your visionary story with clarity and focus on the essence. This practice gears you up to be successful if you only have sixty seconds to share your ideas. |  |

| 8-3 | Verb-alize | Improve your rhetoric skills by integrating a series of powerhouse verbs into your default vocabulary. |  |

| 8-4 | A Picture Is Worth a Thousand Words | Sharpen your imaginary, associative side—a vital skill in communicating colorful visions. | |

8-5   Let Me Tell
       You a Story

Make your visionary
communication truly authentic by
integrating personal anecdotes.
This practice helps you dig into
your database of profound life
experiences.

Notes

INTRODUCTION

1. Robert Ajemian, "Where Is the Real George Bush?" *Time,* January 26, 1987, www.time.com/time/magazine/article/0,9171,963342-2,00.html.

2. "Senate History: George H. W. Bush, 43rd Vice President (1981–1989)," www.senate.gov/artandhistory/history/common/generic/VP_George_Bush.htm.

3. For information on the effects of Bush's lack of "the vision thing," see *This Day in Quotes* (blog), www.thisdayinquotes.com/2011/01/george-hw-bush-and-vision-thing.html.

4. John P. Kotter, "What Leaders Really Do," *Harvard Business Review,* May–June, 1990, p. 5.

5. Unfortunately, this study is biased toward U.S. business leaders only. Nonetheless, given the United States's global dominance in business throughout the twentieth century, it remains a valid research scope to find the keys to successful business leadership, even outside U.S. borders.

6. Anthony J. Mayo and Nitin Nohria, *In Their Time* (Boston: Harvard Business School Press, 2005), p. 354.

7. Arie de Geus, *The Living Company* (Boston: Harvard Business School Press, 1997), pp. 2–3.

8. In addition, he described these organizations in terms of three other factors, which are 1) their strong sense of identity, 2) their tolerance to activities in the margin, and 3) their conservatism in financing. See de Geus, *The Living Company,* pp. 4–5.

9. McKinsey Interview, "Bill George on Rethinking Capitalism," December 2013, www.mckinsey.com/insights/leading_in_the_21st_century/bill_george_on_rethinking_capitalism.

10. Dominic Barton and Mark Wiseman, "Focusing Capital on the Long Term," *Harvard Business Review,* January–February 2014, pp. 45–51.

11. "Short-Termism Has Been 'Hugely Damaging' for Banks, Says Sir David Walker," *The Telegraph,* September 12, 2012.

12. Adi Ignatius, "Captain Planet: An Interview with Paul Polman," *Harvard Business Review,* June 2012, pp. 112–118.

13. Francois Brochet, George Serafeim, and Maria Loumioti, "Short-Termism: Don't Blame Investors," *Harvard Business Review,* June 2012.

14. McKinsey Interview, "Bill George on Rethinking Capitalism."

CHAPTER 1: THE GROUNDWORK

1. Abraham Zaleznik, in a 1992 retrospective commentary on his 1977 HBR article "Managers and Leaders: Are They Different?" in "Leadership Insights," *Harvard Business Review,* 2010, p. 19.

2. Warren Bennis, "Introduction to the Revised Edition, 2003," in *On Becoming a Leader* (New York: Basic Books, 2009), p. xxxiv.

3. Abraham Zaleznik, "Managers and Leaders: Are They Different?" *Harvard Business Review,* May–June 1977.

4. Ibid.

5. John P. Kotter, "What Leaders Really Do," *Harvard Business Review,* December 2001.

6. Kevin B. Lowe and William L. Gardner analyzed the content of research articles published in *Leadership Quarterly* in 2001 and found that a third of them were about transformational leadership.

7. Peter G. Northouse, *Leadership: Theory and Practice* (Thousand Oaks, CA: Sage Publications, 2012), p. 172.

8. Ibid., p. 186.

9. Kotter, "What Leaders Really Do."

10. Aristotle, *Rhetoric,* trans. W. Rhys Roberts, The Internet Classics Archive, http://classics.mit.edu/Aristotle/rhetoric.mb.txt.

11. Michael Maccoby, "Narcissistic Leaders," *Harvard Business Review,* January–February 2000.

12. Ibid.

13. A. Grzybowski and P. Aydin, "Edme Mariotte (1620–1684): Pioneer of Neurophysiology," *Survey of Ophthalmology,* July–Aug 2007.

CHAPTER 2: TAPPING INTO YOUR IMAGINATION

1. I don't know if this story is true. I heard it from someone, who undoubtedly heard it from someone else. That's how good stories come to life. So if you are Edward de Bono, consider it a tribute to the magnificent work you have done on creativity. If you are not Edward de Bono (chances are . . .), don't get hung up on the facts and just enjoy the story. We're in the imagination section, remember?

2. Abraham Zaleznik in a 1992 retrospective commentary on his 1977 HBR classic "Managers and Leaders: Are They Different?" in "Leadership Insights," *Harvard Business Review,* 2010, p. 19.

3. Michael S. Sweeney, *Brainworks: The Mind-Bending Science of How You See, What You Think, and Who You Are* (Washington, D.C.: National Geographic, 2011), p. 170.

4. Fred Polak, *The Image of the Future* (Amsterdam: Elsevier, 1961), p. 19.

5. Ibid., p. 5.

6. J. Davies, C. Atance, and G. Martin-Ordas, "A Framework and Open Questions on Imagination in Adults and Children," *Imagination, Cognition, and Personality* 31, no. 1–2, 2011, pp. 143–157.

7. James L. Adams, *Conceptual Blockbusting: A Guide to Better Ideas* (New York: Basic Books, 2001), p. 8.

8. J. Edward Russo and Paul J. H. Schoemaker, *Winning Decisions* (New York: Doubleday, 2002), p. 21.

9. The friend that Fred meets is not a man, but a woman and the mother of the little girl. Both named Susan.

10. Most notably, the Israeli-American psychologist Daniel Kahneman demonstrated structural irrationality in human beings, and won a Nobel Prize for his work in this field in 2002. His lifetime research was summarized in his book *Thinking, Fast and Slow* (New York: Farras, Straus and Giroux, 2011).

11. Steven D. Levitt and Stephen J. Dubner, *Freakonomics* (New York: William Morrow and Company, 2005).

12. Sweeney, *Brainworks,* pp. 7–9.

13. Robert Reich, "Alan Greenspan by Robert Reich," *The Guardian,* January 16, 2009, www.guardian.co.uk/world/2009/jan/17/george-bush-alan-greenspan.

14. Scott Lanman and Steve Matthews, "Greenspan Concedes to 'Flaw' in His Market Ideology," *Bloomberg,* October 23, 2008, www.bloomberg.com/apps/news?pid=newsarchive&sid=ah5qh9Up4rIg.

15. Leon Festinger, *A Theory of Cognitive Dissonance* (Palo Alto, CA: Stanford University Press, 1957).

16. Paul B. Carroll and Chunka Mui, "Seven Ways to Fail Big," *Harvard Business Review,* September 2008.

17. Adam Waytz and Malia Mason, "Your Brain at Work," *Harvard Business Review,* July–August 2013.

18. Edward de Bono, *The Use of Lateral Thinking* (New York: Penguin Books, 1971).

19. Jeff Jarvis, *What Would Google Do?* (New York: CollinsBusiness, 2009).

20. I'm deliberately steering clear from Apple, as it feels this company has been boasted and hyped enough for its different way of thinking, but that's personal preference. Technically speaking, Apple would qualify.

21. W. Chan Kim and Renée Mauborgne, *Blue Ocean Strategy* (Boston: Harvard Business School Press, 2005).

22. Of course, the interested reader should get a copy of the book; this extremely short summary does not do justice to the powerful ideas introduced in *Blue Ocean Strategy.*

23. "Hotel Concept," www.citizenm.com/hotel-technology-concepts.

CHAPTER 3: DEVELOPING YOUR VISIONARY CAPACITY

1. Sooksan Kantabutra and Gayle C. Avery, "Follower Effects in the Visionary Leadership Process," *Journal of Business & Economic Research* 4, no. 5, May 2006.

2. Steven Johnson, *Where Good Ideas Come From: The Seven Patterns of Innovation* (New York: Penguin Books, 2010), p. 35.

3. Robert Mottley, "The Early Years: Malcom McLean," *American Shipper,* May 1, 1996.

4. Anthony J. Mayo and Nitin Nohria, *In Their Time* (Boston: Harvard Business School Press, 2005), p. 203.

5. "Leading in the 21st Century: An Interview with Ford's Alan Mulally," *McKinsey Quarterly,* November 2013.

6. Ibid.

7. Jerker Denrell, " 'Experts' Who Beat the Odds Are Probably Just Lucky," *Harvard Business Review,* April 2013.

8. Reducing complexity to 2x2 matrixes is something academics and consultants love doing—and for good reason, as explained by Alex Lowy and Phil Hood in their insightful book *The Power of the 2x2 Matrix,* which provides fifty-five remarkable frameworks that share the 2x2 structure. "The matrix is a clear and helpful starting point to achieving balance and clarity. We regard the matrix as one leg of a three-legged stool. The *form* of the matrix needs to be applied in a systematic manner (*method*) and with sensitivity and expertise (*mastery*). The combination of form, method, and mastery imbues 2x2 Thinking with the power to realize more fully what is possible and to generate solutions characterized by what Bill Buxton, former chief scientist at Alias Research, calls *surprising obviousness." The Power of the 2x2 Matrix* (San Francisco: Jossey-Bass, 2004), p. 4.

9. Paul Smith, *Lead with a Story* (New York: AMACOM, 2012), p. 19.

10. Ellen Langer, *Mindfulness* (Cambridge, MA: Da Capo Press, 1989), p. 85.

11. Eileen C. Shapiro, *Fad Surfing in the Boardroom* (Cambridge, MA: Perseus Publishing), 1996, back cover.

12. *The Selfish Cynic* (blog), http://sethgodin.typepad.com/seths_blog/2013/10/the-selfish-cynic.html.

13. Global Information Industry Center, "How Much Information: 2010 Report on Enterprise Server Information," January 2011.

14. Malcolm Gladwell, "Blowing Up," *The New Yorker,* April 2002.

15. Sigmund Freud, *On Sexuality: Three Essays on the Theory of Sexuality and Other Works* (New York: Penguin, 1905), pp. 362–362.

16. Michael Maccoby, "Narcissistic Leaders," *Harvard Business Review,* January–February 2000.

17. Ibid.

18. Walter Isaacson, *Steve Jobs* (New York: Simon & Schuster, 2011).

19. Maccoby, "Narcissistic Leaders."

CHAPTER 4: SEEING THINGS EARLY

1. This is probably among the most unfortunate quotes ever made. It's often used in the context of bad predictions, but it must be said that Ken Olsen was referring to the application of a computer for managing home equipment and facilities such as lights, sound, and automatic doors. Nonetheless, that too has proved to be wrong over time. It feels only fair to also remember Olsen for his contributions to the world: He was acknowledged as a catalyst of innovation, named America's most successful entrepreneur in 1986 by *Fortune* magazine, and ranked number six on MIT's list of the top 150 innovators in 2011.

2. Warren Bennis, "Introduction to the Revised Edition, 2003," in *On Becoming a Leader* (New York: Basic Books, 2009), p. xxvi.

3. Warren G. Bennis and Robert J. Thomas, *Geeks and Geezers: How Era, Values, and Defining Moments Shape Leaders* (Boston: Harvard Business School Publishing, 2002).

4. Dr. James P. Keen is professor emeritus and former chief academic officer at Antioch College in the United States and coauthor of *Common Fire: Leading Lives of Commitment in a Complex World* (Boston: Beacon Press, 1997) and *Leadership Landscapes* (London: Palgrave Macmillan, 2008).

5. W. Chan Kim and R. Mauborgne, *Blue Ocean Strategy* (Boston: Harvard Business Review Press, 2005).

6. Bronwyn Fryer and Thomas A. Stewart, "Cisco Sees the Future," *Harvard Business Review,* November 2008.

7. Sreedhari Desai and Francesca Gino, "Defend Your Research: Adults Behave Better When Teddy Bears Are in the Room," *Harvard Business Review,* September 2011, pp. 30–31.

8. Ibid.

9. A. G. Greenwald, M. R. Banaji, and L. A. Rudman, "A Unified Theory of Implicit Attitudes, Stereotypes, Self-Esteem, and Self-Concept," *Psychological Review* 109, no. 1, 2002.

10. J. A. Bargh, M. Chen, and L. Burrows, "Automaticity of Social Behavior: Direct Effects of Trait Construct and Stereotype Activation on Action," *Journal of Personality and Social Psychology* 71, 2, 1996.

11. With thankful reference to my good friend Tom Cummings, who originally came up with the name when we first started to work with the materials, in the "good ole days."

12. Specifically, the idea was to show that the current policies aimed at separating batteries and subsidizing home solar panels are not nearly enough to tackle the long-term sustainability challenges facing us today.

13. Wayne Burkan, *Wide Angle Vision* (New York: John Wiley & Sons, 1996).

CHAPTER 5: CONNECTING THE DOTS

1. Miles D. White, "The Reinvention Imperative," *Harvard Business Review*, November 2013, p. 42.

2. Stefaan Michielsen and Michael Sephiha, *Bankroet* (BrusselsTielt: Lannoo-de Tijd, 2009), p. 58.

3. As it later turns out, the other two parties are the Royal Bank of Scotland Santander. But Orcel keeps that a secret at this stage. Michielsen and Sephiha, *Bankroet,* p. 62.

4. Nassim Nicholas Taleb, who wrote *The Black Swan* (New York: Random House, 2007), exposed the importance of understanding the impact of highly improbable events, which is metaphorically expressed by the black swan, a variety that did not exist as all swans were white. Until they found one . . .

5. Leon Festinger (1957), Fritz Heider (1946), and Theodore Newcomb (1953) provide the earliest theories in how the desire for consistency acts as a motivator for behavior.

6. Robert B. Cialdini, *Influence: Science and Practice* (Harlow: Pearson Education Limited, 2014), p. 60.

7. Ibid., p. 58.

8. R. H. Fazio, J. Blascovich, and D. M. Driscoll, "On the Functional Value of Attitudes," *Personality and Social Psychology Bulletin* 18, 1992, pp. 388–401.

9. Andrei Shleifer, *Inefficient Markets* (New York: Oxford University Press, 2000), p. 2.

10. Michael Jensen, "Some Anomalous Evidence Regarding Market Efficiency," *Journal of Financial Economics* 6, 1978, pp. 95–101.

11. Dan Ariely's *Predictably Irrational* (New York: HarperCollins Publishers, 2008) is easily accessible. Daniel Kahneman, Paul Slovic, and Amos Tversky's *Judgment Under Uncertainty: Heuristics and Biases* (Boston: Cambridge University Press, 1982) is the classic.

12. Max H. Bazerman and Michael D. Watkins, *Predictable Surprises* (Boston: Harvard Business School Press, 2008), p. 159.

13. J. Edward Russo and Paul J. H. Schoemaker, *Winning Decisions* (New York: Doubleday, 2002).

14. Marc Alpert and Howard Raiffa, "A Progress Report on the Training of Probability Assessors," in Daniel Kahneman, Paul Slovic, and Amos Tversky, *Judgment Under Uncertainty: Heuristics and Biases* (CambridgeBoston: Cambridge University Press, 1982), pp. 294–305.

15. Ellen J. Langer, "The Illusion of Control," *Journal of Personality and Social Psychology* 32, no. 2, August 1975, pp. 311–328.

16. Robert J. Shiller, *Irrational Exuberance* (Princeton, NJ: Princeton University Press, 2000), p. 144.

17. J. Edward Russo and Paul J. H. Schoemaker, "Managing Overconfidence," *Sloan Management Review* 33, no. 2, Winter 1992, p. 11.

18. "Pierre Wack," *The Economist,* August 29, 2008, www.economist.com/node/12000502.

19. Tim Hindle, *The Economist Guide to Management Ideas and Gurus* (London: Profile Books, 2008), pp. 317–318.

20. Napier Collyns and Hardin Tibbs, "In Memory of Pierre Wack," *Netview: Global Business Network News* 9, no. 1.

21. For a comprehensive understanding of scenario planning, I recommend Kees van der Heijden, *Scenarios: The Art of Strategic Conversation* (New York: John Wiley, 1996), and Paul J. H. Schoemaker and Robert E. Gunther, *Profiting from Uncertainty: Strategies for Succeeding No Matter What the Future Brings* (New York: Free Press, 2002).

22. Kees Vvan der Heijden, *Scenarios: The Art of Strategic Conversation* (New York: John Wiley, 1996), p. 17.

23. Ibid., pp. 18–19.

24. André Bénard, "World Oil and Cold Reality," *Harvard Business Review,* November–December 1980.

25. Fred Goodwin, the Royal Bank of Scotland's CEO, was knighted in 2004 in the great British tradition in recognition for his accomplishments. After his leading role in the biggest banking disaster in British history, his knighthood was removed in February 2012.

26. Irving, L. Janis, "Groupthink," *Psychology Today* 5, no. 6, November 1971, pp. 43–46, 74–76.

27. Michielsen and Sephiha, *Bankroet.*

28. Nita Sachan and Charles Dhanaraj, "Organizing for Innovation at Glenmark (A)," Indian School of Business, June 30, 2013.

29. Nita Sachan and Charles Dhanaraj, "Organizing for Innovation at Glenmark (B)," Indian School of Business, June 30, 2013.

30. Clay Chandler, "Leading in the 21st Century: An Interview with Chanda Kochhar," *McKinsey & Company,* September 2012.

CHAPTER 6: YOUR VISIONARY SELF

1. Warren Bennis, "Introduction to the Revised Edition, 2003," in *On Becoming a Leader* (New York: Basic Books, 2009), p. xxv.

2. Ibid., p. xxviii.

3. John P. Kotter, "What Leaders Really Do," *Harvard Business Review,* May–June, 1990.

4. Geraldine Brooks, "Unfinished Business," *The New Yorker,* October 17, 2005.

5. Thomas J. Pritzker, "2003 Ceremony Speech," www.pritzkerprize.com/2003/ceremony_speech2b.

6. Katarina Stübe and Jan Utzon, *A Tribute to Jørn Utzon's Sydney Opera House* (Potts Point, NSW: Reveal Books, 2009), p. 87.

7. "Utzon Family Message: A Word from Jan Utzon," http://jornutzon.sydney operahouse.com/family_message.htm.

8. Stübe and Utzon, *A Tribute to Jørn Utzon's Sydney Opera House,* p. 129.

9. "Leading in the 21st Century: An Interview with Ford's Alan Mulally," *McKinsey Quarterly,* November 2013.

10. Daniel Goleman, "What Makes a Leader?" *Harvard Business Review,* January 2004; *Emotional Intelligence* (New York: Bantam Books, 1995).

11. Bill George, Peter Sims, Andrew N. McLean, and Diana Mayer, "Discovering Your Authentic Leadership," *Harvard Business Review,* February 2007.

12. Ibid., p. 130.

13. Warren G. Bennis and Robert J. Thomas, "Crucibles of Leadership," *Harvard Business Review,* September 2002.

CHAPTER 7: MINDFUL BEHAVIOR

1. Robin R. Vallacher and Daniel M. Wegner, *A Theory of Action Identification* (London: Psychology Press, 1985).

2. For the original story behind Solar Roadways, see http://www.youtube.com/watch?v=KYizzYMr5Y8.

3. Ellen Langer, *Mindfulness* (Cambridge, MA: Da Capo Press, 1989), pp. 16–17.

4. Ibid., pp. 9–18.

5. Robert B. Cialdini, *Influence: Science and Practice*, 5th ed. (Harlow: Pearson Education Limited, 2014).

6. Langer, *Mindfulness,* p. 44.

7. Cialdini, *Influence: Science and Practice,* pp. 65–73.

8. Jonathan L. Freedman and Scott C. Fraser, "Compliance Without Pressure: The Foot-in-the-Door Technique," *Journal of Personality and Social Psychology* 4, 1966, pp. 195–203.

9. Ellen Langer, *The Power of Mindful Learning* (Cambridge, MA: Da Capo Press, 1997), p. 5.

10. John D. Rockefeller, *The Second American Revolution: Some Personal Observations* (New York: Harper & Row, 1973).

11. George Loewenstein, "The Psychology of Curiosity: A Review and Reinterpretation," *Psychological Bulletin* 116, no.1, 1994, pp. 75–98.

12. William James, *The Sentiment of Rationality* (Cambridge, MA: John Wilson and Son, 1897), p. 63.

13. Eric E. Vogt, Juanita Brown, and David Isaacs, *The Art of Powerful Questions: Catalyzing Insight, Innovation, and Action* (Mill Valley, CA: Whole Systems Associates, 2003).

14. With many thanks to Frank Barrett, Ron Fry, and Herman Wittockx, *Appreciative Inquiry: het Basiswerk* (Tielt: Lannoo Campus, 2012).

15. Daniel Kahnemann, Dan Lovallo, and Olivier Sibony, "Before You Make That Big Decision," *Harvard Business Review,* June 2011.

CHAPTER 8: IGNITING YOUR FOLLOWERS

1. Adam Waytz and Malia Mason, "Your Brain at Work," *Harvard Business Review,* July–August 2013.

2. "Leading in the 21st Century: An Interview with Ford's Alan Mulally," *McKinsey Quarterly,* November 2013.

3. Jim Collins, *Good to Great* (New York: Harper Business, 2001), pp. 83–85.

4. Ibid.

5. Viktor E. Frankl, *Man's Search for Meaning* (Boston: Beacon Press, 2006).

6. Collins, *Good to Great*.

7. Garry Wills, *Lincoln at Gettysburg: The Words That Remade America* (New York: Simon & Schuster, 1992), p. 20.

8. "Times Topic: Gettysburg Address," *The New York Times,* http://topics.nytimes. com/top/reference/timestopics/subjects/c/civil_war_us_/gettysburg_address/.

9. With thankful appreciation to David Pearl, who created this comparison on his wonderful blog ("The Gettysburg Address? Speech? Pitch? Promo?" *The Change Gamer's Blog,* http://davidpearl.net/2013/11/the-gettysburg-address-speech-pitch-promo/) .

10. Elizabeth F. Loftus and John C. Palmer, "Reconstruction of Automobile Destruction: An Example of the Interaction Between Language and Memory," *Journal of Verbal Learning and Verbal Behavior* 13, 1974, pp. 585–589.

11. "The Story of a Sign by Alonso Alvarez Barreda," *Purplefeather,* June 17, 2011, http://www.youtube.com/watch?v=HX5aRzXUzJo.

12. Robert B. Cialdini, *Influence: Science and Practice*, 5th ed. (Harlow: Pearson Education Limited, 2014).

13. Daniel Kahneman and Amos Tversky, "Choices, Values, and Frames," *American Psychologist* 39, no. 4, 1984, pp. 341–350.

14. "The Uses (and Abuses) of Influence: Interview with Robert Cialdini," *Harvard Business Review,* July–August 2013, pp. 76–81.

15. George Lakoff and Mark Johnson, *Metaphors We Live By* (Chicago: University of Chicago Press, 2003).

16. Adam Waytz and Malia Mason, "Your Brain at Work," *Harvard Business Review,* July–August 2013.

17. Robin Higie Coulter and Gerald Zaltman,"Using the Zaltman Metaphor Elicitation Technique to Understand Brand Images," *Advances in Consumer Research* 21, 1994, pp. 501–507.

18. Jack Malcolm, "Analogies Are Powerful," *Practical Eloquence* (blog), http:// jackmalcolm.com/blog/2013/05/analogies-are-powerful/.

19. Giovanni Gavetti and Jan W. Rivkin, "How Strategists Really Think: Tapping the Power of Analogy," *Harvard Business Review,* April 2005.

20. Margaret Parkin, *Tales for Change: Using Storytelling to Develop People and Organizations* (London: Kogan Page, 2010), p. 37.

21. Richard Maxwell and Robert Dickman, *The Elements of Persuasion* (New York: HarperCollins Publishers, 2007), p. 125.

22. T. O. Jones and W. E. Sasser Jr., "Why Satisfied Customers Defect," *Harvard Business Review,* November 1995, pp. 88–100.

23. Brené Brown, "The Power of Vulnerability", TEDx, June 2010, http://www.ted.com/talks/ brene_brown_on_vulnerability.html.

Index

ILLUSTRATIONS:
JET STEVERINK